Bridging Divided Worlds

Bridging Divided Worlds

Generational Cultures in Congregations

Jackson W. Carroll

Wade Clark Roof

 JOSSEY-BASS
A Wiley Company
San Francisco

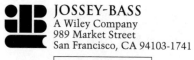

JOSSEY-BASS
A Wiley Company
989 Market Street
San Francisco, CA 94103-1741

www.josseybass.com

Copyright © 2002 by John Wiley & Sons, Inc.

Jossey-Bass is a registered trademark of John Wiley & Sons, Inc.

Jossey-Bass books and products are available through most bookstores. To contact Jossey-Bass directly, call (888) 378–2537, fax to (800) 605–2665, or visit our website at www.josseybass.com.

Substantial discounts on bulk quantities of Jossey-Bass books are available to corporations, professional associations, and other organizations. For details and discount information, contact the special sales department at Jossey-Bass.

We at Jossey-Bass strive to use the most environmentally sensitive paper stocks available to us. Our publications are printed on acid-free recycled stock whenever possible, and our paper always meets or exceeds minimum GPO and EPA requirements.

Library of Congress Cataloging-in-Publication Data

Carroll, Jackson W.
  Bridging divided worlds : generational cultures in congregations / Jackson W. Carroll and Wade Clark Roof.– 1st ed.
    p. cm.
Includes bibliographical references and index.
  ISBN 0-7879-4990-6 (alk. paper)
  1. Church. 2. Intergenerational relations–Religious aspects–Christianity. I. Roof, Wade Clark. II. Title.
  BV640 .C37 2002
  261.8'342'0973–dc21
                                                                                          2001006045

FIRST EDITION
HB Printing   10 9 8 7 6 5 4 3 2 1

Contents

Acknowledgments

This book is the product of two authors whose friendship over the years has led to several other collaborations and who, among other shared characteristics (South Carolina natives and graduates of the same undergraduate college) are now both grandfathers. In a conversation several years ago, we were reflecting on the changing religious scene in which our grandchildren are growing up. How are they likely to be affected by these changes? How will their generation relate to the religious organizations? What kind of congregation, if any, will they be likely to join? How will present-day congregations need to change if they are to respond to the changes taking place about us?

Although these questions are much broader and more long-range than we have attempted to answer in these pages, they motivated us to undertake the research that led to this book. One of us (Roof) has written extensively on generations and religion, especially on the religion of baby boomers. The other (Carroll) has focused considerable attention on congregations and congregational leadership. We have both been students of how broader social and cultural changes are affecting contemporary spirituality and religion, including religious institutions and practices. Thus we decided to bring together our research interests to focus on how generational differences are currently affecting congregational life, and how congregations of various types are attempting to respond to these differences.

Although our focus on the present in the research may not provide direct answers to the long-range questions that we were raising about our grandchildren, it is our hope that we offer insights that will be helpful to students, leaders, and practitioners of religion both now and in the future.

This book has been much longer in the making than the two of us anticipated when we began planning for it in 1995. We are indeed grateful not only for the generous support of grants from the Lilly Endowment that made the research possible but also for the patience of its Religion Division Staff in forgiving the several delays that prevented us from meeting our schedule. Patience was also a virtue exhibited by Sheryl Fullerton and the late Sarah Polster of the Jossey-Bass staff when several times we missed our promised publication deadline. We deeply appreciate their support and assistance as we also mourn Sarah's untimely death.

We must express special thanks to the twenty congregations and campus ministries in North Carolina and southern California that were willing to open themselves so completely to us, allowing study of how they were dealing with the generational challenges in their midst. It was a risk for them to do so, since they had no guarantee that we would always "get it right" in our descriptions of them and no recourse if we did not. Because of this, we have altered the names of the congregations, their leaders, and their members. We have not disguised their location, since that is often pertinent to understanding their stories.

Because we have disguised their names, we are unable to list these individuals here, but this in no way diminishes our gratitude. As we indicate later in the book, we chose finally to present case studies of only nine of the congregations. There were compelling reasons for this limitation, but the members and leaders of the excluded congregations—which are also unnamed—should rest assured the information and insights they shared with us were read with care and have informed what we have written. Indeed, we have cited many of these insights throughout the book.

Although the two of us take full responsibility for the contents of the chapters herein, we could not have written them without the cooperation of several persons who assisted us in the research. They visited the congregations and campus ministries on a number of occasions, observing worship services and other congregational events and writing extended field notes. They conducted in-depth interviews with leaders and members of the congregations, and they provided summary reflections on what they had observed and heard. The student researchers at the University of California at Santa Barbara were Marcy Braverman, Ellen Posman,

Gaston Espinosa, Lynn Gesch, Carolyn Coleman, J. Shawn Landres, Marianna Pisano, Susan Shaw, Coreen Robovin-Hartig, Nina Harlow, Ethan Fassett, Danielle Hammack, and Bryan Roig.

The students and staff at Duke University who we wish to acknowledge were Karen Teague, Jennifer Berentsen Williams, Michelle Wolkomir (then a graduate student at North Carolina State University), Julie Hilton Steele, Regina Sanders, and Matthew Straw. Karen Teague, who for much of the time of the research was research associate at the J. M. Ormond Center at Duke Divinity School, transcribed a number of the interviews and did the initial computer tabulations of the survey data. Her successor, John James, has also assisted with data analysis. Marietta Luna transcribed many of the interviews and spent hours reading the interviews, which ran to more than two thousand pages, inserting codes that would enable us to do computer searches for specific themes. Audrey Brown, Ormond Center secretary, has also been of great help.

Finally, to return to the theme of patience, we must single out two individuals who have exhibited the patience of Job as we plodded along to finish this book. We refer to our wives, Anne Ewing Carroll and Terry Potter Roof. We appreciate their patience, which was strained many times, and we are also deeply grateful for their love, support, and encouragement. It is to them that we dedicate this book.

February 2002

Jackson W. Carroll
Duke University
Divinity School

Wade Clark Roof
University of California
at Santa Barbara

Bridging Divided Worlds

Introduction: Congregations and Generational Cultures

A visitor to the weekly worship service of almost any church or synagogue will come away with many impressions. One in particular is likely, that the worshipers are more of one age or generation than another. Older people typically outnumber younger people in a regular service. Historic "mainline" Protestant congregations particularly have an imbalance of people sixty years of age and older. Jewish synagogues look much the same way, except in rare instances. Roman Catholic congregations usually are more mixed in the participants' age but still made up of a large number of older people. Evangelical Christian congregations have a more even age spread, more so than in other traditions. But as a general rule, even the seating arrangements within a congregation, no matter the religious tradition or part of the country in which located, reflect age-based patterns.

This common feature of congregations is underscored in the comment of a man we spoke with in North Carolina, who said of his church: "I definitely see the seniors sitting together. They are the majority. The youth sit together and are even broken down into senior high and junior high. They are all close in proximity, but they are split up. And the generation X and baby boomer groups are mixed throughout in the congregation."

Another person we spoke with, also from North Carolina, characterized the generations in terms of a declining dress code: coat and ties for the oldest generation, then ties for the next younger one, and finally no ties. The first shift occurred with the boomers, the second with generation Xers. "You're going to see almost everybody in the prewar group in coat and tie, nice skirt and dress," this person said. "You're going to see probably a fifty-fifty split in the baby boomers, those of us who wear a coat and tie versus those who just wear ties. And I think when you get into the generation X, you're going to see another fifty-fifty split, those who wear ties and those who don't."

What stands out most visibly—whether in seating arrangements or dress—about a great many congregations are the two extreme demographic clusters: those sixty years and older and those under twenty. Both the elder and the youth cultures are highly distinguishable in the religious context. Less conspicuous are the cultures of the in-between years, those usually identified as boomers or gen Xers. It is fairly easy to spot these latter groups in the aggregate, but not so easy to draw the line between them, except perhaps an occasional earring or tattoo among Xers. Because they do not sit together as separate generations, as do older people or youths, the two tend to be "mixed throughout in the congregation," as the man from North Carolina points out. But in other ways too, boundaries are blurred. Except for boomers being older, it is not always clear just how they actually differ from gen Xers in values, beliefs, and outlook. Commentators casually point to social and cultural distinctions between them, but these are often little more than stereotypes or generalizations rather than reliable research findings. Added to this, the images of both of these post–World War II generations are to a considerable extent media constructions. They exist in our minds partly as images perpetuated by television, magazines, and other modes of communication. The truth is, we know remarkably little about the actual religious and cultural profiles of these generations—how they are similar and how they differ with respect to beliefs, values, and practices. We know even less about the two within the religious congregation, and how as a generation each relates to the other and to those older than themselves.

This book explores how one generation differs from another both within contemporary society and within a religious congregation. What are the major ways in which they vary in values and views? How do their profiles differ in religious beliefs and practices? What are the contrasts in spiritual styles and ways of relating to organized religion? How does one generation contend with another within a congregation shaping a religious world, engaging in meaningful religious practice, and in setting priorities for the worshiping community? All are obvious questions and yet we do not have good answers.

Defining the Categories

Of course, part of the problem with these questions is that we do not have precise definitions for the generations involved. Limiting ourselves to the century that has just passed, how many generations were there? How many adult generations are there today, generations whose experiences were formidably shaped by events of the twentieth century?

Defining a generation is problematic for several reasons. One is that there is no common basis for identifying and labeling a generation, since it could be named after a national or world event (for example, the Great Depression, World War II, and the Vietnam War); or after a demographic trend (the boomers and "busters"); or after no particular event at all but rather the lack of an identity (such as generation X). Pre-boomers include several demographic cohorts: the GI generation of World War II, the silent generation of the 1950s, and the builders (a label applied to those older Americans who did so much to create and sustain the social institutions of the early and middle twentieth century).

Another problem is that, assuming we can identify the cultural or demographic markers of a generation, there is little consensus as to the cutting point in time where one generation ends and another begins. Boomers were born after World War II, but in terms of birth year where does that generation end and generation X begin? Hence the notion of a generation, though intuitively obvious at one level for distinguishing biological descent, is in a social and cultural sense rather ambiguous and elusive, lacking as it does a consistent set of boundaries and time-specific criteria defining one from another. Not surprisingly, researchers disagree on this most crucial aspect of defining a generation.

Further, the notion of a generation may be fairly simple and straightforward, but researching it is difficult. Sorting out effects of generation from those of life cycle and period is a challenge even with the most sophisticated of social science methods. *Life-cycle*, or *aging, effects* refer of course to the maturation of individuals over time, and *period effects* to influences presumably affecting all people living in a particular time. In contrast, *generational*, or *cohort, effects* refer to the impact of historical experiences and socialization, which tend to stay with people as they age. It is the latter that most concern us, though not at the exclusion of the other effects.

Particularly difficult to sort out when studying religious trends, say, for youth are life-cycle and generational effects. For example, it has long been observed that teenagers are likely to drop out of religious participation in a congregation but tend to return to active involvement once married and with children. That is clearly a life-cycle pattern. But can we necessarily assume constancy of that pattern *across* generations? Might there be a greater number of youths who drop out in a particular generation, or perhaps fewer of them return to church and synagogue later in life as a result of their circumstances and experiences? If so, this would suggest a generational pattern. Far more attention has been given to life cycle in the study of religiosity in the United States than to generation, even though careful and reasoned analysis suggests that both are crucial considerations (plus, of course, period effects). In this volume, we concern ourselves with generations not just because they have been overlooked but because we believe they are of far greater significance in understanding the dynamics of congregational change than is generally recognized by sociologists and other religious commentators. So much of congregational life—programs, styles of worship, and outlook—is linked to generation.

Here we focus on age-based cohorts and take a rather pragmatic approach to defining the generational cohorts under study.[1] We also make the assumption that World War II is a critical marker in the study of religious trends. Previous studies underscore this fundamental point: the greatest cultural and religious divide separating any of the generations in the past seventy-five years in the United States is that between pre–World War II cohorts and all others born since. This marker in history is like a cultural fault line, with religious (as well as many nonreligious) differences before and after 1945 greater than those between age cohorts since then.[2] It is not a surprising observation, although for the study of American religion and congregations there has been insufficient attention given to these age-related patterns. Research points to a wide set of changes, particularly for the white, Euro-American population, in religious attendance, personal beliefs and practices, attitude toward religious institutions, and the role of the individual in making moral and religious decisions that date from this time.

Not all the changes point to quantitative decline in institutional religious life. Indeed, many of the changes are of a positive, qualitative sort, in keeping with spiritual well-being and individuals' assuming greater responsibility for their religious choices. Even outside the United States—in other Western countries such as France, England, Belgium, Germany, Australia, Italy, and Sweden—shifts in religious and spiritual trends are documented in relation to this critical marker, though on a somewhat lesser scale.[3] Patterns are complex but closely bound up with generational changes.

Hence we draw a distinction between pre-boomers and boomers. Indeed, we regard it as essential to analysis of the generations in the United States currently. Pre-boomers are those born prior to 1946; with boomers we follow other researchers in defining their birth years as from 1946 to 1964.[4] This eighteen-year span corresponds to the period of increased fertility after World War II, which created the demographic bulge known as the boom generation. Research also points to subtle but significant cultural trends and some shift in religious and spiritual styles for generation Xers, those born from 1965 to 1980. The end date for this generation is arbitrary, based largely on impressionistic evidence of changing youth identities among college freshmen over the past few years. This simple, threefold distinction among generations has several advantages. It captures what we believe to be the most important cleavage among generations presently for religious study. It yields three living adult generations recognizable by their own self-description. And aside from being able to profile them religiously and culturally, we can observe all three in interaction with one another within congregations at this time.

Carriers of Culture

In a strict sense, a generation is more than simply an age cohort, or an aggregate of individuals all born in the same time period. By the term is implied a set of unifying social experiences binding members into a self-conscious collectivity. German social philosopher Karl Mannheim was particularly influential in helping us grasp the social and psychological dynamics of generational experience. Writing early in the twentieth century, at a time of much social discontent in Europe, he argued that a generation is a carrier of culture that successively redefines worldviews, values, and lifestyles and thus is an important agent of social change within a society. He looked upon a generation as a "social unit," that is, an age-based constituency that shares a "common location in the historical and social process" and has a "specific range of potential experience, predisposing it for a certain characteristic mode of thought and experience, and a characteristic type of historically relevant action."[5] In his way of thinking, the emotional, cognitive, and behavioral aspects of life become integrated in the process of socialization for a given generation.

Mannheim goes on to describe a generation as having a "common destiny" or shared interest much like a social class or ethnic group, and as exhibiting an "identity of responses, a certain affinity in the way in which all move with and are formed by their common experiences." As this view of generation would suggest, it is a constituency held together by a set of shared sociohistorical experiences and, subjectively, by common ways of thinking about, and by responding to, those experiences; consequently, all generations are characterized by some degree of self-consciousness, each distinguished from another. Members of a generation see themselves as different from another.

William Strauss and Irving Howe, whose book *Generations* was published in 1991, go so far as to suggest that a generation has a "peer personality." They underscore three fundamental features of a generation, much like Mannheim: (1) a common location in history, (2) a common set of beliefs and behavior, and (3) perceived membership in a common generation.[6] Sharing a common location in history, members of a generation experience similar historical events and challenges: war, economic depression, assassination of a major figure, new discoveries, national and global catastrophe, famous and not-so-famous personages, and the like. Generational analysis presumes that events and developments in a person's youthful, formative years especially play a decisive role in shaping a distinct, time-specific *weltanschauung,* or generalized set of beliefs and perceptions. The degree of generational consciousness varies, depending on the range and imprint of events binding its members together; hence one generation may be more inclined than another to think of itself as having a common identity and place in history. It is further assumed that the cultural definitions of reality forged by a generation in its formative years are carried, to a greater or lesser degree, throughout the lives of its members. For this reason, generational experience is so important a factor in our lives.

Research demonstrates, in fact, that Americans of all ages, when asked about important social influences on their lives, recall as especially important those memories referring to the time when they were in their teens or early twenties.[7] Memories such as these are lasting in the sense that they are subtle and deeply imprinted; they also encompass a collective attitude about a range of things bearing upon the core of human existence: family life, sex and gender roles, politics, lifestyle, people's hopes and dreams for the future, communal life, notions about the sacred. Mood and ethos as much as anything else are involved. Speaking of the "peer personality" of a generation, Strauss and Howe observe that "it can be safe or reckless, calm or aggressive, self-absorbed or outer-driven, generous or selfish, spiritual or secular, interested in culture or interested in politics. In short, it can think, feel, or do anything an individual might think, feel, or do. Between any two generations, as between any two neighbors, such personalities can mesh, clash, be attracted to or repelled by one another."[8]

Without pushing too far the similarities between generations and individuals, we can think of a generation as a carrier of culture in its broadest sense. It carries particular sensitivities and ways of seeing the world—collective attitudes, cognitive constructions, and feeling-states. The cultural milieu of a generation becomes the lens through which its members see the world and act upon it. The depression generation of the 1930s was sensitive to the perils of a precarious economy and practiced an ethic of frugality and prudence right into old age. The Vietnam generation of the 1960s and 1970s became, and still is, wary of war and ambivalent about rushing into any war unless it is one truly worth fighting. Young Americans who were eye-witnesses to the horrible destruction and loss of life in New York City and Washington, D.C., on September 11, 2001, will carry with them feelings of unease and insecurity brought on by acts of terrorism.

Of course, continuity across generations cannot be overlooked. A generation does not define the world simply through its experiences, but in the context of what it inherits from those who have preceded them. Each generation must in fact reorder what is passed down to it. Religious life—as with cultural values and orientation generally—is always a hybrid mix of the old and the new. Each generation arrives at its own definition of reality and ways of dealing responsibly with the world through some meaningful blending of past and present; it draws upon the cultural resources inherited from forebears in the face of all new challenge and opportunity. In her provocative book *The Transformation of American Religion,* historian Amanda Porterfield writes that "legacies established by earlier generations persist in the lives and ideas of new generations, underpinning and framing everything new, while at the same time, new generations of interpreters constantly create fresh images of the past."[9] Her comment underscores the complexity of human adaptation in every age. We may think of cultural continuity and change as abstractions, as if the two were realities fully juxtaposed with one another, but in actuality the two fuse into a singular process at the very point where every generation forges its own outlook and identity. Nothing could be more fundamentally human—indeed, more a part of every generation's experience—than this ongoing process of cultural reformation and restrategizing.

It seems reasonable to expect that distinct generational cultures emerge during times of widespread social and cultural change. In a stable period of history, generations come and go and are not marked by a huge cleavage between them; children live pretty much by the values and standards taught to them by their parents and in time pass those values and standards on to their own children. But in a period of social discontinuity or rapid technological and cultural change, people's life-worlds are likely to be reshaped—especially if, as has come to be the case for young people, they are differentially exposed to the sources of social innovation. This was the case in the 1960s and 1970s when there was much discussion about the generation gap, a period, surveys show, when discontinuity between generations in the United States did in fact reach a high level—higher than in more recent times.[10] Not surprisingly, historians and sociologists often speak of those decades as a watershed period in a nation's experience.

In varying degrees of self-consciousness, generations define themselves in relation to others before them by either rejecting or reaffirming one or another set of cultural values, beliefs, or aesthetics, and in so doing selectively interpreting who they are over against the past they imagine. In sociologist Robert Wuthnow's words, every generation carries on a "conversation with our past," each one defining itself "in comparison with previous generations by identifying with significant public events, such as a war, an assassination, or a protest movement, and letting these events become defining moments in their emerging conceptions of themselves. More important, people compare themselves with their parents, making assumptions about what their parents believed and defining themselves in relation to those assumptions."[11]

A good example of such a cultural marker and its defining power is popular music. The authors of this book remember fondly, and still enjoy hearing, Peter, Paul, and Mary sing with their passionate lyrics born out of the social protest of the 1960s, but ask gen Xers what they think of this trio and its music! Carry the experiment a step further: ask today's young teenagers, members of the so-called millennial generation, what they think about the music of generation X! Music is just an example, but a superb one, of how rapidly cultural moods and tastes change in contemporary society and how those moods and tastes symbolize perception of a particular time and circumstance. More is involved than simply music: it is a means of defining oneself over and against others, or the construction of an identity. "In an epoch of change, each person is dominated by his birth date," wrote sociologist Norman Ryder in a classic essay that appeared some years ago but aptly describes our situation today.[12]

Generations and Congregations

Why focus on the congregation? We do so for several reasons. First is the simple and obvious fact that *congregations constitute the dominant form of religious gathering in American society.* The *Yearbook of American and Canadian Churches* reports that there are approximately 350,000 congregations in the United States alone. Some 135 million members belong to them, with more than 65 million adults in attendance in an average week.[13] So prevalent is the congregational form of religious participation that faith traditions in which the congregation as we know it in the American experience is not the typical mode of religious involvement—Islam, Hinduism, or Buddhism, for example—have developed congregational forms upon immigrating to the United States. They often borrow patterns of gathering from the existing Christian or Jewish congregation—Sunday school and women's organizations, for example. Doing so demonstrates their legitimacy as a religious group. It is true that for all religions, a host of religious and spiritual practices take place outside of the congregation, in family gatherings, small informal groups, retreats, and private meditation; these practices may in fact have grown in number and popularity in recent decades. Nonetheless, congregational forms remain dominant, and if one's aim is to understand how generational culture is shaping religion in America, then one dare not ignore this primary form of religious gathering.

In addition to the sheer number of congregations is the character of each as a "thick gathering": *each one represents a thick mix of world views, values, symbols, meanings, and practices that participants bring to them.* Gender, ethnic, lifestyle, regional, and social class distinctions are among the most important that are reflected in a single congregation's gathering. The mix also includes generational difference as members of a cohort bring their experiences and expectations to the congregation. This diverse combination of perspectives is often cross-cutting and cross-pressuring, creating a complex set of popular undercurrents beneath the congregation's surface. As a result, what often appear to be similar religious forms—worship services, religious education programs, women and men's groups, coffee hours, potluck suppers, service, and outreach programs—differ greatly depending on the subgroup within a congregation or the particular congregation itself. This variety of religious forms is shaped as well by the particular congregation's culture, including its mix of member perspectives, history, size, location, and denominational heritage.

Because of the overlapping cultures that characterize a thick gathering, *a congregation becomes a staging ground for generational conflict and efforts to mobilize influence.* Social theorists, following the lead of Emile Durkheim, have observed that religion serves to establish and maintain boundaries of collective identity. Thus it is not surprising to find that religious symbols and styles are means by which a group, including a generational cohort, attempts to differentiate itself from another by means of a distinctive religious style. The difference often becomes a source of tension and conflict within a congregation. Consider worship and music as examples. Sharply contrasting preferences in worship style and music have led to what some call "worship wars" in many congregations, with a younger generation asking for contemporary liturgy and music while an older generation finds the newer forms spiritually unpalatable. The choice of liturgy and music is more than a preference, it is a symbolic expression of identity and of religious meaning implicit within that identity.

Who has the authority to make decisions about these things? Usually authority rests with the official leadership, drawn predominantly from the pre-boomer generation, while a growing number of new members are from the younger cohorts, boomers and Xers. Religious leaders often find themselves caught in the crossfire between opposing factions, with one wanting change, the other wanting to maintain the status quo; or clergy may not understand or appreciate the preference of a generation different from their own. One pre-boomer pastor spoke with considerable disdain about what he called the "happy-clappy" worship style of a neighboring congregation that was seeking to attract younger members. Boomer and Xer pastors are equally vocal about the "dull" and "stodgy" worship services of many mainline congregations.

Worship is hardly the only stage for intergenerational conflict. Theological, and especially moral, teachings from one's religious tradition also often set a line of demarcation between generations. Many young Americans, of course, have little if any relationship with a religious congregation because their views on moral issues or practice differ from what is regarded as normative. Correctly or not, they perceive a huge discrepancy between what the church believes and practices and the views they themselves hold. Intergenerational tensions within a congregation often erupt around issues of gender, lifestyle, and sexuality in particular. More than just issues over which people may differ, these issues are emotionally charged and take on great significance as symbolic markers. There are, for instance, few issues that divide Americans at present more than homosexuality.[14]

By appealing to particular teachings and practices, a generational cohort engages in an interpretive battle and seeks to buttress its own views while simultaneously discrediting other teachings and practices said to represent a religious tradition. Because a congregation is a voluntary institution, constituencies within them can easily define themselves and their interests over against others, thereby vying with one another in defining normative faith and behavioral styles. Within virtually all congregations, there is some degree of tension over who holds the authority to interpret, and thereby control, the heritage entrusted to it. Today, those tensions are particularly apparent for congregations whose constituencies are well-educated and feel empowered to act on their own behalf.

Such a battleground is not, however, simply a free-for-all, as if there were no normative boundaries to faith and morality. Generations may differ with one another in their beliefs and practices, but religiously they are more or less embedded within a tradition. The congregation is a crucial *bearer of tradition,* especially for Christians but also for Jews (for whom the family plays an important role). As a bearer of tradition, a congregation is charged with passing it on to its members, and it does so through various practices and institutional forms. Biblical tradition and denominational heritage set normative standards for the gathered community. Even the rapidly growing independent Christian congregations, less constrained by denominational ties, feel pressured to justify their practices and do so by looking to the early Christian community for models described in the Book of Acts. The vast and varied array of institutions and interpretations within Christianity, Judaism, and the other major religious traditions is evidence of the extent to which religious tradition, symbols, and meanings are contested and fractured in the modern world.

Intergenerational conflict, like most other types, within a congregation thus involves a conversation of sorts with a religious tradition. How far can a congregation go in changing its practices without losing or compromising distinctive religious claims? Can practices and beliefs be changed primarily to satisfy a new generation's preferences? Ardent advocates of tradition say no. They are likely to agree with G. K. Chesterton's comment that "tradition means giving votes to the most obscure of all classes—our ancestors. It . . . refuses to submit to the small and arrogant oligarchy of those who merely happen to be walking around."[15] But there are advocates of contemporary practice who sit lightly with inherited tradition (other than Scripture) and appeal to the religious and spiritual preferences of younger generations. Lyle Schaller, for example, argues for what he calls "made in America" models of the church fitting to those born since 1945 in contrast to inherited, European hierarchical models appealing to those born before that time.[16] Thus the very structure of the congregation is contested.

Between these two extremes are others who propose a more self-conscious mediating approach: adapting rather than scrapping traditional practice and institutional form to meet new demands and challenges, both generational and otherwise. Such a position takes tradition and the need for innovation seriously and aims at achieving a blend of past and present living traditions, sustained through reflexive conversation that keeps each in dialogue and tension with the other.[17] It is the position advanced in this volume.

Finally, as the discussion of tradition versus innovation implies, *congregational forms are not static and unchanging.* Although they often resist innovation, congregational leaders and their members must—if they are to survive—adapt to new challenges as the population and cultural context change. Religious adaptation is commonplace in the contemporary world, a major reason being the pace at which new generational cultures now evolve. A major task for any religious community today is thus to "bridge" worlds—that is, to understand the various life experiences and outlook of its followers, to negotiate with one another over competing interpretations, and to carry on a larger dialogue with historic tradition. Of course, a religious community is always engaged in a process of ongoing world building that cuts across all cultural divides. This is a process that often occurs without much awareness of it actually happening, much the same as with the cultural reordering that every generation engages in as mentioned earlier. Gradually, if not always very visibly, religious institutions reinvent themselves.

The power of a religious definition of reality lies in its inherent capacity to create an inclusive, persuasive universe of meaning, tapping deep sentiments and bonding people together. But in our view, this task of bridging should become a more self-conscious undertaking within a religious community; indeed, we regard it as essential under conditions of rapid social and cultural change. Rather than passive acceptance of, and accommodation to, diverging generational cultures, the religious community is challenged to exercise agency, defining and forging an inclusive world of meaning and practice that bridges those boundaries.

Plan of the Book

In the chapters that follow, we explore why attention to generation is so important for the study of congregations. Our observations are based upon research conducted in North Carolina and southern California in the mid-1990s, involving a large-scale survey with scores of questions, interviews with dozens of pastors and members of churches and synagogues, and ethnographic accounts of twenty congregations in the Research Triangle area of North Carolina as well as in southern California. The choice of the states was determined, of course, by where we as researchers live, but for our purpose the selection was not inappropriate. North Carolina being more traditionally religious and California a place of rapid social and cultural change, the two offered an excellent contrast in religious context for examining congregations and generations.

As we shall see, the dominant story we tell is one of generations and how they relate to the congregation. But we also observe variation in those patterns relating to setting. Our aim has not been to write a how-to manual for religious leaders concerned to minister to generations in their midst. The congregations we examine were not chosen as model or exemplary ones. Instead, they are, to a greater or lesser extent, the stories of ordinary congregations struggling to respond faithfully to their understanding of their mission or calling. They represent a range of possible responses. As such, our hope is that leaders and members of other congregations find these stories helpful as they struggle to be responsible in their own setting. We hope also that our reflection on generations and congregational responses to them proves of interest to students of American religion and will encourage them to delve further into these issues.

Chapter One explores the shaping influences on the three generations we examine (pre-boomers, boomers, and generation Xers). It looks as well at the nexus between religion and other social institutions, particularly education, family, and communication systems and technologies. We cannot understand the life space and experience of generations without some grasp of how all these major institutions, and relations among them, have been fundamentally restructured over the past seventy-five years. The cultural values and meanings, outlook, and ways of knowing that people bring to a congregation are shaped in great part by these societal transformations.

In Chapter Two, we examine current religious and spiritual trends, especially the social psychological typology of dwelling and seeking—two contrasting spiritual styles. To dwell is to live in a religious place, formed by its habits and traditional practices; to seek is to explore new vistas, to cultivate from within, and to be open to spiritual wisdom from various sources. Conditions of modern life such as religious pluralism, greater privatism, and detraditionalizing influences bear directly on our religious authority; the contemporary context for religion opens many uncertainties but also new and challenging opportunities for enriching faith and spiritual life. The younger generations in America especially are caught up in these shifts of religious mood and style.

Chapter Three presents a social and religious profile for the three generations. Here we look at generational identity and family experiences, as critical dimensions on which pre-boomers, boomers, and gen Xers must be carefully arrayed. Next we examine in some depth shifts in religious identification for members of each generation from the time they grew up to the present. The crucial role of generations in reshaping the American religious landscape over the past half century becomes apparent in this comparative analysis. We also document trends regarding belief in God, extent of religious individualism, and the churched and unchurched sectors for the three generations.

In Chapter Four, we focus on the congregation. We begin with a historical perspective making clear that congregational forms have not been static but have regularly undergone adaptation to change in the broader social milieu. We then turn to data from our telephone interview survey to consider how these generations view the congregation—which institutional characteristics they do or do not prefer and how, if at all, this varies with the two regions that we studied. The survey data also help us look in greater depth at a range of characteristics affecting congregational involvement for each generational cohort. Finally, we introduce the congregations that we studied, grouping them, for sake of analysis, into three types that we call the inherited model, the blended congregation, and the generation-specific congregation.

Chapters Five, Six, and Seven include profiles of three congregations in each chapter. In Chapter Five, we introduce three congregations that we believe fit the inherited model—that is, ones whose practices are primarily guided by their inheritance from the past, both their own and the broader traditions they represent. Even if they are diverse generationally, this diversity is not of great concern in how they order their life. Chapter Six presents profiles of three blended congregations, ones that do not neglect their inherited tradition but at the same time are considerably more attentive to generational diversity than is the inherited-model congregation.

They have self-consciously sought to adapt their life and practices to the generations in their midst. Finally, in Chapter Seven, we consider three congregations that we call generation-specific. They have made a conscious decision to tailor their programs and practices to the characteristic interests and needs of a specific generation, even though other generations may be present in the congregation. At the end of each of these chapters, we reflect briefly on some of the important themes and dynamics characteristic of the profiled congregations.

In an Epilogue, we offer brief concluding observations stemming from reflection on the preceding chapters. What are some of the primary conclusions that we draw from these earlier chapters? What are the strengths and liabilities of the three types of congregation? What might it mean for a congregation to live reflexively in a pluralistic society? We regard these as crucial questions not just for congregations themselves, but for all who want to understand the subtle transformations now under way in American religion.

In the main body of the book, we have tried to keep statistical tables and graphs to a minimum. We have, however, included in the Appendix a full report of the data from a survey on which many of our interpretations are based. Additionally, the Appendix includes a description of our data collection strategies and other methodological matters.

Chapter One

Generations as
Cultural Waves

The dictionary definition of *wave* includes, aside from a moving swell on a body of water, such notions as a "rapidly growing trend," a "spreading condition," a "mass movement." Socially speaking, a generation may be likened to a wave, coming one after another, each bearing cultural changes that reverberate throughout society—particularly in regard to values, beliefs, and social outlook. At times these changes are subtle and gradual, perhaps even imperceptible; other times they are much more broadly encompassing and so obvious that ordinary people can easily spot them. Just as one can stand by the ocean and observe the waves battering the shore, one can look out upon society and observe the generations and their distinct lifestyles. The terms "generation" and "change," in fact, easily become conflated. From a religious vantage point, people are quick to describe change in generational terms by commenting that young people "don't go to church as did their elders" or "aren't as religious as people once were."

Such was the case with a Southern Baptist pastor we interviewed in the Research Triangle area of North Carolina. A pastor of a conservative church in a section of the South now undergoing widespread social and cultural change, he had no difficulty spotting the generations (even if somewhat stereotypically). Asked about what separates the generations religiously, he pointed immediately to the huge cleavage between pre-boomers and boomers: "Our seniors were raised in church. Born and bred in church. Probably went to church all their life. Their parents were churchgoers. Basically, people [born] before the fifties were church-minded."

Commenting about those born after World War II, he observed: "The baby boomers were either raised in church or weren't raised in church. It just depended on where you were from regionally. I was raised in the South, which tends to be steeped more in Baptists anyway—we used to be known as the Bible Belt. You can't say that anymore really. But there is—you know I grew up with some kids whose parents went to church sometimes. So the kids were there sometimes. So I've got some friends, people I grew up with that were semi-raised in the church, but not totally."

About boomers in his own church, he said:

> They are transients here. Probably half and half. Half our members were raised in this area from birth, have lived here. The other half are transplants from other areas because of their jobs. They are functionally unchurched, because of the questions they ask—"Why do you do certain things?" . . . Most of them are well educated. You are looking at people who work in the technical field, in technological work with IBM, pharmaceutical companies, the power companies. So they are all technical-minded . . . they have some kind of technical background. They did not drop out of high school or just finish high school and go on. The wives are probably the same way. They are probably educated, although it would probably be more half and half; some of them stay-at-home mothers, but we probably have more working mothers than stay-home mothers.

And what about generation Xers? "Fired up. They are workers. The ones we do have are visible. You see them. You know they are there."

But in the same breath he adds that many in this generation are not present in the church. "They are what we call the 'CE people,'" he says, "your Christmas and Easter people." Asked about how his church relates to this latter constituency, he admits it has been somewhat a failure. "Well, right now probably our biggest flaw is with the generation X group. We just don't have much of a ministry for them."

This pastor's comments are insightful. Thinking of generations as successive movements, he can identify a stability and anchoring within the church for pre-boomers that does not exist for more recent generations. A taken-for-granted religious world that once held, and still does for many elders, seems to have fractured. Further, boomers and generation Xers are deeply divided, religiously and culturally. The locals differ from those having moved into the community from elsewhere, especially in education and lifestyle. Some women stay at home raising children; others pursue professional careers. Whether one is churched or unchurched is readily apparent in the wider culture; even *within* the church some are, as the pastor says, "functionally unchurched." That is, they may participate but they do not know much about the church—its history and tradition, doctrines, and moral teachings. Often they lack grounding in a religious heritage and a shared faith. Compared to older generations, they appear to drift and are less certain of what they believe.

Yet we should be careful not to assume a simple pattern of religious decline across the generations. There are fewer Xers than boomers active in his church, but those who are involved are more involved—more "fired up," as the pastor says. Actually, the situation is more complex than what meets the eye: there is an overall pattern of declining involvement in religious institutions for the three generations, but also a shift toward a more conservative style of religious belief and commitment for the youngest generation. As in every circumstance, religion is multidimensional in expression and cannot be reduced to a single trend or indicator, and certainly not to a single trend or indicator of institutional religious loyalty. We risk oversimplification of religion and generational change if we fail to recognize this fundamental point.

Moreover, religious patterns for generations are one thing within a particular congregation, and something quite different for society as a whole. Some congregations are far more exposed to the larger social trends than others, just as waves in the ocean vary in height and force depending upon the shores on which they splash. All of these are important caveats to keep in mind in this chapter as we probe the social and cultural changes or the generational waves now reshaping American religious life.

Shaping Influences

Major events in society during an individual's adolescent and early adult years shape his or her outlook, in subtle and enduring ways. More than just a definition of social reality, a person's values, sensitivities, and emotions are fundamentally affected by such experiences. The term *consciousness* captures a broad range of individual human processes—cognitive, evaluative, emotional—formed by the social environment. What happens during the youthful years is thus significant not just in forming how one sees the world but in solidifying social identity. This being the case, we must ask the straightforward but crucial question, What were the major social events and crises that played a decisive role in forging a generational consciousness among pre-boomers, boomers, and generation Xers?

For pre-boomers, the Great Depression looms large in memory. Growing up during the 1930s and early 1940s, they have vivid memories of living under conditions of scarcity. Even those not yet born at the time grew up in a world that, until World War II, was characterized by economic stringency, and they carried the imprint of their parents' views. For Americans at the time, it was a world of frugality; of living close to one's means; and, perhaps most important of all, of purchasing only what one could afford to buy. Installment purchasing began in the 1930s, but as a practice it was limited to a relatively small proportion of the middle class. Economically, it was production, not consumption, that defined how the world operated; capitalism was based on a moral system of reward rooted in an older Protestant culture that held together values of hard work, self-denial, and belief in God. Indeed, as the great sociologist Max Weber so eloquently argued, the Protestant work ethic was closely bound up with a notion of divine approval and salvation. Among pre-boomers, even today one hears a good deal of talk about hard work and its rewards.

For members both of the GI generation and the silent generation, no event would have a greater impact than World War II. The war exposed them to new political dangers on the world stage and drew them out of narrow isolationism. But most important, it pulled these people into an all-encompassing cultural drama of us versus them, of democracy pitted against the threat of totalitarian regimes aspiring to conquer the world. The war solidified notions of God, country, and the American way of life, creating an ideology that dominated the late 1940s and the 1950s. Triumph over evil empires reinforced national self-confidence and pride. When Tom Brokaw speaks of the "greatest generation" (as he did in 1998), it is these pre-boomers he has in mind for whom sacrifice for one's country in World War II is crucial to their identity, and for whom duty to God, democracy, and family took on an overarching symbolic significance.

Indeed, this matrix of values fundamentally altered the nation's social institutions—economic, political, familial, and religious. American life held together around a renewed sense of unity and purpose. Cold-war ideology and return to normalcy after the war led members of these generations to see themselves as "builders," those responsible for creating the new economy, strong families, and loyalty to God, country, and apple pie.

Boomers, in contrast, grew up after the war in a more expansive economic era. The period immediately following World War II witnessed unparalleled growth of the middle classes and a level of affluence never known before by so many people. People were moving to the suburbs and buying new homes, acts both closely linked with family symbolism. People were starting their lives over, going back to school and moving into better jobs, creating larger families. For many it was the best of times. The American Dream was alive and well—at least in the early years for boomers.

It was also a new world of television, of mass marketing and advertising, and, most significant of all, of increased consumption. Installment buying was more common than ever and was soon surpassed by a quicker, more efficient means of making financial transactions: the credit card. This little card was the perfect answer to a growing discontent, a reason to buy more and to trade in the old for something new and better. Yet the middle-class assumption that the material conditions of life could continue to improve, that the present was less desirable than the future, was confounded for this generation by the trauma of national and world events and resulting loss of confidence in social institutions. Events of the 1960s and early 1970s—political assassinations, civil rights, the Vietnam War, the environmental movement, and a gender revolution—all profoundly shaped a sense of social solidarity and urgency for creating a better world. For many young Americans, idealism and optimism were thwarted by disillusionment that such a world was indeed possible; an era of social protest and activism faded, and many of this generation turned inward in the hope of finding a more authentic self and a deeper spiritual life.

Generation Xers have grown up in a world inherited from the boomers, yet they have their own distinctive experiences. Trends toward greater consumption, environmental consciousness, and gender role changes are largely taken for granted; indeed, most of them can hardly imagine a world not shaped by these influences. They have also inherited a high level of distrust in public institutions, religious as well as political. Gen Xers are especially suspicious of religious leaders, having grown up in an age of televangelist scandal and publicity about the sexual abuse by priests. Though bound together less by dramatic social events in their formative history, those born from the mid-1960s through the early 1980s can lay claim to a particular set of experiences. They have known more family disruption than the two previous generations. They have watched more television than any generation in history, leading them to be, as is sometimes said, "entertainment-conscious." Technology looms large in their experience; they grew up with computers and are more online and cyberspace-savvy than their predecessors. More often than not, they are known for who they are not rather than for who they are: they are not boomers.

More so probably than any other generation, they recognize their fate to be inextricably linked to technology; they know that it can bring about quick and at times detrimental consequences for the workplace—and even displace them. Psychologically, they suffer from following so large and highly touted a generation as the baby boomers. They grew up knowing that many who might have been born into their generation were aborted. Generation X writer Janet Bernardi describes the depth of feelings within her generation about how it is perceived in relation to the earlier generation:

> My generation has been called various things by our elders, not many of them positive. We have been described as lazy, useless, ill educated, and shallow. We are considered a Peter Pan generation, unwilling to grow up, slow to start careers and launch families. We are defined in contrasts to the generation that immediately preceded us—and that likes us least—the Baby Boomers. In their eyes they are the world's boom and we its bust. Thus we are called the "Baby Busters." We have also been called "Generation X" because it was thought that we stand for nothing and believe in nothing.[1]

To a considerable extent, generation X identity is shaped by strong feelings about those older than themselves. Xers understand themselves in an open-ended and evolving manner but are acutely aware of their ambiguous relationship with a larger, more celebrated, generation that helped to shape the world they inherited.

Social Meaning of Age

As pointed out in the Introduction, the aging process is a complex phenomenon. Aging is of course a human universal, yet how we age and the meaning we attach to each phase of aging vary enormously across time and cultures. Were it not so, we would have little difficulty predicting religious trends: a woman twenty-five years old will embrace religious and cultural features pretty much as her fifty-year-old mother did by the time she reaches her mother's age. Life would recreate itself through a process of cultural duplication. But obviously, such is not the case in a rapidly changing society. The cultural meaning of age varies in keeping with changing social and cultural circumstances. To understand this better, we must consider the social contexts that shape people's identity as youths, and how those experiences can differ greatly from one generation to another. Particularly with boomers and gen Xers, there is a huge break in their identity formation as youths when contrasted with pre-boomers.

Consider this paradox: young people today grow up faster, but also slower, than did their grandparents. They grow up faster in the sense that the onset of puberty now occurs earlier. Improvements in health care and nutrition are generally credited with bringing about earlier sexual maturity. But young people also grow up slower, remaining dependent much longer on parents now than was true in the past. This is obvious financially in noting how many young people return to live with their parents after a period of having left home—the so-called boomerang effect. This return movement came about not as a matter of choice in most instances, but rather as a result of major structural changes in our society forcing young people to adapt to them. Changing job opportunities and upgrading of professions, thereby requiring a high level of education, have greatly altered life circumstances for younger generations. What we have, in effect, is what sociologists James E. Cote and Anton L. Allahar describe as "an enforced and prolonged dependency,"[2] unlike anything experienced by previous generations.

This greater dependency is rooted historically in the industrial era, but it has manifested more recently in the transition from an industrial to a postindustrial economy. From the beginning, industrialization devalued the labor of the young; children could no longer be incorporated into the workforce as easily as they had been in an earlier time within an agricultural world. With the shift to a postindustrial economy, dependency was further intensified. Expectations on the part of young people were raised in the hope of finding a position within the rapidly expanding service and information sectors, but often to a far greater extent than could be met. That there would be discrepancies was virtually assured.

Particularly in the past several decades, within high-technology industries (notably computer programming and telecommunications), the pace of change, owing to a premium being placed upon product innovation combined with intense competition and frequent corporate takeovers, has resulted in considerable workplace uncertainty. Many boomers in their prime young adult years experienced downsizing, or loss of a job as a corporation or business adjusted to a recessionary economy. Many generation Xers have known uncertainty in jobs throughout much of their adult lives, relying on what they dubbed "McJobs," or a low-paying, dead-end type of employment. Often their aspirations go unmet, as they are unable to get sufficient education or, even if they have a good education, face the reality of "education inflation," the ever-rising level of credentials deemed necessary for a decent job. Either way, they fail to achieve the level of independence and security they would like in early adulthood.

Not surprisingly, under social conditions as these a definition of *youth* emerged in the latter half of the twentieth century that marked off a new and distinct phase of life. A more clearly defined conception of youth reinforced the possibility that life experiences for people of comparable age across generations would differ. As developmental psychologists say, youth was defined as a "liminal phase" characterized by "role diffuseness" as opposed to "role specificity," thus giving rise to youth cultures known for their freedom and expressiveness. This possibility of an extended, transitional period of one's life is bound up with other, far-reaching social changes in postindustrial society. Prolonged economic dependence combined with the advent of the birth-control pill encouraged postponement of committed relationship and marriage, which had the effect of further delaying the social responsibilities of adulthood. Nowhere is this more apparent than in religious participation. Involvement within a congregation tends to increase once people are married, have children, and are settled into the routine of family life. But postponement of marriage on average by six to seven years—as occurred over the span of our three generations—has produced some noticeable effects on the congregation: fewer young people present, and fewer married couples without children as well.

Add to these economic and demographic factors the cultural changes of the past half century, and we begin to grasp even better the impact upon religious and civic organizations. Involvement in many of the older, more established organizations—both religious and otherwise—has declined.[3] Value shifts stemming from the 1960s and 1970s having to do with gender and lifestyle, attitude toward war and government, and rebellion against bourgeois conventionality all helped to solidify a view of youth as a phase of life open to pursuit of individual options, and largely freed from traditional role obligations. Youth as a distinct period of the life cycle became more fully established, and its duration was also greatly extended. This is true for both boomers and generation Xers, but especially for the latter generation, brought up with less exposure to religious institutions than was true for either of the preceding ones. As customs and social expectations have changed, so has people's familiarity with congregational life. As one person in California told us, "My parents went to church out of habit; you just did it. But my generation, well, we have to find our way into it if we are going to do it."

Religion and Education

Much has changed with the nation's social institutions and with the links among them over the span of three generations. With rapid technological innovation and growing global connection, no institution is left untouched. Indeed, so encompassing are these shifts that a best-selling book published in 1995 by Hedrick Smith was entitled simply *Rethinking America,* his point being that we must think anew about the links among schools, business, government, and local communities.[4] Old modes of thinking and getting things done must be replaced by newer ones. Smith did not examine religious congregations, but obviously they—like other voluntary organizations—are caught up in the restructuring of society. Here we look at religion and education and how, as inevitably happens, a shift in one institutional sector within society leads to new ways of organizing social experience within another.

To begin with, we pick up on a theme from the previous section. Enforced and prolonged dependency for young people is linked to expansion of higher education and normative pressure created by credentialism and upgrading of professional qualifications. Gen Xers feel that for opening the door to a job a college education is a credential equivalent to a high school education for pre-boomers (or possibly less so). Added to anxiety surrounding economic disenfranchisement and loss of status for youths are other psychological maladies, among them a higher-than-average level of depression and suicide rate.[5] At stake for many young people is the American Dream itself, the vision that has long inspired generations in this country to believe that hard work leads to success and happiness. Born out of an earlier Protestant theology that took root in a plentiful and seemingly ever-resourceful American environment, that vision in its now largely secular version is blurred for many who cannot imagine that they will have materially what their parents had.

In no small part, the vision that inspired so much hope in the past is eroded by an expanding gap between having things, or what people deem necessary to meet their "needs" in a consumption-oriented society, and finding satisfaction and happiness in their lives as ordinarily experienced. Caught up in this gap, many young adults express their doubts about living out the American Dream. Of all the people we talked to, an older woman in a Baptist church in North Carolina best captured the current dilemma:

> Now, I would say the message given to society is more complicated, that it is necessary to have things to make you happy. The American Dream—it's a fallacy. It's like going to the beach and building a sand castle and it's real pretty, but you know the water is going to come and going to wash it away, so the American Dream is like a sand castle. . . . By the same token, that's what we live by. That's our Bible. I think they [generation Xers] are looking for a piece of the American Dream. I think we in the Christian community have to rethink that, because we are living it. My generation is living it. The younger generation is living it. Generation X is living it. And then we have the children that are being born now and teenagers are liv-

ing it. It is getting things and things that [has] become the symbol of happiness. And everybody can't afford the American Dream as it stands now.

As she makes clear, religion is deeply implicated in this cultural myth of success and happiness. But the American Dream is as fragile as a sand castle and, unfortunately, religious communities often fail to rethink it. Worse still, religious communities are themselves so enmeshed in the dream—living it—that they lose the power of a critical theological perspective upon it. So there is, as she says, a fallacy, a disjunction between "what we live by" and religious affirmation about what is truly important in life. Religion is hardly alone, of course, since other major social institutions—education, the media, and the advertising industries—are all caught up in a spiraling pattern of increased consumption, creating (paradoxically) considerable distress and misguided hope for many Americans. The religious community has a particular responsibility in society, however, considering that its task is to address the fiction by which we live and to bring meaningful perspective to the human situation.

In other ways, too, the changing connection between education and religion is very important. The expansion of higher education over the past half century was greater than for any previous period in American history. This meant a huge increase in the number of young Americans attending college or university, especially in the proportion attending large public institutions, which have an intellectual agenda quite different from that of small, religiously affiliated colleges. Science and technology are at the forefront of these institutions, not advancement of religious conviction and principles. To the extent religion finds a place in the curriculum of such an institution, it is best described as "religious studies," not as normative discourse devoted to theology, ethics, or the Bible.

Consequently, students in the post–World War II era have had an increased opportunity to learn about the great world religions and new religious and metaphysical movements, as well as enjoy exposure to critical Biblical scholarship and to feminist, gay and lesbian, and minority approaches to religious interpretation. This has added to knowledge about religion (particularly about its humanly constructed and contested interpretations) but not necessarily to enhanced faith or trust in a religious institution. Of course, the proportion of young people obtaining a college or university education has increased, producing a large demographic base for a growing cleavage in outlook, values, and belief between college graduates and those who are less educated. This growing gap cuts across denominations, and across congregations within a denomination, posing a new challenge for meaningful and unifying religious interpretations.

The sheer size of the contemporary educational institution bears consequences. A large number of youths living in a dense enclave around a university creates influential peer cultures. For a growing number of Americans, coming of age involves life in a setting with strong pressure from one's own age cohort, and thus the added reinforcement that comes from bonding among peers. Much more than a classroom experience, education for millions of young Americans is immersion into a subculture with its own distinct values, norms, and lifestyles. That so many people under the age of fifty-five say they believe in reincarnation today, for example, reflects to a considerable extent the diffusion of Eastern religious themes into youth cultures built up around educational centers in the period since the 1960s. Likewise, Wicca, paganism, and New Age philosophy all flourish in these surroundings. Psychologically, the impact is substantial, perhaps best grasped with Erik Erikson's notion of a "psychosocial moratorium" in mind.

Accordingly, the argument is that youth culture creates the resources that allow postponement in dealing with fundamental questions about faith and identity; or an extended period in which to explore religious ideas, beliefs, and practices without feeling undue pressure to arrive at closure on such matters. In Erikson's terms, the structural basis for an "identity diffusion" is virtually assured by the youth cultures formed around an educational institution, especially for white, middle-class Euro-Americans. Racial and ethnic minorities differ in having a stronger identity-support system, and of course those with a less privileged background generally cannot afford the luxury of so extensive a period of self-exploration. Neither do they have the resources others have for travel and for therapy and counseling that many people in today's psychologically oriented culture associate with ego development. The links between educational opportunity, social class, and the notion of a psychological moratorium are thus fairly obvious.

Moreover, education emerged in the latter half of the twentieth century as a significant basis of religious and cultural differences: those better educated and exposed to symbolic and metaphorical interpretations of religion were more likely to abandon literal interpretation of text and doctrine that had been passed down to them and to seek psychological means of adjustment. The impact of education in an age of science and information technology reaches deep, reshaping people's worldviews and sensitivities. Some scholars suggest that it has given rise to a new social class, the so-called knowledge class, for whom the symbolic and humanly constructed aspects of religious systems are more generally recognized and accepted.[6] Members of this class, if they articulate such matters, tend to give attention to an inner self and to spiritual concerns of a deeply personal sort. Over against those in the knowledge class are the more conventional members of the working and middle classes, for whom traditional religious beliefs, practices, and institutional involvement are readily embraced and defended on the grounds of a transcendent authority.

These two poles of organizing religious life—the inner and the outer, or the immanent and the transcendent—need not be opposed to one another in religious life, but in popular religious and spiritual culture they often are viewed that way. Among members of the post–World War II generations, and for a considerable number of older Americans, the basis of religious authority is very much contested: an inner self and sense of the sacred, informed by intuition and psychology, versus an outer, transcendent God as affirmed by traditional biblical faith. Though hardly a new distinction theologically, it has been reinforced by the social and cultural changes of our time and takes on considerable significance; despite much rhetoric about its deepest meanings, there is often confusion.

However understood, what is important is that the division reaches deep within American religious consciousness at the beginning of the twenty-first century. The polarization of religion into liberal-progressive and conservative-orthodox camps, as we have come to describe it, resulting in "cultural wars," rests largely on this dispute over religious authority.[7] Does one "know" God as mediated through inherited scripture and creeds in a communal setting? Or is the divine known primarily through personal experience, biography, and self-awareness? We examine these questions in the next chapter; here it is important only to point out that this rupture along educational lines is deeply entrenched. It is a divide accentuated by developments related to the expansion of higher education, namely, the rise and widespread appeal of popular psychology and trends toward a therapeutic culture generally. Without some appreciation for the full expanse of these developments, we cannot grasp the breadth or the depth of generational change in our time.

Religion and Family

As everyone knows, religion and family are basic institutions, integrally linked in any society. Religious symbols and blessings bring legitimacy to marriage and offer support for families; family constitutes the basic unit of society where religious teachings and values are practiced and therefore transmitted from one generation to the next. As the primary nurturing institution for the young, the family has a role in inculcating moral and religious values that is obviously crucial. People may leave behind the faith communities in which they were raised, but they carry with them throughout life much that they have learned about God, love, trust, responsibility, and giving to others from those early years. Here is where the generational bond is formed and continuity of cultural heritage is institutionalized. Here is where fundamental social identity—including religious identity—is shaped and sustained.

But the well-being of the family is itself an important issue today. Families are undergoing enormous change, as is evident in the high level of divorce and the rise of many single-parent and blended families. Add to this the proportion of people choosing not to marry, or to marry and not have children, as well as gay and lesbian unions, and the fact that we live in a world with many acceptable types of intimate relationship and family arrangement becomes ever more apparent. In fact, the growth in the number of people living in a family arrangement outside of the two-parent nuclear family over the time span of our three generations is nothing short of astounding. In 1970, 40 percent of Americans lived in a nuclear family with children present under the age of eighteen. By 1990, the percentage had fallen to barely one-fourth of all families. The implication is simple: family disruption is much more common for children and young people now, and the experience of moving in and out of a family or some type of family arrangement is much more frequent today. As sociologists Barry A. Kosmin and Seymour P. Lachman write, "There are more transitions as people form, dissolve, and re-form households and families"[8] than was true for earlier generations. Many young Americans have grown up not knowing stable family ties and without the emotional nurturing that only can come from such ties. It was during their growing up that the term *dysfunctional family* entered into public discourse and serious worries surfaced about family values. Nor is it surprising that in much gen X music today there is a discernible "longing for belonging" mixed with themes that are cynical, irreverent, and at times nihilistic.

Implications for religion, or what is sometimes called the "the religion and family connection,"[9] are considerable. At the most fundamental level, religious socialization for children is severely weakened under conditions of family disintegration. Children particularly suffer from lack of moral and religious role models. Many boomers and gen Xers have grown up without a firm grounding in a religious tradition and therefore display a high level of illiteracy with regard to the Bible, doctrinal heritage, and religious ritual. Fundamental religious identity (Catholic, Lutheran, Presbyterian, and the like) is often in name only; it may hold some meaning as a "religious preference" but not be deeply embedded religiously. One recent study of young Catholics in the United States describes them as having a "weak," "hollowed out," and "vague" sense of Catholic identity,[10] terms that could easily be applied to young non-Catholic religious constituencies as well.

Religious boundaries are already blurred in contemporary society as a result of religious pluralism and other modernizing trends, and the current family situation further intensifies the situation— particularly the problem of how faith traditions are transmitted from one generation to the next. What we have in many instances is a great deal of confusion, shallow commitment, and uncertainty about the meaning of inherited faith and identity. As philosopher Alasdair MacIntyre points out, deprive children of stories arising out of religious tradition and you leave them "unscripted," known by their "anxious stutters."[11]

Research demonstrates that the level of religious participation is relatively low for singles, the divorced and separated, and so-called nonfamily households. Traditional religious teachings are closely associated with family life and symbols, so much so that in many churches, synagogues, and temples those living in an unconventional family or arrangement frequently are unwelcome or feel out of place. This does not mean, of course, that they have less personal faith or fewer spiritual concerns. Survey evidence suggests that such populations, like Americans generally, hold fairly well-defined beliefs about God or the sacred as part of their privately religious lives. But it does mean that ties to a religious community are often rather fragile. This can have double consequences for the individual. On the one hand, it adds to the loss of community that so many gen Xers feel, or what one pastor of a church in California describes as an "unmet relational need." On the other hand, because of lack of strong and meaningful contact, feelings of distrust and skepticism about the religious community are easily perpetuated. Family and religion are so deeply and subtly connected as institutions, emotionally and cognitively, that it is virtually impossible to sort out the overlap between them.

The mixed-faith marriage marks another important change as well. Although there have always been such marriages, normative expectations shifted significantly during the past half century. Normative pressures were stronger in the past for maintaining religious homogeneity, even if that meant one marriage partner should switch to the faith of the other, or that the couple should adopt a new faith altogether. Especially if there were children, a family was expected to have a common faith. Today, of course, the situation is different. Individual choice in religion is highly valued, and mixed-faith couples are much more likely to respect both faith traditions and want to bring up their children with knowledge about, and exposure to, those traditions.

Beginning with the boomers, there is considerable respect for the autonomy of all members of a family in matters concerning belief and practice. More than a decade ago, one study on the boomer generation found that when asked about the importance of attending church or synagogue as a family, 55 percent of respondents said it was important to do so as a family unit, and 45 percent said family members should make the choice individually.[12] A "shared religious" family is still a majority ideal, but not by much. In the years since the study, the mixed-faith marriage has become even more accepted, and increasingly we see much attention directed toward planning for such weddings and finding ways to respond creatively to religious diversity within the family. As one fifty-eight-year-old woman said while being interviewed for this project, pointing to her son's wedding picture in her living room, "My son, being Catholic, married a Methodist girl . . . in her church. And we had her minister marry them and our priest [celebrate], I guess they call it. I think that's wonderful, and I don't think that happened back in the fifties at all." Marriage and celebration of that sort was certainly rarer then; to state it differently, what was then extraordinary has now become ordinary. When this happens, as is the case in so many instances of religious and cultural change, a congregation must adapt and mold new styles of family rituals.

Generations and Communication Technology

Much of religious change historically has been closely linked to the emergence of new forms of communication. We cannot imagine the Reformation without the printing press; as historian Leonard I. Sweet points out, the "priesthood of believers" meant a "priesthood of readers."[13] One can enumerate a long list of consequences for religion stemming from the print industry; surely none is more important than fostering individualism and democratization, with all that this has meant for authority, interpretation, and participation within a religious community. After print came the telegraph, radio, film, television, and most recently the Internet. In fact, within the time span of our three generations, an enormously significant shift has occurred in the predominant form of communication from print to image, or from book culture to electronic culture.

We are still very much in the midst of this transition and yet to grasp fully what it may mean for religious traditions (especially for organized religion). Certainly, many of the historic changes have been for the better, and we should proceed cautiously in our judgment. With new technologies often comes worry initially that a social institution may be adversely affected, but in time the impact may be less severe than expected and the consequences mixed— some positive, some negative. One suspects that the same is the case for a congregation adjusting to changes in communication forms now under way. People are more adaptable than religious leaders often recognize.

We began this chapter with the metaphor of the cultural wave, conceptualizing society as a series of new, but overlapping, realms of experience. Nowhere is this more the case than with the impact on each generation of media and communication technology. Boomers were the first to grow up on television, and thus to be exposed so extensively to an image culture. The impact was not just quantitative but qualitative. Television brought the cataclysmic events of the sixties and seventies instantaneously into the living room, in all their horror and messiness. Likewise, these people were the first to be targeted as an identifiable market from the time they were children with distinct needs and wants, the first to be brought up so thoroughly on consumption as a way of life. Almost from the beginning of life, for them image superseded word in shaping a distinct social identity, separating that generation from the pre-boomers, who were far more oriented to print culture and the radio.

Later, gen Xers grew up with computers, video games, cable television, MTV, and cyberspace, which made for a much more encompassing and interactive set of visual experiences. Images began to flow not just one way to the receiver but omnipresently in the world of both the sender and the receiver, involving simulation of reality and not-quite-real communication, or "virtual reality"—all contributing to what one commentator calls an "image-heavy generation."[14] Increased interactivity also means greater subjective involvement and increased choice of worlds of meaning.

What does this all have to do with religion? Much has been written about media as epistemology, or the fact that any definition of truth—including religious reality—is shaped, at least in part, by the character of the form of communication. In a print culture, for example, pulpit oratory and theological debate flourish, as was certainly the case for American Protestantism in the nineteenth century. As a religion of the book, Protestantism resonated with the times in no small part because of a historical synthesis with Enlightenment rationality, that is, correspondence between divine and human reason. There was at that time, as Neil Postman describes, a "typographic mind,"[15] one that was imprinted by the written word and the oratory based upon it, and oriented to coherent arrangement of ideas, beliefs, and practices that sought justification in their clarity and forcefulness. Rational order and linear thinking were hallmarks of the typographic mind, and important as a foundation for congregational worship as a sequential or linear set of practices and experiences. It produced a mind-set expressed well by one pre-boomer we interviewed as he described what, practically speaking, goes on in his mainline Protestant church: "People want to go in there, get their hymns, the Lord's Prayer, Scripture, and get the sermon, give their offering, get the benediction, drink coffee, and go home." Thus worship as an experience, both for individuals and congregations, is highly structured and predictable.

Once electronic culture is superimposed upon print culture, obviously we have a much more multitextured religious context, responsive to differing modes of knowing. "Seeing is believing" and "feeling is believing"; both adages take on the status of an epistemological axiom, along with "reading is believing" and "hearing is believing." Compared with print communication, the visual relates more to affect and evokes understanding of religious and spiritual life as a process. Because feelings are deeply involved, the body is engaged as an intimate and integral part of the total response.

Electronic culture also marks a shift from rhetorical logic to what is termed "logic of consciousness."[16] Visual logic dominates the latter, that is, reliance upon the image as creatively connected to narration and music for the purpose of enhancing imagination. This involves a strong sense of movement and simultaneity of experience, neither of which is bounded by the linear logic of typography. Because of the affinities between this mode of knowing and mysticism, it is not surprising that so many young Americans talk about spirituality in terms of their own experience and often move rather easily across vistas of time and place, combining insights from a variety of sources. Religious discourse becomes multilayered as people speak in, around, through, and against various vocabularies all loaded with meaning. By virtue of exposure to various epistemologies, each generation brings a particular mind-set to the worship setting and responds quite differently to congregational symbols and activities.

A congregation that blends generations is thus one in which religious language and symbols are understood from quite differing angles of vision. It is a "thick gathering," if for no other reason because sermon and ritual take on a variety of meanings depending on the cultural frame brought to them. Truth seems to be less objectively grounded and more subjective, defined more in its personal

meaning. This greater emphasis on subjectivity can open up the possibility of an expansive spiritual consciousness, and also of a popular and negotiated religious language that incorporates differing
angles of vision, slants, or experiences.

But we should not assume that this comes easily. Such negotiation can be a source of tension within a congregation, even among
young traditional believers themselves. Ambiguity in trying to rec-
oncile differing modes of knowing are not at all uncommon, even
in a traditional religious setting. This was well articulated by a twenty-
five-year-old fundamentalist Christian we interviewed in North Carolina. When asked about the approaches to truth associated with his
generation, he offered a carefully guarded response:

> We really distrust truth, the systematic study of theology and God's
> Word. We feel like it is going to be heartless and fake. We very
> much have an aversion to rebuke and exhortation and feel very un-
> comfortable doing that with each other or having that done to us.
> We are very worshipful in the sense we appreciate worshipful expe-
> riences like singing, our music is very expressive, and it focuses a
> lot on the experiences of God. I think that's a positive thing and in
> my opinion it becomes negative when we become worshipers in
> spirit but not in truth and we start to see the experience as primary
> and the truth of what's being said as optional.

Finding the balance between experience and proclaimed truth
is what baffles many people today. It is a balance obviously not limited to his generation, or necessarily to all religions, but at present
a source of tension and negotiation in many congregations, be they
Jewish, Christian, or whatever. Sociologist Peter Berger once wrote
of the "heretical imperative,"[17] or the situation we face in the contemporary world of sorting out religious truth claims and the epistemologies on which they are made. In a world of rapid change in
communication technology, and of increased awareness that we
live with and rely upon multiple modes of knowing in everyday life,
it seems reasonable to assume we can expect such tension for the
foreseeable future.

As we have seen, many cultural and religious changes in American life are bound up with how the generations relate to a congregation. Each generation bears the distinct imprint of a huge set of
influences shaping its outlook, sensitivity, and institutional style. To

speak of a generation as a carrier of culture is to use shorthand for describing myriad influences, and as a means of sensitizing us to the approaches people take in relating to God or the sacred—without passing judgment on those approaches. To speak in this way is not at all to distract from the congregation but rather to acknowledge that it is, biblically speaking, a treasure in an earthen vessel. Generation is but one aspect of the humanness, or the earthen vessel. With this awareness of the human side of religion in better focus, we now turn to the religious and spiritual themes themselves that have surfaced within congregations in recent times.

Chapter Two

Dwellers, Seekers, and Hybrid Souls

Religious and Spiritual Change

When asked to describe a class for young married couples in his church, a Presbyterian pastor in Los Angeles said that "there are about fifty people or so, who are kinda core members of the group who are committed to the life of the church. They're very active in the church. Then we have a group of anywhere from eighty to one hundred people that come sporadically. They're sort of seekers. They are wrestling with life. They are trying to find the meaning of their work life and their relationships and things like that."

He is hardly alone in pointing to a boundary that can be observed in many a religious gathering, essentially that of regular participants versus spiritual seekers. It is a better distinction than active versus inactive members, or even believers versus nonbelievers, if for no other reason because it places a positive valence upon both types of individual. Committed members are loyal supporters of the church (Presbyterians in this instance) who find its established beliefs and practices meaningful. Spiritual seekers are looking to find meaning in life but are less sure about the beliefs and practices. The distinction does not rest upon a firm boundary since believers have their moments of seeking, and seekers hold to some beliefs; many people might be described as hybrid souls, part participants, part seekers.

Commenting upon this situation, sociologist Robert Wuthnow distinguishes between "dwellers" and "seekers."[1] Dwellers live in a stable place and feel secure within its territory; for them the sacred is fixed, and spirituality is cultivated through habitual practice within the familiar world of a particular tradition. Not that they are untouched by social change, but they are relatively well anchored amid the flux. By contrast, seekers explore new vistas and negotiate among alternative, and at times confusing, systems of belief and practice; for them, the sacred is fluid and portable, and spirituality is likened unto a process or state of becoming. The language of the journey fits their experience.

Wuthnow observes that we are witnessing at present a considerable shift "from dwelling to seeking." Like the Los Angeles pastor, he points to a state of spiritual flux and changing ways in which people view their relation to religious symbol, narrative, and practice. A questing mood is in vogue, inside and outside established religious institutions. All of this is happening at a time of other significant religious changes as well. Older religious and cultural markers, such as those distinguishing among the historic Protestant denominations and faith communities, are blurred and less important than they once were; yet other types of distinction, many experiential in character, now take on significance. There is considerable ferment at the grassroots level. In this rather fluid, open-ended context, people are restructuring their spiritual lives and realigning their institutional commitments. In this chapter, we look further at this shift in mood, building upon what was already said in the previous chapter about social-structural change reshaping our institutions. Our focus is upon the three generations and how they relate to, and embody, these specific religious and spiritual themes.

Religious Pluralism

Any mapping of religious change over the span of time covered for our three generations must deal with religious pluralism. Pre-boomers grew up in a time when Protestantism held a cultural hegemony that no longer exists. More is involved than simply the number and type of religious communities. By cultural hegemony we have in mind not just a widely accepted set of beliefs and practices but power—social, economic, political, and, perhaps most important, cultural. This further suggests a web of interlocking connections, be they based upon marriage, ethnicity, friendship, membership in a voluntary organization, or structure of community leadership. Personal as well as institutional networks figure prominently in exercising and maintaining power. In a more subtle sense, power implies the authority to define and enforce values and norms; to shape notions of propriety, taste, preference, and style; and to legitimate a way of life. So-called mainline Protestantism enjoyed an influence that was outwardly visible and that reached deeply into the experience and life space of Americans, showing up, as historian Dorothy C. Bass says, "in places like Henry Luce's *Time/Life* empire, in leading educational institutions governed by quotas and certain ethnic habits, in the dominance of some groups in public office, as well as in many other subtle ways."[2]

But that was a pre-1960s religious and cultural reality. The boomer generation came to adulthood in a nation increasingly aware of its diversity, and by the time generation X had grown up religious pluralism was deeply embedded in consciousness—indeed, simply taken for granted. There are several ways in which this shift in consciousness might be viewed. One is to invoke Peter Berger's classic description of modernity as a transition "from fate to choice." What had at one time been largely a taken-for-granted religious world now has less of a hold upon consciousness; that is to say, modernity pluralizes human experience and creates greater subjective space for alternative meaning systems. In terms of religion, this means more options, whether in a range of religious traditions or internally within a single tradition.

Yet another way to think of this expanding pluralism is as a series of historical challenges to the white, male, Anglo, Protestant hegemony that reigned in the early decades of the twentieth century. Since the 1960s, movements for racial and gender equality have greatly altered the range of religious options and interpretation. Liberation, feminist, and womanist theologies are examples.

In still another view, American history could be read as a series of "religious disestablishments." To begin with, there is legal disestablishment, which laid the groundwork for religious pluralism early on in the nation's history. The free-exercise-of-religion clause, combined with the nonestablishment clause in the First Amendment, opened the way for radical pluralism, through creating the possibility for a cultural (as opposed to a strictly legal) style of religious establishment. Protestantism throughout the nineteenth century enjoyed such an establishment. The second disestablishment, following World War I, is sometimes described in terms of an example of how a cultural establishment can be undermined: in the face of large-scale Catholic immigration and growing Jewish diversity, Protestants were forced to recognize the claims of other faiths. As Will Herberg wrote so persuasively in the mid-1950s, by then the United States had become largely a "Protestant-Catholic-Jewish" country.

It is argued that there was a third disestablishment during the 1960s and early 1970s, a period characterized by loss of moral, cultural, and religious consensus in the United States, and simultaneously a greater level of individualism, personal choice, and ideological polarization.[3] Religion was on its way to becoming whatever one *chose* as one's own, including the possibility of greater internal pluralism, or varying popular versions from within a single faith tradition, plus the opportunity to pick and choose religious and spiritual themes from various traditions and ideologies, thereby creating an eclectic mix suitable to one's taste. Personal autonomy and meaning gained emphasis at the expense of institutional authority. Trends since that time have only enhanced these possibilities.

Whether thought of as a shift from fate to choice, or as a challenge to white Protestant males, or as a series of religious disestablishments, the outcome is much the same. It was not until the 1960s and early 1970s that expanded pluralism really took hold in the minds of ordinary Americans. Many events occurred during that period to reinforce the shift in consciousness. The election of John F. Kennedy, the first Catholic president, was deeply symbolic of a new era. Likewise, a Supreme Court decision ruling that public school prayer was unconstitutional undermined an older civic piety that had long rested upon close ties between the public schools and Protestant culture. Civil rights, the counterculture, the women's movement, the Vietnam War, Watergate—all exposed tension and contradiction in the larger culture and ushered in a level of diversity unlike anything the country had known during the age of the WASP. Visibly, a new religious America was emerging.

Within religious institutions, too, crucial changes were occurring. The historic, mainline Protestant churches were at the beginning of a downward spiral in membership and public presence; evangelical, fundamentalist, and charismatic movements were ascendant. The largest religious institution in the country, the American Catholic church, was itself in the throes of massive reform, brought on by Vatican Council II and its call for *aggiornamento,* or updating of the church in the face of modernity. Youthful Americans were also experimenting with new religious movements and discovering, or rediscovering, metaphysical traditions in the American past such as theosophy and New Thought, with resultant broadening of the base of religious pluralism. Boomers were at a formative age when all of this was happening and thus would be caught up in the religious ferment. For Americans generally, this was a period of considerable transition, one that would be remembered as a marker in the nation's religious and cultural history.

While all these cultural and institutional changes were occurring, there was yet another development that would radically alter the nation's religious demography. Not fully realizing the implications of its action at the time, the U.S. Congress in 1965 passed legislation lowering barriers to immigrants of non-European origin. Few decisions of the Congress have had so significant an influence on the normative religious climate of the country as did this one. Following that vote, Latinos, Asians, and Middle Easterners began to enter the country in record numbers, bringing with them the religious ideas and practices of their homeland. Latino Catholicism, itself varying considerably from one Central American or South American country to another, was vastly different in style from what previous Catholic immigrants from Europe had brought with them in earlier years. Asians and Middle Easterners brought traditions that, though not totally new to Americans, were new in their increased visibility and presence. Moreover, the legislation opened the way to "new immigrant" religious leaders, especially spiritual gurus from Asia, who found the nation's unregulated religious marketplace a fertile environment for recruitment.

Given the unsettled period of the 1960s and 1970s and challenges to an older WASP establishment, spiritual teachings from the East were particularly attractive to many youths. Middle-class young people particularly were drawn to emphasis upon the inner life and to meditative practice, features of Eastern spirituality that were readily interpreted and packaged by a new cadre of religious entrepreneurs and directed at those disenchanted with the prevailing religious meaning systems. It is particularly important that exposure to Asian teachings led to greater clarity about how Eastern and Western religious psychology differ, and to awareness of the growth in religious options. Whatever else the new religious pluralism was, it was now more diverse than anything Americans had known in the past.

This was also a pluralism on a scale much grander than the older Protestant denominationalism or even a Protestant-Catholic-Jewish America. Even those young Americans who embraced the American way of life with the same fervor as did their parents, or who might have been alarmed by the growing presence of Eastern spiritual teachings, could not dismiss the fact that there were new players on the nation's religious field. The resurgence in evangelical Christianity was in no small part a reaction to this changing cultural and religious environment. Conservative Protestants sought to restore a religious past that was rapidly fading.

Hinduism, Buddhism, Islam, Sufism, Sikhism, Baha'ism—indeed, all the world's major religions—took on far greater public presence within the United States than ever before. Though often conceived as monolithic, Latino Catholicism and Protestantism, Buddhism, Hinduism, and Islam were all internally diverse as religious populations; each consisted of subpopulations formed by ethnicity and nationality background. Recognition of this reality was itself important. What had once been thought of as small, often weird, cultlike groups on the margins of the culture were coming to be understood as variations of the older religious traditions—in much the same way that Protestant denominations and Catholic parishes had emerged in an earlier era.

In effect, a global and increasingly transnational world was bringing into being an expanded scale of religious pluralism, arguably a development for the nation's future of equal importance to the cultural and lifestyle changes of the 1960s.[4] Unlike earlier waves of European immigration, this later wave involved traditions that were neither Christian nor Jewish, thus breaking with the nation's two historic faith traditions. The "Judeo-Christian heritage," a religious construction that took on particular prominence during the cold-war years of the 1940s and 1950s, became increasingly strained, unable to sustain a sufficiently comprehensive sacred canopy binding all American believers. Not surprisingly, the nation's civil religion, or the historic set of Biblical myths and symbols by which Americans have understood themselves, came to be highly fractured and openly contested between liberal and progressive on the one hand and conservative and reactionary on the other. At the same time, the presence of new immigrant religions opened the way for creative possibilities in search of a more encompassing civil religion.

Pluralism in the United States is something of a religious orientation itself, in the sense that it encourages respect for, and tolerance of, faith traditions of many kinds. It produces an ethic of civility, which frowns upon lack of respect and appreciation for the religious claims of others and thus makes suspect the moral and faith claims of any one religion as binding upon the society as a whole. It is an ethic that imposes limitations on particularistic religious tradition, undermining especially the role and authority of those traditions insofar as they seek to influence or control the public order. As one commentator writes, "Not only are individuals required to be *tolerant of others;* individuals must also be *tolerable to others.* . . . This ethic is an ethic of gentility and studied moderation. It speaks of a code of social discourse whereby religious beliefs and political convictions are to be expressed discretely [sic] and tactfully and in most cases, privately. Convictions are to be tempered by 'good taste' and sensibility. It is an ethic that pleads 'no offense.'"[5]

Pluralism brings about transformation not just of discourse and sensibility but of religious consciousness. People begin to define their religious worlds differently, or feel some pressure to do so, out of respect to others. There is evidence to suggest that these definitions of religious reality vary by generation. For example, Americans born since World War II are more likely than those born before that time to hold to a universalistic religious orientation and regard all religions as equally true and good. The full impact of this shift in outlook is as yet unknown; nor do we know if this reflects a lasting trend. But it is quite likely that norms of religious tolerance and civility are more widely diffused throughout the society now than at any other time in American history.

In a context like this, a faith community increasingly enters into dialogue with others; indeed, many theologians, sociologists, and political scientists argue that it is essential in a democracy that such a community be open to the voices of others. In this way, people's beliefs and views are tested, affirmed, and critiqued—and as a result often reformed. Sometimes through dialogue people sharpen their own sense of group difference, but they often discover similarities or are forced to reassess which group differences are important and which are not. This need not necessarily lead to moral or ethical relativism, or even to loss of religious distinctiveness, but it does mean that faith communities come to respect, and to some extent even learn from, one another.

In this regard, religious pluralism as we know it today poses a new challenge for the traditional congregation and the theology on which it bases its existence. As one theologian writes, "Communities of faith must come to recognize the compatibility of deep and abiding commitment to the truth claims of one's tradition and openness to and respect for the claims of another tradition. Truth-claiming and an acceptance of pluralism are not inconsistent."[6] Although many Americas may find it difficult to accept the premise that one can hold to one's truth claims while also embracing pluralism, still it cannot be denied that in a highly differentiated society there is strong pressure in the direction of encouraging dialogue and exchange of ideas and principles, all essential in developing a common basis of understanding.

Privatized Religion

From a psychological standpoint, religious pluralism encourages the "privatizing" of faith. As particularistic faith becomes more problematic in the public arena, the private sphere retains (and may take on even greater) significance as a realm of meaning and expression. Religion is not necessarily less important to an individual, but its center of energy shifts. Here in this more inner, personal world, religion generates force and vitality. This dichotomizing of social life into the public and private becomes more salient generally as people organize and interpret their daily experiences. The legal separation of church and state lays the groundwork for this bifurcation, but it is reinforced by contemporary religious and cultural trends. Aside from the growing number of quite different religious traditions defining their own private worlds, there are broader cultural trends reshaping the private realm (such as the increased powers of the state and its control over the public sector and the prominence of a therapeutic ethic emphasizing individual autonomy and personal initiative as a means of solving dilemmas in everyday life). Under such conditions, religion is likely to manifest itself, Berger points out, as "public rhetoric," yet to be meaningfully adhered to as a deeply personal faith, or as he says, "private virtue."[7]

Privatization as a religious trend cuts across religions and social strata, but it is most pronounced among educated, middle-class constituencies. These are the population most exposed to the secularizing influence of modern society, where individualistic and humanistic orientations tend to clash with the theistic. Even the more recent arrivals on the American scene, such as Islamic communities, face these confrontations. This is especially true for second-generation Muslims and members of other new-immigrant communities who are now rapidly assimilating into American life. Asked about the shared beliefs and practices of her religious community, a second-generation Muslim student at one of the University of California campuses objects to drawing easy communal stereotypes, emphasizing instead the important role that individuals themselves play in shaping a religious outlook. "I think everybody's religious in their own way," she says, "because it's what your heart believes. You can never judge anybody because they dress a certain way and say they're not religious, or if they do a certain thing then they are religious. Because it all depends on what they think inside." Aside from accommodation to American-style religious individualism, her comment reveals internal, as opposed to external, validation for conviction and determining what is authentically religious. In a university setting, how quickly this accommodation occurs.

Privatization transforms religion in ways that are not always so obvious. For one thing, it often generates countertendencies, or a trend seeking to restore a public religious presence. At times, as in the case of fundamentalist Christianity, these efforts are dogmatic and aggressive. Because religion seeks to offer an encompassing and integrated worldview and thus is not likely ever to become fully privatized, religion's efforts at reclaiming a hold on the public arena are to be expected. Today, we witness strong movements seeking to restore one or another ideological version of religion's moral and ethical presence in the public arena. The proliferation of special-purpose groups and religious movements, many of them born out of ideological polarization, generates considerable tension in the public arena, or culture wars as the phrase has come to be used. The congregation itself easily becomes a battleground between warring factions over such highly charged issues as abortion, women's ordination, and gay and lesbian lifestyles.

Even within what seems to be the most harmonious of congregations, tensions often exist just beneath the surface, ready to erupt, and they frequently do along generational lines. Whereas in an earlier era conflict and tension might have arisen over issues of doctrine or a charge of heresy, today they arise largely over gender and lifestyle issues, that is, over personal matters that have escalated into public dispute. Of course, the dispute is often bound up with generational differences in outlook. Members of a generation not only hold distinctive cultural values and points of view; they also filter their religious perspectives through those values and viewpoints. Not surprisingly, the boundaries between what is defined as private and that which is public are themselves contested and revised in the process.

A congregation may thus be thought of as an arena of conflict, as a setting in which contestation over moral and lifestyle issues as well as styles of religious belief and practice may erupt at any time. For this reason, the symbolic world uniting members of a congregation is precarious and rests upon a complex set of social processes. Unity within a congregation, and especially unity across the generations, depends upon local tradition, and perhaps most of all upon skillful manipulation on the part of religious leaders of the "ties that bind." Pastors know there must be ongoing negotiation of those ties and work at unifying the social bonds within a congregation. Savvy pastors know they must deliberately try to build bridges of understanding across generational lines. This is evident in the comment of a Catholic priest we spoke with, who had served several parishes and knew about differences among them. Extolling the virtues of his present parish, he says "people who are attracted here or stay here do so because they like the progressive nature of the community. So the tension that I would feel, for example, or have felt in other congregations when you had a large group of traditional Catholics that pretty much had a static notion of faith and its development versus a younger community that would have been educated differently and look at life differently—that kind of conflict just isn't present." Our survey of congregations in North Carolina and California revealed this awareness of conflict on the part of clergy, though more often understood as an underlying, latent condition than as a manifest reality. Worry often was simply how to avoid its eruption.

Second, there is the impact upon the individual's religious psychology. That cultural and religious pluralism undermines the taken-for-granted certainty in one's own beliefs has long been advanced by sociologist Berger; from lack of social reinforcement, or of a strong "plausibility structure," he argues, religious worlds are likely to become fragile. "Cultural plurality is experienced by the individual," he writes, "not just as something external—all those people he bumps into—but as an internal reality, a set of options present in the mind. In other words, the different cultures he encounters in his social environment are transformed into alternative scenarios, options, for his own life."[8]

It is not easy to subject Berger's theory to empirical validation, however there is a considerable body of research suggesting this is the case. The evidence from polls and surveys suggests that the great majority of Americans today understand faith less as adherence to particular belief (or even as certainty of belief) than as an evolving, meaningful relationship with God or the sacred. This is an important distinction, though often overlooked. Findings from a major study reveal that even though 70 percent of Americans say faith is important to them, and another 25 percent agree it is fairly important, when asked further about what faith is to them fewer than one-fifth regard it as involving a particular "set of beliefs."[9]

The rhetoric of faith is one thing of which there is much in America, but certainty about its content is something else. It is not known if historically this is truer today than in the past, although that is likely the case. Teasing out the more interesting and positive nuances in how Americans view faith, sociologist Jerome Baggett writes that "more than half understand it as 'a relationship with God'; for another fifth of the population, faith is defined as 'finding meaning in life.' Religious beliefs are clearly no more than a part of living a life of faith. Nor are they necessarily unchangeable, or primarily derived from a religious institution. Three quarters of

Americans believe that faith is actually 'strengthened by questioning early beliefs,' and a full four-fifths agree that 'an individual should arrive at his or her own religious beliefs independent of any churches or synagogues.'"[10] Survey as well as anecdotal evidence suggests that faith and doubt are not bound to a zero-sum equation, that a living and expansive faith entertains doubt and skepticism as healthy features.

Are there generational trends associated with privatization? The evidence suggests the answer is yes. Research from an earlier study of boomers shows that traditional religious doctrines are of less importance than authenticity in one's faith, or being true to oneself in what one holds as true; the ethical aspects of faith are also privileged over other aspects of religious commitment.[11] Compared with those of their parents' generation, doctrines that once distinguished one denomination or faith tradition from another have receded in importance while concern about ethics and personal integrity appears to have increased. Specifically, when asked about the qualities of a "good" Christian, among mainline Protestants—those arguably the least certain of what to believe—commitment to social justice is more important than firm belief in the divinity of Christ. Only 8 percent of mainline boomers say one can be a good Christian without concern for the poor, whereas three times that many agree that a good Christian need not believe in the divinity of Christ. Even among conservative Protestants, more insist upon concern for the poor than upon traditional doctrine about Christ in defining their operative faith, which itself is a telling commentary about contemporary religious construction.

Also, this same study documents trends across generational cohorts on many religious attitudinal indicators. There is a discernible five-to-fifteen-point spread on such key items as "strength" of religious preference, whether attendance at church or synagogue services is viewed as necessary for being a good Christian or Jew, the importance attached to arriving at one's own beliefs, and personal views about the rules of morality as practiced within church or synagogue. In general, there is a weakening hold of traditional religious norms across the cohorts, comparing those born before 1946 with those born after that time. As is pointed out in that study, the end of World War II is like a cultural fault line; the religious attitudinal gap between those born before and after that major historical event is greater than those between senior citizens and the younger GI generation or between first-wave and second-wave boomers.[12]

Unquestionably, younger generations of Americans are exposed to a variety of religious and spiritual possibilities. Given increased cultural contact, mass communication, and the rise of a new cadre of entrepreneurs now packaging and marketing spiritual teachings targeted to them as consumers, it is no surprise they are open to mixing and matching religious elements—often combining them from quite differing traditions. Because their ties to a particular tradition are often not as strong as for their elders, they appear to be less concerned about having a coherent, singular religious orientation; quite diverse, pastiche-style belief and practice seem fitting to life in a religiously pluralistic society. They recognize, to use Martin E. Marty's phrase, the "merits of borrowing" from other religious traditions and spiritual leaders.

The diffusion of belief in reincarnation is a good case in point. With upwards of one-fourth of the post–World War II population in the United States affirming such belief, there is clearly a blending of Eastern and Western religious themes across major religious populations today, even to some extent among conservative evangelical Christians. Although we do not know just how widespread Eastern spirituality was in earlier generations, unquestionably it is better known and more accepted among the younger generations. Careful attention to religious rhetoric suggests as well a more personalized, individually tailored religious style on the part of the young. Both those adhering to a particular faith and those borrowing elements from across traditions speak rather freely of their "needs," of their "experiences," of their "journeys," of "searching for a congregation in which [they] feel comfortable or that [they] like," and more so generally than do pre-boomers. The meaning systems by which they live tend to be multilayered and eclectic, in diverse environments. As sociologist Wuthnow says, "People become heteroglossic; that is, they gain the capacity of speaking with many religious voices."[13]

Posttraditional Society

Throughout our previous discussion on pluralism and privatism, the emphasis was upon how in contemporary society an individual exercises considerable *choice* in matters of religious faith and practice. American society historically has been characterized by a great deal of religious individualism, but the massive social and cultural changes of the past fifty years brought these expressions of personal religious preference into even greater focus. This became especially evident in 1978 when pollster George Gallup Jr. reported that eight out of ten Americans agreed with the statement that "an individual should arrive at his or her own religious beliefs independent of any churches or synagogues."[14] On a related item, Gallup found that almost the same number agreed that "a person can be a good Christian or Jew if he or she doesn't attend church or synagogue."

With national figures hovering around 80 percent on both items, obviously no major subgroup of Americans was immune from what at the time was labeled "religious individualism," or "Sheilaism" to cite the self-reported description of a nurse named Sheila Larson described in *Habits of the Heart,* the widely read book by Robert Bellah and his colleagues written in the mid-1980s. Today, such individualism is taken for granted, accustomed as we are to widespread choice and diversity in religious life; indeed, we are surprised when we hear of religious groups that are just the opposite—that is, groups characterized by a fanatical sense of "we-ness" or strong communal solidarity. Given all the cultural and religious trends we have described, it could hardly be otherwise.

A helpful way of thinking about religious individualism is from the vantage point of a posttraditional or detraditionalizing society. These terms imply massive social-structural changes affecting religion, changes that have been under way since the Enlightenment but have accelerated in the latter half of the twentieth century, all affecting the hold of tradition upon people's everyday lives. Historically, tradition exercised strong binding power in the sense of orienting people around common values and practices and of routinizing their day-to-day lives. In an age when the pace of change was much slower, what one would do tomorrow would be pretty much what one did today. To put it differently, tradition involves habits, or repetitive patterns in social life, which function to undergird a sense of order and continuity in human experience. As British sociologist Anthony Giddens likes to say, order and continuity create for the individual a sense of "ontological security."[15] Without some degree of this life would of course be impossible.

To speak of a process of detraditionalization is not to suggest that all this disappears, or that the force of tradition is no longer operative in offering such security, but "rather to say that something important is happening in the way that we relate to traditions, including religious traditions."[16] Detraditionalization as a result of increased attention to science and rationality, the enormous impact of mass media, and popular cultural trends affects us all in fundamental ways: it disembeds the self from its historic, communal context and displaces older views of truth and authority. That is to say, tradition in the modern world is caught up in major upheaval and transformation (observable in loss of habit and memory) and is thus felt at the deepest levels of personal identity. In the extreme case, even the simplest of things we take for granted in everyday life are affected. Again, to quote Giddens on the character of this transformation engulfing us, "The question, 'How shall I live?' has to be answered in day-to-day decisions about how to behave, what to wear, what to eat—and many other things—as well as interpreted with the temporal unfolding of self-identity."[17]

Detraditionalization as a process sheds a great deal of light upon religious change. Loss of historic authority means that we are thrown back reflexively upon our own religious choices, upon our own sense of the proper fit between the beliefs and practices we adhere to and the circumstances of our lives. Religious belonging becomes less ascribed than simply given as a crucial part of one's social inheritance; likewise, religious meaning in a more cognitive sense must be worked out, for it cannot be assumed that one is born into strong religious identity. Americans have long used the language of religious preference to describe who they are in a pluralist society, but the subjectivity associated with the rhetoric of preferences becomes even more pronounced under such conditions. An expanded menu of choice means not just institutional options, but also pluralist interpretations within a single tradition. For many boomers and generation Xers, there is a great deal of exploration, of looking for something to be part of, as one African American woman, age twenty-two, told us. She emphasizes what is well known but bears repeating about many young Americans today: "A lot of people are going to different religions and trying out different things. And trying to find a place of belonging as far as religion's concerned. Judaism to Islam to Jehovah's Witnesses. And they have a lot of questions about different religions, and how do we know that? How do we prove this? What are the facts that are behind this? And so forth."

Her description bespeaks the information-oriented age in which we live. What are the religions available, and what do we know about them? Epistemological questions loom large in such a context, as does worry about finding a place where people can belong and feel comfortable. Inundated with information and media-oriented, they often do not know what to believe or where to turn to obtain reliable knowledge about religious groups. Information overload combines with a high level of subjectivity, making for a plethora of religious interpretations. In a milieu of image and questionable reality, it is not surprising that people we spoke with often said they were "looking for the church to be real" or that they are "searching for reality."

There is considerable skepticism about truth—including religious truth. For a great number of Americans, there is no such thing as an absolute, objective point of view in matters of morality and religion. Especially for affluent, middle-class Xers—those with a good education and cosmopolitan in outlook—there is much less certainty regarding what one can accept as religious truth. As one university chaplain told us, "When you get into discussions about truth and things like that, then you see skepticism. Epistemological skepticism. What can anyone know?" Such skepticism is broadly based for the generation but tends to be articulated differently for those with less social class standing and economic security. Asked about how members of this generation approach religious truth, the pastor of an evangelical generation X congregation had this to say:

> That was a generation not raised with boundaries. Dr. Spock told their parents, "Let them become. Don't give them walls around them. Let them just discover who they are." So they grow up with no discipline really, nobody telling them what to be and how to live. So now they grow up and they go, "What the heck am I? Who am I? What do I believe and who am I? Nobody ever told me what is true!" So the pope or a conservative church says, "This is what is true and we believe this." And they go, "Yeah, I need someone to help me to be able to see that because no one ever did before." And so the Bible becomes as a word of truth. And they go, "Oh great! Something that's true!" You know, they don't say it quite like that, but you feel a sense of relief. But on the other hand, they were raised, as someone says, "in a busted world," and it's very clear to

them that things are not well. And because things are not well, we've gotta work with that. . . . This generation is gonna show the world that there can be truth, but that we can work with people on a very appropriate level interpersonally, and those two are not incompatible.

From this pastor's comment, it is clear that at least within this congregation sensitivity in dealing with questions of religious authority and what it means to live in a "busted world" of human relationships are both crucial for many young Americans. Affinity between these two realities points to a distinctive world of experience combining great awareness of human frailty, appreciation for personal experience, and honest acknowledgment of doubt and uncertainty in matters of faith. Our interviews reveal this to be a combination characterizing many Americans, though more pronounced for the younger generations. The latter perhaps simply give greater voice to these realities.

Among generation Xers especially, there are mixed feelings about tradition. There is a longing for answers to religious questions—for a "bedrock against this whirl of change," as one person told us—yet an insistence on tolerance, understanding, and openness to other points of view even while asserting their own point of view. In a deeply psychological sense, there is a paradox in their many spiritual expressions, described simply as wanting simultaneously to be both grounded and fluid, of very much wanting an anchor for their lives yet not wanting to be overly tied to it—the dilemma of the "protean self," as described by Robert J. Lifton.[18] This protean quality comes through in many ways, nowhere more so than in the ambivalence surrounding worship styles. In an evangelical church, for example, there is tension between strong affirmation of religious authority and how best to express that authority in an idiom that is culturally current, and thus meaningful for that generation's life experiences. Mixed feelings are voiced, especially within those churches where much effort has gone into creating worship service using contemporary music, a screen for lyrics, video clips, and other teaching and preaching techniques that, though not antithetical to religious authority, often seem rather arbitrary and contrived.

Then, too, there is the problem of the seemingly constant change in contemporary worship styles. For a generation whose religious roots are often shallow to begin with, and whose lives have been shaped from the time they were born by rapid and constant cultural change, it comes as little surprise that worship style is so fragile. It can be a source of frustration to religious leaders, as was expressed by a pastor of a generation X congregation whom we interviewed: "This is a generation that doesn't have a great deal of love for tradition. So things get old here and it doesn't take more than three or four months before [they say] 'Aaah, this is old.' And in other churches it might take three or four years for the same thing to get old."

Aside from pressure for ongoing reformulation of cultural expressions of faith, there arises the question as to what are its essentials, as opposed to the nonessentials. This same pastor goes on to say: "So there's a real drive for creativity, but what we are discovering is, OK, what are the nonnegotiables? Actually we've been around for ten years and we are now beginning to identify what those nonnegotiables are."

Ten years may be a meaningful span in the life of a congregation, but against the backdrop of Christian history and its long, protracted struggle within the tradition over heresy and doctrinal interpretation, a decade pales in significance. Modernity, it seems, leaves such transmutations of time in its wake. Because of the privileging of what is new and innovative, contestation over faith and its institutional expression now becomes telescoped into a much shorter span of time. Strategies of church growth and of making faith relevant to personal experience and evolving niches of lifestyle and meaning change often, sometimes abruptly. In a detraditionalized world, religious people are confronted with having to make choices as to which portion of Scripture and story to privilege, and then having to make difficult and somewhat arbitrary interpretations. There is no secure, agreed-upon narrative framework, except in the most general sense, that goes without debate. Whereas for boomers an apologetic of choice seems like a workable argument, Xers are likely to push, as one commentator says, for "an embodied apologetic, a flesh-and-blood, living and breathing argument for God.[19]

Worry about what is negotiable in matters of faith and morality and what is not creates a distinctive dynamic in many congregations. For sociological as well as religious reasons, people often look to connect with others. In religious terms, this plays out in a search to find others who share with us a similar universe of meaning, those with whom we can agree on doctrinal and lifestyle issues. Banding together, in a small group or in a larger lifestyle enclave, gives rise to a distinctive religious rhetoric and reinforces conceptions of reality, both of which constitute a basis for internal difference within an institutional structure. Thus within the same congregation there can be a plurality of religious worlds and loosely organized constituencies, which often are not visible to outsiders.

Even among members of the same generation, there can be a plurality of religious worlds. Skilled pastors and religious leaders recognize the necessity of careful negotiation within and among such widely discrepant religious worlds, especially in large congregations that attempt to institutionalize opportunity for religious choice. Packaging the religious message thus becomes an essential skill, along with a reflexive grasp of why (and whether there should be) a range of interpretive approaches to religious truth within the same congregation. Sometimes the challenge in this respect is quite formidable. As one pastor told us, it is a "serious task" trying to navigate in his preaching between "firm believers willing to be impacted by the truth" and others in his congregation "who have killed the concept that truth is absolute . . . and who kind of think, 'Well, maybe it's true, maybe not.'" Hardly a new distinction in the history of congregations, but certainly it is one that has become particularly pronounced in our time.

From Dwelling to Seeking

The themes described in this chapter are in keeping with Wuthnow's claim of a shift from dwelling to seeking in recent times. It is a subtle but significant reordering within the culture, he says, wherein "a traditional spirituality of inhabiting sacred places has given way to a new spirituality of seeking . . . people have been losing faith in a metaphysic that can make them feel at home in the universe and [now] increasingly negotiate among competing glimpses of the sacred, seeking partial knowledge and practical wisdom."[20] In Wuthnow's usage and in ours, the notion of seeking is understood within a broad perspective more in keeping with Ernst Troeltsch's view of mystical or spiritual religion than in the narrow sense sometimes applied to people prone to join a cult. Our assumption is that a quest culture in the sense of searching for deeper meaning flourishes today, giving rise to hybrid souls and restless seekers.

Although this shift in dominant style of spirituality applies to individuals, it is important to recognize the implications for a religious institution and how it relates to its social environment. Congregations and religious organizations of many kinds today have permeable boundaries; aside from other social attributes that apply to them, they are shaped by the popular cultural mood of our time. But religious groups are hardly alone in this respect, since people's connections to social institutions generally are in many respects rather loose. In fact, there is a close affinity between this shift in spiritual mood from dwelling to seeking and the fluid institutional loyalties of Americans across all sectors of society. In a world of flex time and telecommuting, work is less and less assigned to a particular space and time; information flow and financial transactions initiated on the World Wide Web all occur within cyberspace, unbounded by the constraints of physical place; the local and the global no longer seem so far apart. Dwelling is simply not easy in a world where fluidity overshadows fixity, where stability has given way to movement.

Distinguishing between settled and unsettled times is helpful in grasping the shift in religious and spiritual styles. In relatively settled times, a dwelling spirituality sustains people with its emphasis upon habit, familiarity, and security. People's lives are ordered around sacred space and time; faith is lived out in established routine. Carefully drawn symbolic boundaries define the sacred world, separating it from the less hospitable and often intrusive secular world. There is coherence of personal meaning and social belonging. But in unsettled times, a seeker spirituality is likely to emerge, aimed at finding meaning in a seemingly strange, if not chaotic, set of circumstances. Mobile lives mesh with a concern for personal discovery, for journey and growth; pilgrimage within a tradition gives way in the extreme to the tourist who gazes from the outside and picks and chooses those aspects from one or another traditions as he or she likes. The symbolic boundary between the sacred and the secular loses importance as people look for spirituality in all sorts of life experience, in hope that it can be found. Belonging and meaning in a person's life easily become disjointed and pose a challenge of reestablishing a connection.

Helpful, too, is sociologist Ann Swidler's view of culture as a "tool kit" of symbols, stories, rituals, and worldviews, which people may use in varying configurations to solve different kinds of problems, and particularly her notion that cultural "strategies of action" vary for settled and unsettled times.[21] Elsewhere, one of us has summarized Swidler's perspective this way:

> In settled times, culture provides materials from which people construct broad, well-established strategies of action that become traditions that anchor and integrate their lives. The strategies or traditions are like well-worn paths that one travels to get from here to there. One does not have to stop and think about them. Even when people do not always act in the ways that their traditions dictate, their lack of consistency does not call the traditions into question. They continue to be taken for granted as right and inevitable. They are accepted as authoritative even when they are not fully followed.
>
> In contrast, in unsettled times, older cultural patterns are found wanting and are jettisoned. Entrepreneurial leaders draw from the cultural tool kit to develop and create new meaning systems, new cultural styles, new strategies of action to meet the challenges of unsettled times. As an example of "cultural entrepreneurs," Swidler cites the Reformers, especially John Calvin. Furthermore, in unsettled times, innovations in ritual practice or doctrine become highly charged emotionally, because "ritual changes reorganize taken-for-granted habits and modes of experience" (p. 279). They sometimes require a break with established, embedded, traditional ways of life; thus it is not surprising that conflicts, often severe in intensity, arise between those who promote new cultural models and practices and those who are reluctant to abandon familiar strategies of action.[22]

If we think of recent decades as an unsettled time, the enormous scope of the religious change now under way becomes clearer to us. The older, well-worn paths of tradition seem less able to prescribe a course of action grounding life in a meaningful whole, for the post–World War II generations especially. Religious habits once associated with a sacred, transcendent dimension of life seem to have lost much of their sustaining power. Strong religious identity institutionally formed and sustained over the life course is not as common as it once was. These were all strategies of action fitting a more stable time, when the community was more intact, when the boundary distinguishing the sacred from its surroundings was better demarcated, and when social institutions exercised greater control over people's lives. But with the rapid change brought by globalizing and detraditionalizing influences of modern life, people experience a less tightly bounded world and with it a great deal more personal unease, and not infrequently a sense of homelessness.

But two important observations need to be made. One is that despite the demise in older religious forms that some feel, it does not follow that people are left spiritually bereft. A detraditionalizing trend is not just liberating and secularizing; it also forces upon the individual greater responsibility for his or her own life. We must confront the choices before us and reflexively make decisions that otherwise we might not make in a more institutionally structured context. There may be a great deal of loose attachment and experimentation—"church hopping," as it shows up in the congregation—but there can also be honest searching, self-conscious deliberation, and creative reinterpretation of tradition as it relates to people's own lives.

In the context of a seeker culture and its more open and expansive strategies of action, many people are inclined to ask serious questions about the meaning of their lives and to address doubt and uncertainty relating to faith; they are forced into "working on God," to use Winifred Gallagher's apt phrase.[23] Lacking the strong anchor of tradition and institutional support systems, many seekers must rely upon their own effort at cultivating spiritual practice. Although many younger Americans especially revel in the freedom of an unsettled era, they also often come to realize that spiritual formation and guidance do not come easily, and that much work is required to achieve a deeper spiritual understanding of themselves. Herein of course lies an important challenge for congregations.

Also, the seeker culture has contributed to the rise of an expanded, far more diversified "spiritual marketplace."[24] A new cadre of entrepreneurs now competes with religious leaders in marketing spirituality to consumers, among them best-selling authors, motivational speakers, independent spiritual advisors, and radio and television talk-show hosts. These new suppliers cater to the questing mood in a variety of institutional settings: through the book publishing industry, as it redefines popular spiritual categories; at retreat centers, with their expanding topics of personal development; in hospitals, with growing attention to healing the body and the mind; in seminars sponsored by corporations and businesses; and on the Internet or through a toll-free telephone line. Religion in the United States has long thrived within an open, competitive marketplace; this latest market expansion reflects changes in technology, the growing consumer mentality, and the innovative strategies of the entrepreneurs. With people shopping for spirituality, the difference between what a religious congregation offers and that provided by these new suppliers is often blurred. Further, there are members of every generation, not just the younger members, within congregations now who bring to their religious involvement ideas, orientations, and concerns shaped by the larger popular culture. In effect, institutional boundaries are porous.

Thus we see that the religious and spiritual transformations of our time are profound and far-reaching, in terms of both personal psychology and institutional structure. Americans generally, even those claiming no religion, are affected to one degree or another by these changes. Congregational life within all religious traditions is also affected, though it responds variously to these changes. In this respect, there is no religious retreat from the massive detraditionalizing trends of modern life. Inevitably, how people relate to religious symbols, beliefs, and practices becomes quite varied and nuanced. It is our argument that the generations are differentially exposed to these trends, and further that to understand the contemporary congregation we must take seriously how these trends play out within it. Hence we turn next to a social and religious profiling of the three generations to get a better picture of the highly differentiated, multilayered religious reality increasingly found within this institution.

Chapter Three

Portraits of Three Generations

Identity, Life Experience, and Religion

"Each generation is a new people," observed Alexis de Tocqueville when he visited the United States in the 1830s. Coming from France, Tocqueville was struck by the freedom people had in this country to recreate and shape anew the American experience. In a country built upon principles of democracy and individualism—and unlike the more tradition-oriented, hierarchically based European nations— changes from generation to generation were much more obvious. Of course, Tocqueville was far from alone in observing the malleability and evolving character of American society. Throughout the nineteenth and twentieth centuries, commentators repeatedly pointed to populist trends in American life, noting the diversity of ideas and organization, the powerful force of public opinion, an emphasis on needs and experiences of the people, and fluidity of grassroots attitudes and sentiments. Rather than tradition, authority, or divine revelation, pragmatics in its many forms is a powerful driving force shaping all of society, including its religious life. Nor has the country lost this quality. Recent commentators such as William Strauss and Neil Howe underscore the point made by Tocqueville and others when they say that in America there is continuing, strong susceptibility "to generational flux, to the fresh influence of each new set of youth come to age."[1]

What has long impressed commentators is subtle change in values, mood, and sentiment—the cultural orientations that in one way or another shape people's views and experiences. Each successive generation in America develops to a greater or lesser extent its own distinctive personality and thereby reshapes the nation and its future. Religion is very much bound up with a people's mood, values, and emotions; thus it too is always in a state of flux and evolving. The configuration of meaning and interpretation—what anthropologist Clifford Geertz calls "webs of significance"—inevitably varies depending upon social circumstance and the life experience in question. This being the case, we are led to look carefully at the three generations that form the centerpiece of this book. How different are the pre-boomers, boomers, and generation Xers in their social and religious profiles? What are the major religious differences between the generations, and between which generations? On what issues do the generations differ most, and on what least?

To answer these questions, we make use in this chapter of both the interview materials and the survey data collected in southern California and North Carolina. Here we paint a portrait in broad strokes of the three generations, focusing on generational identity; social and family background; and religious beliefs, attitudes, and practices, leaving for the next chapter explicit attention to involvement in the congregation.

Generational Identity

To begin with, we look at generational identity. As was discussed in the Introduction, the notion of generation is intuitively obvious, yet somewhat elusive as a basis of self-definition because there is so little consensus with regard to label. Consider the many events and experiences that, for example, pre-boomers living today remember as having a formative influence upon them when they were young. Depending on whom you ask within this generation, some of those events had a far greater impact upon them than did others. Even so, survey research has uncovered considerable statistical consensus on the major defining events for pre-boomers: the Great Depression, World War II, and in the case of Jews the Holocaust.[2] Much consensus also holds for boomers who remember the disruptive and eventful 1960s and 1970s, although in the case of generation Xers there is somewhat less agreement as to formative events and developments. For them, there simply have not been the decisive and unforgettable markers that stand out for the other two generations.

As a generation gets older, how it views the past is influenced by selective memory and shared stories. That is to say, a generation's identity is to a considerable extent a narrative construction as people age and look back upon and interpret their experiences. An individual's own story is cast within a larger story of the cultural markers defining a generation's experience. Certainly the Great Depression and World War II are crucial to the stories now told by pre-boomers, but so too are features of the popular culture remembered from the 1920s and 1930s. Narrative constructions, often enhanced by film and television, create for this generation a common identity and sense of belonging; media representations of the past help as well to reinforce the distinctiveness of a generation's experience and to define it over against others. This comes through in the response of a seventy-three-year-old man who was asked about what made his generation unlike others:

> Well, the fact that most of us grew up in the Depression, and that's something you all can't grasp because you weren't there. We also went through World War II and that binds people together. . . .
> I was watching *South Pacific* the other night on TV. I don't know if you can relate to those boys on that island, those nurses . . . that's my generation. You know, half of them [the soldiers] didn't come back, and if they did they were wounded, and it's something that makes you relate to each other. And then the swing period, the music also keeps you going. And the next generation down can't feel that, I don't think.

Memories and emotions are powerful, which may explain why the pre-boomers we interviewed were more likely to say they belonged to a particular generation than either the boomers or generation Xers. Fifty-five percent of pre-boomers in our survey agreed. Somewhat fewer boomers, slightly less than half, said so. Only 31 percent of generation Xers felt they belonged to a distinctive generation. No doubt age is a crucial factor in explaining depth of belonging. But also, many in the younger generations are sensitive to what is said in the media about them and are often likely to distance themselves from it. So they reject such labels outright, or offer a cautious, more reserved definition of themselves. For example, a thirty-four-year-old Catholic responded to the question about generational belonging by saying he was "certainly aware of the generation X stuff" but qualified his answer by noting that he did not have any "deep knowledge of it." Having grown up in the shadow of the boom generation, which received so much attention because of their huge number and claims of having lived through the turbulent 1960s, many Xers simply resent being categorized as an "unknown" generation or as busters, with a seemingly diminished profile. This means they are less likely to think in generational terms.

Pre-boomers are more likely to say they belong to a generation, yet they are the least likely of the three generations to agree upon a label describing them. When those saying they belonged to a generation were asked to name it, the majority of pre-boomers identified themselves as the "senior citizen" generation, though some also mentioned being in the "fifties," "World War II," or "Depression" generation. Their identity is bound up with many shared historical experiences. In contrast, boomers and generation Xers were more likely to recognize themselves by using ahistorical labels. The overwhelming majority of boomers identified themselves as such, although some referred to themselves as the "sixties" generation. Whatever else may define them, they have known from the time they were children that they had numbers on their side; after all, they got their name because of a demographic boom. Similarly, more than half of Xers who identified themselves generationally did so by referring to themselves as generation Xers or baby busters. A small number spoke of themselves simply as the "modern" generation. Thus both the aging process and choice of label contribute to a generation's distinctive consciousness. With labels attached to generations, there is more than just an issue of majority consensus; there is a positive or negative valence surrounding them.

Family Experiences

As we saw in Chapter One, family-related changes are crucial to our understanding of a generation and its experience. The magnitude and sheer pace of change over the past half-century are staggering, producing chaos and shock; some people become caught up in nostalgia for a way of life that no longer exists and concerns about moral decay and family values, while others celebrate the individual freedom and choice they now enjoy. These family-type changes, too, overlap with the lives of the three generations we are examining in this book. Pre-boomers and the oldest wave of boomers remember the television programs of the 1950s and 1960s that celebrated the American dream of a happy, secure family life: "Father Knows Best," "Leave It to Beaver," "The Adventures of Ozzie and Harriet." Even then, TV did not portray how most Americans actually lived, but as sociologist Arlene Skolnick points out it gave us images of "idealized families in idealized settings, successfully masquerading as 'normal,' 'healthy,' 'typical,' 'average.'"[3]

Many within the boom generation grew up recognizing the mismatch between a Norman Rockwell America held up as an ideal and the strains that families faced in actual, everyday life. Those were years of cultural confusion and stress, of changing norms governing intimate relationships and family patterns; white middle-class youths in particular felt this tension since many of them had parents who held deeply to conventional expectations of, and dreams for, a future family that would resemble what they had known in the past. Every generation knows some disparity between cultural ideals and realities, but this generation especially was caught in its grip.

If boomers felt the stress of an impending rupture, it would be the gen Xers who would feel the pains of family disruption. Forty-five percent of this younger post–World War II generation (as compared with 26 and 23 percent of boomers and pre-boomers, respectively) experienced either divorce or separation of their parents or were raised by a single parent. The level of family disruption while growing up is slightly higher in California than in North Carolina, but not by much; the family as an institution everywhere was in disarray. Statistics substantiate the fact that in the 1970s and 1980s especially change within the family was omnipresent. Divorce, births out of wedlock, and the absence of the father within the family all spiraled during these years.

These trends in family patterns are often associated with boomers, but it is really the generation following them who from the time they were children have known, more than any other, about single mothers, illegitimacy, and absent fathers. They grew up with the label dysfunctional family bandied about, and it signaled a deep message to them. Even if both parents were in the home, most likely they were the children of two-job families—yet another trend that marked the gen X experience. In our interviews, boomers often talked about, and at times celebrated, their experience in alternative family arrangements. But it was the Xers who experienced growing up without emotional support from their parents; they were most likely to express those feelings of loss.

The shift in family experience occurred rather quickly for those born at the tail end of the boomer generation and for older Xers, and not without subtle, far-reaching psychological consequences. A Catholic we spoke with in North Carolina, forty-one at the time, described just how much the world had changed between the times when she and her sister, just nine years older, were in high school: "When she was in high school, you know if you got caught smoking in the bathroom you were in big trouble. When I was in high school there were girls going to school who were pregnant, and there were kids getting stoned on the football field. So a lot had changed. Things were very much more open. When she was a teenager, if a girl got pregnant they sent her away to somewhere and she had the baby and they gave it up. It was different, just totally different."

Her account testifies not just to a changing school setting but to a shift in sexual norms, drugs, and family expectations. With "things . . . much more open," as she says, people become more vulnerable psychologically, as evident in themes of abandonment and loneliness so common in the popular culture and music for this youngest sector of adult Americans. National surveys suggest they have become more negative than older persons about people and human nature. Having lost trust in people and institutions, they feel disconnected from society. Some express worry about the prospect of a happy marriage, though in general they are not necessarily more pessimistic about their personal lives.[4]

Just as families themselves have changed, so too has the nexus between family and religion. Pre-boomers are most likely to report having parents who were involved in congregations when they were growing up, generation Xers the least. This is not very surprising, although the differences across the generations are not huge and should not be exaggerated. Anecdotal evidence from our interviews suggests that in every generation an intact family is inclined to report parental religious involvement, but the catch is, there is a declining proportion of such families across the three generations. It is likely as well that retrospective measures for one's parents are subject to bias in reporting and that older persons are more sentimental or nostalgic when thinking about their parents as moral and religious role models than younger persons. Although the actual level of religious involvement appears not to have declined greatly, probably normative expectations of religious involvement have declined. Pre-boomers were more likely to tell us they had parents who brought them up to attend church or were religiously observant than either boomers or generation Xers.

There are subtle psychological religious changes as well bound up with the shift in the family-religion nexus. Whereas pre-boomers often still have warm feelings about togetherness and a time when the congregation was filled with intact families and children, many younger Americans have not had this depth of experience. These latter report more bad experiences with both family and religion. Some boomers remember the church of their childhood and often go looking for a congregation partly in search of "family talk"[5] (discourse driven by rich memories and emotions) but are often frustrated by what they find. The gap between memory and actual family experience is overshadowing. For still other boomers and many generation Xers, there is a recognized need for community even though organized religion does not always provide what they are looking for.

Because they have been deprived in stable primary relationships, many do however look to cultivate close, personal ties within a religious community. As one thirty-four-year-old North Carolinian told us, reflecting upon her generation's emotional deprivation and difficulty in settling down as adults, "we are concerned about relationships and especially value friendships and community." Many in her age cohort talk of hanging out with friends—a rhetoric arguably born out of loneliness and deep hunger to belong. Identity can become deeply rooted within a close social network, including that formed within a religious community. Whether one's personal identity is transformed in a congregation or in another type of religious fellowship greatly depends, as sociologist Richard W. Flory says, on the opportunity for "creating a more or less unique individual identity that is rooted in the confines of the religious community."[6] Striking a balance between shared faith and individual freedom is necessary, in which instance the religious group takes on qualities of a healthy surrogate family. A good family is one that nurtures both togetherness and personal development. This type of loose connection is evident in lifestyle enclaves such as gay and lesbian support groups where individuals deal with their own struggles; in Latino, Asian, or other ethnic congregations organized around heritage but that also encourage individual initiative; and in Shabbat services for Jewish singles where members share a great deal of common life yet are able to express their individuality. It also happens in more conventional religious settings under the right conditions. An atmosphere of openness, opportunity for sharing group experiences, respect for one another's spiritual journey, and ease in locating oneself in a larger religious narrative are all essential.

At a time when grand narratives reflecting a unified vision of reality are suspect, a strong religious identity is possible if there is an experiential approach to knowledge and recognition of the truth and insights arising out of a distinctive sociobiography. Commenting on his Sunday school class, comprising mainly generation Xers, a twenty-eight-year-old United Methodist says, "We're a very open group and I think as far as keeping an open doctrine St. Luke [his parish] does that. . . . We can disagree in a respectful way; you know not everybody agrees and we're not going to agree. I think the difference is, not taking the ideas personally, but trying to keep in focus that we're all together in the family of Christ regardless of race, sex, politics—Christianity transcends all those boundaries. And I think that is something that I feel St. Luke has upheld, and certainly the group that I identify with."

Noteworthy is the "family" image. Religious community is like a family in the sense of caring and sharing, and in the importance of close attachments and a feeling of belonging. Religious community is like a family in the sense that the bonds holding it together arise out of deep feelings and rest not just upon dogmatic affirmation or creed.[7] Community rests less upon right thinking than upon shared activity and experience. Under such conditions, the chances are that an individual will take on a communal identity and recognize the importance of suppressing disagreement in the interest of accepting and supporting one another. Like a family, a congregation of this sort may not avoid controversy but still have the resources to minimize its disruptive potential. Asked about homosexuality, for example, this same Methodist comments, "We believe as Methodists it is wrong, it is a moral wrong; however, even though it is wrong, we are not in any position to be condemning. We are not in a position to be better than another person. We are all subjects to Christ and everybody is deserving of that grace and of that service. . . . We don't promote that lifestyle but then again, we're not condemning as well."

The comment suggests an affinity between close congregational bonding and religious style among those most deeply committed. Suspicious of hegemonic versions of absolute truth, many Americans born after World War II work at reconciling their values and lifestyles in relation to religious teaching but insist upon honoring and preserving the truth that arises out of subjective knowing. This latter mode of knowing, as opposed to propositional truth, privileges feeling, intuition, relationship, pluralism, and perhaps most of all idiosyncratic insight from human experience. It is an epistemology that cautions against rigid dogmatics and moralizing. Not that the search for higher forms of knowledge and moral principles above those found in individual experience should be abandoned, but subjective and pragmatic truth is now understood by many young Americans as integral to meaningful religious life.[8] Any congregation that would relate to them must grasp this fundamental point.

Religious Identification: Past and Present

Compared with most modern societies, in the United States the level of religious belief and activity remains quite high. Affiliation or identification with a religious organization is remarkably high within the country, unlike in many parts of Europe. Polls and surveys find that roughly 90 percent of Americans continue to identify with some religious group or tradition. Over the period of the nation's history, the proportion holding membership in a church, synagogue, temple, or mosque has actually increased. At the same time, there have been some important shifts in religious involvement among recent generations. According to the National Opinion Research Center (NORC), national surveys over the past quarter century show that the young today score lower on a number of religious indicators than did Americans of a similar age twenty or thirty years ago; they attend weekly religious services less often, are less likely to identify with a particular religion, and are less prone to believe that the world reflects God's goodness. An exception to this downward trend is that youths are more likely to believe in an afterlife now than was previously true.[9] As measured by this item, the young are actually more religious today than even the oldest cohorts of Americans—itself a fascinating observation. If nothing more, it underscores the fact that one should be careful in making any simple, sweeping interpretation of religious change in the United States.

It is often said that the United States is a denominational society, that religious identity remains particularly important for reasons both historical and cultural. Now, as has long been true, the great majority of Americans claim a religious affiliation and find it easy to describe themselves as Catholic, Jewish, Presbyterian, Southern Baptist, or some such label. More than just a personal belief system, or set of faith commitments, religion plays a role in helping Americans define and locate themselves socially, which is especially important because it is freely chosen in a voluntary religious order. That is to say, belonging—not just meaning—is integral to religion in a highly pluralist society where religion offers a large set of communal structures readily available for identifying oneself. Americans also switch from one faith tradition or denomination to another fairly often, and seemingly do so with a good deal of ease. The prevalence of so much switching suggests pragmatic, individualistic religious styles, often related more to social circumstance and life situation than to ecclesiastical or doctrinal commitments. Still, there is considerable evidence to suggest that for many people religious switching involves a conscious and responsible decision and is not to be viewed as necessarily reflecting lack of a faith commitment.

What about generational trends in religious identification? This is an important question, one that goes to the heart of religious change in the United States. With respect to the public role of religion in the country, few indicators give us a better clue as to what is happening within the culture at large, and over time, than the broad shift in patterns of religious preference. This is clear from the trends evident in Figures 3.1 and 3.2. Shown are tabulations from the basic questions: "What, if any, is your present denomination or faith tradition? Which religious denomination do you personally feel closest to?" and "Which religious denomination did you personally feel closest to growing up?" By comparing responses to these two questions, tapping people's views now and when growing up, we arrive

**Figure 3.1. Religious Background and Current Preference,
Three Generations: North Carolina.**

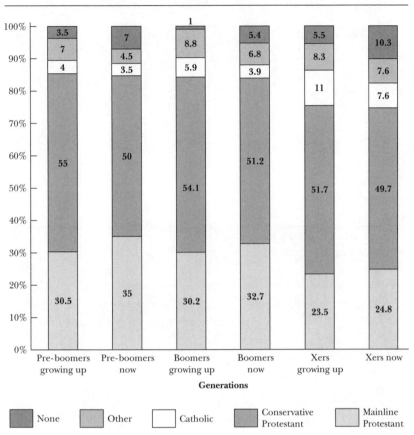

at a measure of the extent of the shift in popular preferences and
the direction of those changes. The figures depict trends for Roman
Catholics, conservative Protestants, mainline Protestants, other religions, and none, for the North Carolina and southern California
samples. We found it necessary to omit from the analysis respondents belonging to historic African American denominations because there were too few cases to break out by generation or state.

Several observations can be made. First, there is a discernible
shift to "none" for all three generations. For pre-boomers as well as
generation Xers, the proportion roughly doubled toward "none"

Figure 3.2. Religious Background and Current Preference, Three Generations: California.

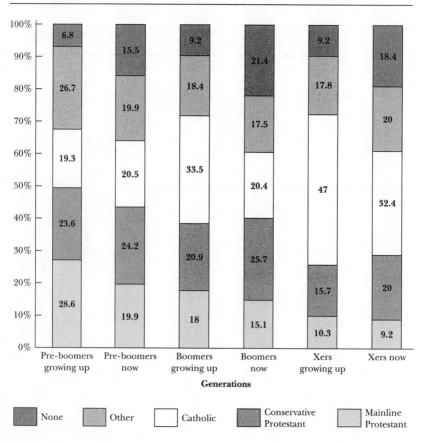

from the time they grew up to the present. By far, the greatest shift in these preferences occurred with boomers. Countercultural trends for that generation continue to show up in surveys. The proportion generally claiming no preference is considerably higher in California, but the trends vary for the two states. Whereas in North Carolina there is the predictable pattern of Xers currently rejecting organized religion more so than boomers, in California the reverse actually holds. Though many Xers claim no religious affiliation, they are overshadowed in this state by the huge number of boomers also having made that choice.

Second, for Catholics there are two interesting trends. The overall proportion growing up Catholic has increased with each generation—not surprising in view of considerable Latino immigration. In California, a staggering 47 percent of the Xer population grew up Catholic. In North Carolina, 11 percent of Xers grew up Catholic, higher actually than might be expected in a southern Protestant environment. Except for pre-boomers in California, current preference for Catholicism is less than when growing up. The decline in Catholic preference is relatively minor for pre-boomers in North Carolina, but considerable for boomers and generation Xers in both states. Without doubt, the greatest break in identification comes between pre-boomers and boomers, consistent with what some commentators have said about the impact that Vatican II has had on Catholic youth during the mid-1960s.[10] Data here make for a strong argument about generational-based religious change.

Third, the number growing up in a mainline Protestant tradition has declined proportionately across the three generations, and especially in California. Hardly news anymore, the fate of this once well-entrenched religious and cultural establishment is one of the big stories of religious change in the United States during the latter half of the twentieth-century. Particularly striking is the large decline for generation Xers currently identifying with moderate-to-liberal Protestant denominations: 9.2 percent in California and 24.8 percent in North Carolina. The religious environments for the two states are obviously different, which is also apparent in switching trends: pre-boomers, boomers, and generation Xers all switch into these high-status denominations in North Carolina, but in California they switch out. A mainline Protestant establishment exists in this decidedly "low-church" southern state that is respected and attractive, especially for those who are upwardly mobile.

Fourth, a conservative Protestant tradition is espoused by half the population in North Carolina, but less than one-fourth within California. Trends for the two states differ significantly: with the former there is some slight decline in current preference compared to the number growing up within these faith traditions, whereas in the latter there is a marked increase in such preference, especially among boomers and generation Xers. Popular evangelicalism has grown rapidly in California over the past half century, although in a highly pluralistic and individualistic ethos not all switchers necessarily accept the doctrines of the tradition into which they switch.[11] Not just conservative Protestant denominations benefit from this popular trend; so too do many independent, nondenominational and community churches that promise a return to primitive religious teachings without the cultural and theological baggage often associated with denominational heritage. Again, the evidence points to major generational-based changes in the religious landscape.

Fifth, generational trends for non-Christian, non-Jewish religious and spiritual traditions differ for the two states. Contrary to expectation, the proportion growing up in other religions has declined across the three generations within California. Historically, the state has been receptive to religious imports from Asia and elsewhere, and a seedbed for new syncretistic religious movements. In North Carolina, there has been a slight increase in preference for other religions. In both states, there is a pattern for people who grew up in other traditions to shift preference later in life, except among generation Xers in California. Of course, the latter have had fewer years in which to change their preference, but at present fully 20 percent of the members of this generation in this state embrace a faith or spirituality belonging to the "other religions" category. This may signal a more established non-Christian, non-Jewish religious sector in a state already known for its span of religious possibilities.

Religious Involvement

To gain further perspective on generational styles of religious involvement, we asked several questions in our surveys. We inquired into current religious involvement using multiple items all having to do with such institutionally prescribed religious practices as attendance at worship services, Sabbath, or Sunday school; prayer; Bible or Scripture study; and participation in a men or women's group within a congregation. Although religion is hardly limited to such expression, what is publicly defined as religious in a society and thus highly institutionalized is important to study. Combining items into a scale, we find significant differences by generation in the direction we would expect: pre-boomers the most involved, boomers next, and generation Xers the least. Fully half of the pre-boomers are "very religious" on our scale, compared to 36 percent of boomers, and 26 percent of generation Xers. As already noted, evidence from various sources shows that the greatest break in religious involvement occurs between pre-boomers and the two younger generations.

We consider religious involvement in more detail in the following chapter. Here, however, we want to look especially at self-reported changes in religious involvement. One obvious predictor of a person's current involvement in a religious group is the extent of his or her religious involvement growing up. People whose parents brought them up within a faith, or who choose it on their own when they are young, tend to remain active in later years; that is to say, youthful religious exposure is likely to stick even if predicting when it might reassert itself is impossible. It is but one of many factors of course shaping a person's involvement in a congregation.

But does religion's early sticking power vary for the generations? Our rather limited evidence suggests that to some extent it does. Forty-five percent of pre-boomers who were "somewhat" or "very" involved religiously when growing up are now "very religious," as measured on our multi-item scale. By comparison, only 32 percent of boomers who were religiously involved when growing up now fit into this most active religious category, and only 26 percent of generation Xers do so.

It may be that in time, as the younger generations pass through the life cycle, they will approach the level of religious involvement observed for pre-boomers; should this be the case, then life cycle better explains these patterns than does generation. However, studies of religious change lead us to suspect that organized religion's sticking power may have declined somewhat over time. The NORC surveys previously mentioned point to declines in involvement for the young of this sort in the period since 1985. Other evidence suggests that many boomers actually drop out of active involvement in church, synagogue, or temple in midlife once their own children grow up, a pattern that goes against the more traditional life-course expectation that people having raised their children in a congregation remain active throughout their lives.[12] Generations vary in religious expression and especially so in how they relate to congregational life.

Beliefs About God

An important battery of questions in our survey had to do with God, both belief in God and discerning the presence of God in everyday life. Both types of question have proved to be promising in religious research. Previous studies show that Americans are quite diverse in their images of God, and they also underscore a great deal of variation in the strength of conviction. The vast majority of Americans of all ages say they believe in God, however what they mean when they say that and how intensely they hold to such belief is an open matter. Research makes clear that the setting and life circumstance in which people experience the presence of God vary a great deal. The great psychologist of a century ago, William James, spoke of the "triggers" of religious experience; what may be a trigger for one person is not necessarily so for someone else. We know that religious imagination is crucial to the power of faith and wide-ranging in its sweep and also that the depth and breadth of the imagery is deeply influenced by a person's life situation and by selective appropriation of the content of a particular religious tradition. Hence it is difficult to generalize about the imagery that comes into play describing a person's meaningful relation with God or the sacred, but we can reasonably expect some difference by generation.

On the question about belief in God, the responses are interesting for what they tell us both about similarity and difference for the generations. Eighty-eight percent of all respondents indicate they definitely believe in God or a Higher Power. Pre-boomers are more likely to report a definite belief in God, at 90 percent; boomers are next at 89 percent, and generation Xers are at 84 percent. As such, the differences are quite small. A somewhat more striking contrast turns up when we look at strength of belief. Generation Xers report they are "uncertain" in their belief, at 15 percent (19 percent in California), followed by boomers at 10 percent and pre-boomers at 9 percent. Boomers and pre-boomers are three times as likely to say they are uncertain but "lean toward believing"; generation Xers are more closely divided on whether to believe or not to believe. Again, sorting out how much of this is generation and how much is age, or life cycle, is impossible.

But clearly there is an expanding sector of young Americans who openly acknowledge their uncertainty in theistic belief, yet who are seriously exploring and debating within themselves what to believe. Abstract formulations of deity seem cold, distant, and unconvincing to them; experience and feelings are the means of discerning the reality and presence of God. "Generation X is the first postmodern worldview generation," a pastor of an evangelical church in California told us. Commenting on the younger members in his congregation and their epistemological skepticism, he notes that "they are a little more flexible in their views. I think a lot of them are still searching and haven't become dogmatic yet." Only 2 percent of the respondents in our survey say they "don't believe in God or a Higher Power," more of them proportionately boomers than for either of the other two generations. In California—a trend-setting state culturally and religiously—a greater number in every generation say they don't believe than is the case in North Carolina; but patterns of overwhelming belief or considerable uncertainty and a small number of atheistic responses are much the same. Region of the country is important in understanding religion, but more important it seems is generational change.

More than 90 percent in our survey believe that God is personally involved in their lives. Interestingly, the difference by generation here is not statistically significant. Boomers are slightly less likely than either of the other two generations to claim personal involvement with God. Over the past several decades, there has been a movement within religious communities to recover the personal and experiential—as spiritual style and as mode of religious knowing—and many Americans, including young Americans, seem to be rejuvenated. Call them postmodern, as does the pastor just quoted, or simply having undergone a shift in cognitive universe, away from the objective toward the subjective, away from the doctrinal to the spiritual, from the head to the heart. What appears to be happening is that in all generations—but perhaps most strikingly among generation Xers—people find, as one commentator says, "the religious in personal experience" and as a result of a "constant yearning, both implicit and explicit, for the almost mystical encounter of the human and the divine."[13] No doubt the person saying this is correct in pointing out, too, the emphasis upon the personal has close affinity with the sense of freedom and responsibility they feel in regard to managing their own spiritual lives. Truth, however defined, must be validated by experience; it must give assurance to believers they can trust their own lead and follow their judgment. Without this, no matter how dogmatically it is proclaimed, it risks becoming hollow.

Where do people experience the presence of God or a spiritual power? There are some differences as reported by the generations, but by and large similarity across generations outweighs whatever contrast there may be. Pre-boomers are actually more likely to say they experience the presence of God or a spiritual power while meditating than either boomers or generation Xers are. This may be surprising, given all that has been said about boomers and their interest in meditation in their earlier years, but such practices have come to be widely diffused in the United States. Boomers do engage in meditation at present more than Xers. Pre-boomers are most inclined (and boomers next) to report a spiritual experience during a moment of great joy, in sorrow or tragedy, in nature, while reading an inspirational book, or in acts of service to others. Deeply embedded cultural narratives in America define these settings and activities as conducive to experience with the divine or the sacred. It may be that pre-boomers report a greater number of such experiences simply because of their age, and thus exposure to such narratives. Some research suggests that as people age, they have more mystical and paranormal experiences.

With regard to feeling the presence of God in a worship service, there are no significant differences by generation. This may seem surprising considering that pre-boomers would likely have greater affinity with a worship service than the other generations. But worship service is not restricted to a conventional church: many people we spoke with belonged to megachurches that had contemporary services, or attended folk masses, or were members of an informal fellowship often meeting in people's homes, and all were quite likely to say they encountered the presence of God in such a setting. Worship is hardly limited to a particular form. Generation Xers stand out in their claims of having a spiritual encounter when visiting a shrine or other sacred place, and in the significance they attach to dreams, visions, and encounters of one sort or another. Almost half say they have had such an encounter of this kind, and almost a quarter report feeling a spiritual presence in dreams, visions, or revelations. Miracle, epiphany, prophecy, signs, and other claims of supernatural encounter all fit into their more open, engaging approach to piecing together religious notions from a variety of sources and their emphasis on the deeply personal, experiential aspects of religion. They attach more importance to exploring differing religious teachings, and to learning from them, than do even the boomers, who were often labeled as spiritual dabblers when growing up. It appears they are reclaiming primitive encounters and experiences that are associated historically with faith and spirituality but that often are downplayed within the religious establishment. In this respect, religious heritage is a resource that is being rediscovered.

Religious Individualism

Much has been written about religious individualism in American life. Historically, this has been the way Americans typically approach religion, although many observers argue that the level of personal autonomy has increased in the period since World War II. What we do know is that the post–World War II generations express greater individualism in matters of faith than was true for those born in the twentieth century prior to that watershed period. The argument some years ago by Bellah and colleagues about religious subjectivity and attention to self in this period—what they called "Sheilaism"[14]— is not without merit. For example, when asked about whether "an individual should arrive at his or her own religious beliefs independent of any church or religious group," 47 percent of generation Xers, 40 percent of boomers, and 34 percent of pre-boomers "strongly agree." Not surprisingly, endorsement of religious individualism is greater overall in California than in North Carolina, but the spread on this question is unambiguous in both states. So clear a trend in two quite dissimilar states within the country reveals what is an unquestioned religious reality today: Americans want—indeed, insist upon—great latitude in arriving at their beliefs.

Other items yield similar conclusions. When asked whether "a religious person should follow his or her conscience, even if it means going against what his or her religious tradition teaches," 60 percent of both generation Xers and boomers agree, compared to 52 percent of pre-boomers. Asked if "the rules about morality preached by most religious groups today are just too restrictive," 42 percent of generation Xers strongly agreed; 30 percent of boomers and 27 percent of pre-boomers did. On yet another strongly-worded item

("People who have God in their lives don't need a church or religious group"), 44 percent of generation Xers, 40 percent of boomers, and 35 percent of pre-boomers agreed. Combining positive responses to these four items to create a scale on religious individualism, we find a decisive spread in mean scores: 3.3 for generation Xers, 3.0 for boomers, and 2.8 for pre-boomers. Religious individualism finds expression in every age, but for many younger Americans it is defended as a religious style. It might even be said that this is an example of a "period effect," when Americans of every generation are deeply touched by an individualistic religious ethos; yet it is clear that gen Xers, at least at this moment in their lives, embody the trends more so than the other two generations.

Even so, there are countertrends that deserve attention. The trend away from excessive individualism is most apparent when comparing generation Xers and boomers in their involvement in organized religion. Whereas 50 percent of boomers say a religious congregation is very important in their life, 53 percent of generation Xers say the same. Obviously this is a small gap, yet it is significant that the Xers are also more likely than members of the generation immediately before them to say they have "a great deal" of confidence in churches and organized religion. Similarly, they express a greater level of trust in the U.S. Congress, the U.S. Supreme Court, and organized labor. Again, differences between the generations on these questions are by no means huge, but the consistency of responses cannot be overlooked. They point to some shift away from the high level of alienation and distrust of social institutions associated with boomers.

If there is an explanation of this slight reversal in trends it is that though generation Xers are highly individualistic in spiritual styles, they also yearn for religious community, for the support and nurturing that can come from the presence of others who share similar commitments. It is important, too, that gen Xers are much more likely to be involved in a congregation that makes use of media such as popular music, video, and art, thereby offering culturally current and engaging opportunities for sharing and worship. The importance of this observation lies not simply in the powers of communication and conviction that come with accommodating faith messages to what is culturally current. It may be that in such a setting anti-institutional sentiment is deflected, and communal identity and participation are greatly enriched, with the result that religious involvement takes on greater affect and a more positive sense of group belonging.[15] If so, we then have to conclude that the religious culture of a generation is puzzling, even paradoxical at times. Xers in some congregations may have more in common with pre-boomers than they do with many alienated, anti-institutional boomers. Broadly speaking, it also means that the relationship between individualism and community is complex indeed, and hardly one to be characterized as zero-sum.

The Churched and the Unchurched

In this final section of the chapter, we look at the churched and unchurched populations for the three generations. It is a distinction often drawn by sociologists of religion pointing to two quite divergent cultures in the United States, one communally oriented and closely tied to a church, temple, synagogue, mosque, or other religious institution; and the other less religiously based and oriented to personal freedom. Often the distinction is used to describe a growing divide between "traditional-religious" and "cosmopolitan-modernist" cultures.[16] Whereas the former is identified with family and conventional moral values rooted within a faith tradition, the latter is much more oriented to secular, technological values and more receptive of social and cultural change. Commentators note that such a divide is reinforced by the expansion in higher education and the changing values, orientations, and lifestyles over the past half century. As we saw with the participation patterns discussed earlier in this chapter, pre-boomers have a higher proportion of members belonging to the churched culture than either of the other two generations.

The churched population is more conventional and traditional-minded than the unchurched across all three generations. Questions we asked inquiring into the respondent's attitude toward social, political, economic, religious, and personal moral issues all revealed, quite predictably, the churched population to be more conservative. Contrary to what we might have expected, we do not find greater divergence between the two cultures among the youngest Americans. Moral and religious boundaries obviously change from generation to generation, but the statistical spread in views and attitudes between the churched and the unchurched seems not to have increased much. The stable churched culture is diminished in size for both boomers and generation Xers, but perhaps more important for the latter especially is a trend cutting across that generation toward somewhat greater moral and political traditionalism. For sure, there is no evolving, ever-widening gap between the churched and unchurched cultures of the sort that proponents of secularization would argue. American religion is much too fluid, evolving, and populist-based for so simple an analysis.

Religious themes are blurred across the churched-unchurched divide since love of God and religious faith, practice, and charity cannot be contained within the walls of organized religion. This is very much the situation with Xers, the generation most in the news at present and the most paradoxical religious in terms. When Catholic writer Tom Beaudoin says that the most common sentence he heard in his interviews with members of this generation was "If you want to talk about church, I'm not very interested," clearly he is describing the unchurched who, as he says, are irreverent, deeply skeptical, and suspicious of religious institutions, yet religious often in their own way.[17] At the cultural extreme, they mark themselves by tattoos and body piercings, sending a visible message of their opposition to the conventional styles of the traditional religious community; theirs is a strong signal to the effect they are not Wuthnow's dwellers settled comfortably into a place but seekers looking for authentic religiousness, but unsure if or where it might be found.

Even more so than with boomers now in midlife, Xers invest a great deal of emotion and meaning in the distinction between being religious and being spiritual, opting for the latter as an expression of lived theology and a critique of organized religion. But this portrait of the generation is at odds with the moderate views of many Xers who have not written off all congregations and parishes. There is a churched version of the generation X culture that is definitely milder, more open to the possibility of discerning the mystery of life wherever it may be found—even in stodgy places like congregations and parishes. *Milder* and *more open* do not mean, however, that this culture does not reach far or permeate the boundaries of the congregation or parish. Xers are generally skeptical, suspicious, and at times irreverent, but if we dig beneath this exterior appearance we discover real people who often are eager and anxious, as one young person in a California congregation told us, to "start working on God." As already mentioned, writer Winifred Gallagher brought out a book about this same time entitled *Working on God*,[18] capturing the notion of religion for neoagnostics as a process of negotiation and formation of faith. She suggests there is a counterpart to the noisy, external appearance of doubt and suspicion: an internal, much quieter quest for something deep and vital. Call it a quest for the sacred; what distinguishes the churched from the unchurched in this instance turns on the willingness to entertain the question, "What if religion could be about something more, essentially about getting real with life?" Those who can say yes to this question are spiritually seeking, hybrid souls as we say, religious on their own terms, even if the word *religion* conjures up negative feelings.

It is a question presupposing that life has no easy answers. It is also recognition, articulated better by some than by others, that if there are answers they are likely to come in the context of sharing within a faith community. The truth is many young Americans do discover an institutional space for working on God and negotiating religious styles within mainline Protestant and Catholic congregations, within Jewish synagogues, even within contemporary evangelicalism. They find authentic religiousness not handed down to them by religious authority, but as something worked on and shaped through personal and shared experience in relation to Scripture and religious teachings, within these settings or in the specialized context that these settings make possible. Beaudoin allows as much when he says "wandering the edges of the institution" may be the way young Americans come to terms with themselves and discover this fuller realization of life.

On some fundamental religious questions, there is a crucial difference by generation, which shows up within the churched population. For example, when asked about the significance attached to a particular denomination or religious tradition, 41 percent of the churched gen Xers and 40 percent of churched boomers say it is important, compared to 54 percent of the churched pre-boomers. For churchgoers, clearly there is a discernible change of outlook toward religious heritage and its role and authority for faith commitment on the part of the post–World War II generations. As popularly understood, faith communities have lost much of their distinctiveness of history and theology. This becomes all the more important considering that among the unchurched, generational differences on this item are not striking; the unchurched of all ages and generations have a rather uniform, secular outlook. What we have is an instance of vanishing boundaries, finding its fullest expression among the unchurched.

Those views having evolved broadly in society, we also begin to see something of the same pattern in the connection between religion and morality. When asked if "most importantly, religion teaches good moral life," boomers and generation Xers are less likely than pre-boomers within the churched sector to embrace the notion that religion is a source of a good moral life. That religion and morality are connected seems to have been widely accepted in an earlier era and is still reflected in the views of many pre-boomers. However, the younger generations (even within churches today) do not adhere as strongly to an older bourgeois culture that presumed a close connection between the two. This breakup of an older cultural pattern has long been reflected in the expansion of the unchurched sector, but now it finds expression within the congregation with the younger generations. In no way does this suggest that these church members and participants lack strong views on moral issues; indeed, the great majority of them do. Rather, the point is that each and every moral issue must now be dealt with on its own terms. Old-style generalization about religion and morality has given way to specifics in an age of single-issue politics. Consequently, it becomes more difficult to peg people on a liberal-to-conservative continuum of religious ethics than was once the case.

But such changes have also opened up new opportunity for the congregation. A good example is the evolving ways in which churches, synagogues, and temples are now relating to marriage and family styles. Historically, throughout the twentieth century at least, those who were divorced or separated (and single parents in particular) often were less involved in the congregation than those in an intact marriage and family. White, middle-class Protestant congregations especially functioned as a bastion of familism. Church teachings, programs, and ethos all sanctioned the nuclear family; those engaged in a sexual relationship outside of marriage or those from a broken marriage typically felt out of place or were forced to be less than honest about their lifestyle and status.

This heritage persists in many congregations today. But in a growing number, too, new programs for singles (including those who are divorced and single parents) have led to greater involvement. Corresponding to these programmatic initiatives is an environment of greater tolerance in regard to lifestyle, various forms of family arrangement, and changing patterns of sexual intimacy. People who might otherwise be alienated from a congregation are drawn to a religious setting that, as one divorced woman told us, is "nonjudgmental and very accepting." The popularity of evangelical Christian singles' groups for those currently unmarried is a case in point of greater openness and acceptance.

Despite their conservative moral teachings, evangelical and "new paradigm"[19] churches are quite successful in creating a more accepting environment. Popular culture places great emphasis on the interplay between the body and the sensual and upon the mystery of human experience, including sexual experience—themes that are rich spiritually and theologically, and increasingly embraced in a creative way by religious leaders. Redefining moral and religious norms relating to sexuality is highly contentious, but the impetus to do so and to explore further its connection to spirituality is very much a growing grassroots sentiment. As one California pastor said to us about ministering to single-parent families, "We must listen now more than ever to who the people are, not only in the congregation but in the world . . . and I've seen in the last year or two more of a movement that says, 'You know, we've gotta change to make a difference in people's lives,' and yes, that is happening, there's more of an openness to people's real lives."

What all these changes imply is that the boundaries once distinguishing the churched from the unchurched are in a great deal of flux. Although members of the younger generations are as inclined as pre-boomers in our survey to say they want a "sharp distinction between the religious and the secular," they mean something else by the comment. They want lines drawn less in keeping with a Norman Rockwell world where religious experience and practice are clearly demarcated and rigidly institutionalized, preferring instead a world with permeable boundaries where an individual's own experience and journey are privileged as a spiritual trajectory over rigid structures and expectations. Certainly they thrive upon a blurring of older religious and cultural dichotomies such as sacred-secular, spirit-body, and public-private, in the search for reconfigurations in keeping with a more holistic human vision.

In keeping with our earlier discussion on the importance of familial and communal themes in the congregation, many people today—and not just young adults—are looking for a deeper level of spiritual bonding built upon the sacred potential of human experience, be it intimate or simply a relationship with fellow believers. Fundamentally, the old cultural and theological boundaries separating the human from the divine may themselves be under revision. Beaudoin must be on to something when he observes that what many people, and certainly many gen Xers, are looking for is a lived theology that engages experience at the intersection of the human and the divine, one that takes seriously "exploring the experiences of the incarnation, that is, finding the divine in human form."[20] If so, our very categories of churched and unchurched may need to be recast and shorn of their older, culturally embedded assumptions. Certainly our conceptions of the congregation must be sharpened, a concern we take up in the next chapter.

Chapter Four

Generational Divides in Congregations

In the romantic comedy *Keeping the Faith,* two friends—members of generation X, one a Catholic priest and the other a rabbi—set their respective congregations astir as they introduce various innovations, which we might describe as postmodern or posttraditional: introducing contemporary music into traditional congregational worship; worship practices that mix and match borrowings from other faith traditions; interfaith and intergenerational programming; and a general religious style that sits loosely to their inherited traditions. The film presents one perspective on the cultural world of generation X, in terms of both religion and morality. Regarding the latter, the two young clergy struggle with ethical issues—especially around sexuality—that test integrity and fidelity to their calling. Although all works out happily in the end (as befits a romantic comedy) the film presents an authentic, if slightly exaggerated, insight into how generational differences affect a congregation, leading sometimes to acrimonious conflict and sometimes to significant change.

In the previous chapters, we have considered the meaning of generational cohorts and examined the social and cultural worlds of three generations: pre-boomer, baby boomer, and generation X. We've tried to show how these three cohorts differ from one another, especially when it comes to religion and spirituality. In this and the remaining chapters, we turn to "So what?" questions:

- What are the consequences of these generational worlds for the church and synagogue?

- Do generational groups differ in what they look for in a congregation?
- What factors affect their involvement in a congregation?
- How, if at all, are congregations attempting to respond to these generational challenges?
- What might the congregation need to change in its practices if it is to attract members of the different cohorts into their membership?
- What tension or conflict does generational expectation create for a congregation?

Later in this chapter (and in the ones to come), we draw on several sources of data to suggest answers. First, however, we need to note what may seem obvious but is nevertheless important to recall: just as generations differ in important ways, so also do congregations. Some of these differences have historical roots. Thus, before turning to our data, we take a brief historical excursion.

The Congregation in American History

In the Introduction, we pointed out that congregational forms are not static and unchanging. We noted that congregational leaders and their members must constantly adapt to challenge as populations and social settings change. Such adaptation is nothing new; American religious history makes this clear. Writing about congregations in the United States, historian Brooks Holifield points to four congregational models that have emerged over time in response to changing social and cultural milieu.[1]

The first, which he calls the *comprehensive congregation,* was the dominant model from the early settlement of America roughly to the establishment of the republic at the end of the eighteenth century. It was so named because the ideal was to have only one congregation per community, a congregation that would comprehend the whole community. Its primary reason for being was conducting public worship. There were no Sunday schools or other church organizations as we now know them. If they fought over issues—and there certainly were church fights—a congregation's conflicts were primarily over worship: Who could take communion? Who could be baptized, and how? Should the congregation sing hymns?

These comprehensive congregations were also public institutions, responsible for giving aid to the poor in the community and also for exercising discipline.

As the new nation grew, as towns became larger and more diverse, the comprehensive congregation gave way to what Holifield calls the *devotional congregation*. Now a town could have not one but several congregations of differing denominations, which developed a variety of new patterns and programs: worship and music styles, Sunday school, prayer meetings, Bible class, and mission societies. The diverse congregations often competed to offer the best programs, and social class distinctions developed among them.

Near the end of the nineteenth century in large urban centers, a third model emerged, the *social congregation*. This was similar to what today we might call a seven-days-a-week church. In addition to Sunday worship and the various programs introduced in the devotional model, the social congregation sponsored Sunday school concerts, church socials, women's meetings, youth groups, girls' guilds, boys' brigades, sewing circles, benevolent societies, temperance societies, athletic clubs, scout troops, and many other activities. They built gyms, schools, and boarding houses for single women; they engaged in many outreach activities in the surrounding community. Preaching and worship continued to be emphasized, as in previous models, but there was more use of congregational singing, shared prayer, and responsive reading.

Finally, in the latter half of the twentieth century, a fourth model emerged, the *participatory model*. It is characteristic of most present-day churches. Continuing many of the emphases of earlier models, this congregation designs its programs to meet the needs of an increasingly diverse and well-educated laity—different "audiences"—who are self-conscious about their participation and choose to be involved on their own terms and not necessarily those set by a leadership elite. Lay initiative and participation in all aspects of congregational life, including decision making and corporate worship, are emphasized. Church architecture, especially worship space, also bears witness to the shift to participation, away from earlier practice where worship was a performance before passive observers. The shift to the participatory congregation is a way of responding to the broad trends that we analyzed in Chapter Two: religious pluralism, privatization, detraditionalization, and the growth of a seeker mentality.

Such a congregation offers a space where numerous voices may be heard and responded to. At the same time, it also increases the likelihood of tension and conflict as diverse perspectives strive to be heard.

Though Holifield's analysis carries us through the 1980s, it only barely touches on an even newer model: what has been variously called the posttraditional or new paradigm congregation,[2] intentionally designed in response to the social and cultural changes we have discussed in previous chapters and often with a specific generation in mind as its target audience. The posttraditional model is in many ways simply an extension of the participatory, and it also has some of the characteristics of the social congregation—especially its seven-days-a-week emphasis. Typical is Willow Creek Community Church in Great Barrington, Illinois. Now twenty-five years old, Willow Creek, with its "seeker-sensitive" worship, emphasis on small groups, and multiple congregational ministries that have been characterized as "mall-like," has spawned a growing group of emulating congregations across the nation (as well as numerous detractors).[3] On the one hand, expectation of participation in congregational life and ministry is minimized for those who are considered seekers. Everything is made to be user-friendly, including instruction to visitors or seekers that they are guests and should not feel pressured to contribute to the offering. Likewise, traditional hymns, liturgies, and Christian symbols are either played down or entirely absent from the church architecture and worship services designed for seekers. Here is how one writer described the changes he observed in congregations following the new paradigm model, which he called the "next" churches: "No spires. No crosses. No robes. No clerical collars. No hard pews. No kneelers. No biblical gobbledygook. No prayerly rote. No fire, no brimstone. No pipe organs. No dreary eighteenth-century hymns. No forced solemnity. No Sunday finery. No collection plates. . . . Centuries of European tradition and Christian habit are deliberately being abandoned, clearing the way for the new, contemporary forms of worship and belonging."[4]

On the other hand, the posttraditional congregation does have high expectations for those who move beyond seeking. Their aim is to make them "fully devoted followers of Christ"—shortened in some instances to *FDFX* on T-shirts that we observed. Through weeknight worship services with traditional hymns, teaching sermons, and observance of sacraments; through small groups in which all who move beyond seeking are expected to participate; and through emphasis on discovering and using one's gifts in ministry, the intention is to lead members into ever growing and deepening discipleship. Although this pattern varies from one congregation to another, the posttraditional model has been especially designed with boomers and gen Xers in mind. We see examples of this kind of congregation in the chapters that follow.

As Holifield shows, each of these models—including the fifth one that we have added—built on its predecessors, adapting some of the practices of the preceding model while also innovating to meet the challenges of social and cultural change. These models form the historical stream in which contemporary congregations swim. Their diversity reminds us that there is no single congregational model to which one can point, and that congregations have regularly adapted to new contexts. Those that have not adapted have dwindled in membership and influence, and many have ceased to exist.

At the same time, because the legacy of the past continues to inform the present life of the congregation, inherited patterns make adaptation and change difficult. This is especially true for the older congregation (here we refer to congregational age, rather than members'). All congregations, particularly those that have been in existence for some time, have a distinctive culture—beliefs, rituals, symbols, stories, and practices—developed out of the inheritance from its own history and the denomination's. These cultural patterns are highly valued; especially in older congregations, they often set limits on how much adaptation is possible. A new congregation that has yet to develop strongly valued cultural patterning—other than widely shared views of what a congregation should be—is less constrained. It is not surprising, as we shall see, that the congregations that have most readily adapted to generational difference are the newer ones.

Consequently, in asking what a congregation might do today to bridge generational worlds, we are asking not only what kind of continuing adaptation is necessary but also what is possible given a congregation's history and present makeup. How can tradition, of which the congregation is a bearer, remain a living tradition, connected with the personal narratives and experiences of new generations as well as the older cohorts in their midst? The film *Keeping the*

Faith offers one possible answer. Our data suggest others. Thus we turn now to two kinds of data: our telephone interviews with random samples of the population in North Carolina and southern California, and, importantly, our data from selected congregations in the two regions. We look first at the telephone survey data before turning in this and the remaining chapters to a closer look at the congregations.

How Generations View the Congregation

In the preceding chapter, we used our telephone survey data to consider how the generations differ from one another personally, socially, and religiously. Now we extend that analysis to ask about their valuing of congregations and their preferences regarding the type of congregation.

How important is their congregation to the members of the three generations? Excluding those who indicated that they were not involved at all in a congregation, we asked the remaining interviewees about the importance of their congregation in their lives. A majority of all three generations told us that their congregation was very important to them. This was especially true, as might be expected, for those who reported high involvement in various aspects of congregational life. Nonetheless, there were significant differences among the three generations, and by region. Reflecting the strong religious culture of the South, North Carolinians of all generations—especially pre-boomers (72 percent)—affirmed that their congregation was of great importance. In contrast, 40 percent of California boomers—still a high percentage—indicated that their congregation was of great importance.

But what kind of congregation do the generations value? What do they look for in a congregation? In the interviews, we listed a number of congregational characteristics that we suspected might be more or less attractive to members of these generations and various religious traditions. Several of the characteristics reflect distinctions that other research has highlighted. For each characteristic, we asked about its positive or negative impact on the individual's participation. For those not currently involved, we asked how the presence or absence of the characteristic would affect possible involvement. Table 4.1 shows the average (mean) scores for each characteristic by gen-

Table 4.1. Preference in Choosing a Congregation by Generation and Region (State).

Congregational Characteristics	Generation X		Boomers		Pre-boomers		Significance
	Calif.	N.C.	Calif.	N.C.	Calif.	N.C.	
Particular denomination or tradition	2.96	3.14	2.95	3.11	3.19	3.19	ns
Clear rules of morals and ethics	2.99	3.14	3.00	3.21	3.19	3.28	* #
Sharp distinction between religious and secular	2.79	2.75	2.47	2.82	2.73	2.80	*
Emphasizes social action and justice issues	3.07	3.05	3.14	3.06	2.97	2.92	#
Emphasizes helping needy people	3.77	3.73	3.76	3.78	3.70	3.83	ns
Emphasizes witnessing and faith sharing	3.22	3.40	3.12	3.37	3.05	3.46	*
Emphasizes individual decision making	3.05	3.09	3.03	2.78	2.79	2.74	#
Emphasizes shared leadership	3.05	3.27	3.24	3.32	3.31	3.42	* #
Preference for contemporary worship and music (scores vary between 1 and 2)	1.56	1.47	1.61	1.48	1.47	1.35	* #

Notes: Higher mean score = more favorable response.

* = between-state difference at <.05.

= between-generation difference at <.05.

eration and region (state). We consider first those comparisons that are statistically significant either between regions or among generations. We also note some comparisons by denominational family, which we have not shown in a table.

In the preceding chapter, we considered religious or denominational preference, both when growing up and at present, and we saw much evidence of denominational switching by the respondents. Here, however, we asked not about the respondent's denomination but rather whether the denomination or faith tradition of the congregation mattered for actual or potential involvement. Given claims about the declining significance of denominationalism,[5] we were surprised to find denominations faring as well in both regions and in all generations—at least when it comes to the denominational affiliation of the congregation. The typical response was that the congregation's denomination has at least a somewhat positive impact on people's involvement. Less than 25 percent of all groups gave negative responses. There were no significant differences between regions or among generations.

We looked further at denominational family groupings. Catholics of all generations generally rated denomination as more important than did the other denominational families. What this suggests is that when people, regardless of generation, choose a congregation, the denomination (or at least its denominational family) still matters. That is, the prospective member typically affiliates with a congregation that at least reflects a particular denominational family or tradition (for example, mainline Protestant or conservative Protestant). Where the declining significance of denomination may be most felt is not at the congregational level, but in the relationship of the congregation and its members to their regional and national denominational organizations. We did not, however, explore these relationships.

As with the declining importance of denomination, much has also been written about the attractiveness of the strict or strong congregation, that is, one that has strict membership standards and makes belief and behavioral demands on the members. Such a congregation, as Dean Kelley once argued, generates an ardor that "catches up [members' lives] in a surge of significance and purpose." In contrast, a weak congregation produces lukewarmness, individualism, and reticence to share one's faith.[6] Though not disagreeing that many prefer a strict congregation, Nancy Ammerman has argued that there are many "golden rule Christians," as she calls them, who avoid such congregations and are much more content with a less demanding one; they want its assistance in raising their children, want to be related to Something or Someone that transcends human life, and want to be involved in serving others.[7] Although our survey touches only lightly on this issue, we did ask about preference for a congregation that states clear rules of morals and ethics (one aspect of the strict church). The majority of our respondents prefer such a congregation, although there were significant regional and generational differences. Preference for a strict congregation was generally high for all generations, however Californians were less positive in their evaluation of such congregations than North Carolinians were. Pre-boomers were generally more likely than Xers or boomers to be attracted to such a congregation. When we took into account the denominational family to which respondents belong,[8] we found, not surprisingly, that conservative Protestants and African Americans in all generations expressed strong preference for a strict congregation, as was also the case for pre-boomer Catholics. Mainline Protestants in all generations were the least likely of the denominational families to prefer a strict congregation.

Whether the congregation made a sharp distinction between the religious and secular aspects of life was evaluated as moderately positive by all generations, although Californians were slightly less positive about such congregations than North Carolinians. Both Xers and boomers were more likely to be positive about a congregation that emphasizes social action and social justice issues than were preboomers. Region made little difference. Black Protestants and Catholics of all races and generations favored such a congregation. All generational cohorts were favorably attracted to congregations with programs that reach out to those in need. Responses also did not vary significantly by region or denominational family.

Congregations that emphasize witnessing and faith sharing were generally positively evaluated by all three generations, with no significant differences. Californians, however, were significantly less positive about such congregations than North Carolinians. Conservative and African American Protestants in all generations were most likely to be positive. Catholics and mainline Protestants were slightly less favorable, though still generally positive in their evaluation.

In a reflection of the predilection for religious individualism that we noted in the previous chapter, Xers and boomers were significantly more likely than pre-boomers to prefer a congregation emphasizing that individual members should make their own decisions about doctrinal and moral issues. This finding is, on first glance, in some contrast to the previously noted preference for a strict congregation. Further analysis shows, however, that responses to the two items are negatively correlated, and that those who are less religiously involved are the majority of those preferring a congregation that emphasizes individual decision making. (We return to this issue later in the chapter.) The regional differences were not statistically significant. The denominational family to which respondents belong also made little difference.

The one characteristic in which boomers and pre-boomers were more like each other than like Xers was in preferring a congregation that emphasizes sharing of leadership between clergy and laity. Although Protestants have long stressed the "priesthood of all believers"—one meaning of shared leadership—it has sometimes been more a matter of lip service than actual practice. Nonetheless, shared leadership has been more strongly emphasized in recent years in Holifield's fourth congregational type, the participatory congregation; it also receives emphasis in what we call posttraditional or new paradigm congregations, which encourage lay members to use their gifts in some form of appropriate ministry. Similarly, Catholic parishes since the Second Vatican Council have come more and more to emphasize shared leadership as a way of giving expression to the council's emphasis on the church as the work of all of God's people and not just that of the bishop or priest. North Carolinians of all generations gave more importance to shared leadership than did Californians. Denominational family made little difference in evaluation. We suspect that shared leadership is not as high a priority for Xers because, being younger, many of them would not have had—or been given—much opportunity to be involved in congregational decision making.

Finally, what of the worship and music styles practiced in a congregation? Few issues in recent years have been so hotly contested or contributed so greatly to congregational conflict as the style of worship and music. Should a congregation adapt its music and worship—even its architecture—to meet the tastes of younger generations? What we call the posttraditional or new paradigm congregation has been at the forefront of such change, as have many other congregations following or adapting the Willow Creek model or innovating on their own.

Table 4.1 includes responses to questions about preference for traditional versus contemporary music style. We combined the responses to create an index that varies on a continuum between traditional and contemporary preference. Scores could vary from 1 (favoring traditional) to 2 (favoring contemporary).[9] Both generational and regional differences were statistically significant; however, the average scores in the table mask an interesting split. Just over one-third of the respondents preferred traditional worship and music styles; another third preferred contemporary; and just under one-third fell in the middle, preferring both styles. Californians of all generations were more favorable to a contemporary style than were North Carolinians. Boomers and Xers, especially Californians, were more likely to favor a contemporary style, in contrast to pre-boomers, who mostly favored a traditional worship style and music.

When we looked further at generational differences by denominational family, both mainline and conservative Protestants as well as Jewish Xers expressed stronger preference for contemporary worship and music than was true for African American Protestants or Catholic Xers. Xers with no religious preference also strongly favored contemporary worship and music styles. African American Protestant boomers and boomers with no religious preference indicated the strongest attraction to contemporary style. African American and conservative Protestant pre-boomers were more likely to lean toward contemporary expression, although most pre-boomers, especially Catholics, were strongly traditional in their preferences.

What Affects Generational Religious Involvement?

With these various similarities and differences in congregational preference as well as other comparisons that we took note of in the previous chapter, can we say anything more from our data about the factors that affect religious involvement for each generation?

Figure 4.1. Religious Involvement by Generation and Region.

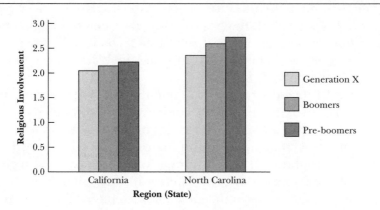

To answer this question, we used the index of current religious involvement referred to in Chapter Three, an index that reflects the amount of participation in several religious practices: worship attendance, Sunday school attendance, prayer and meditation, and Bible reading. Respondents' religious involvement is the average of their scores on each practice and can vary from 1 (low involvement) to 4 (high involvement).[10] Figure 4.1 shows the involvement profile by generation and region. Californians are less involved in religious practices than North Carolinians. Also, involvement increases from younger to older generations.

We also compared involvement scores among the five denominational families plus those indicating no religious preference. The results are shown in Figure 4.2. In the denominational family comparison (except for the "other" group), pre-boomers had the highest level of involvement. Gen X and boomer involvement is roughly similar for mainline Protestants; but for all other denominational families, boomers occupied a middle position between Xers and pre-boomers. Although, as might be expected, those with no preference were the least involved, Catholic religious participation was generally lower than for the other denominational families, though not far different from that of mainline Protestants.

Given these profiles, we used the statistical method of multiple regression analysis to examine the effect of various factors on religious involvement. Included were background factors (such as gen-

**Figure 4.2. Religious Involvement by Generation
and Denominational Family.**

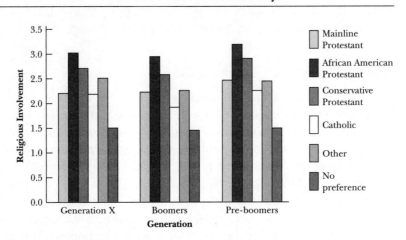

der, race, and level of education) and a number of factors more directly associated with one's religion. Several of the items that we
considered previously—for example, congregational characteristics and worship and music preferences, and so on—are also included. Multiple regression allows us to see how much a particular
factor affects involvement when the effects of all the other factors
are taken into account at the same time. We conducted a separate
regression analysis for each generation. (For those interested in
the statistical findings, Table A.2 in the Appendix summarizes the
results. Here we describe the relationships that were statistically
significant at the 95 percent level of confidence or greater.[11])

In some sense—surprising given previous findings—one relationship that turned out not to be statistically significant when the
other variables were considered along with it was region or state.
This does not mean that the regional differences noted earlier are
not real or important for many purposes; rather, it means that when
considered along with the various other factors in the regression
analysis, they do not help us explain religious involvement. Other
factors are more important.

Before considering what these other factors are, we note that the
overall regression model predicts religious involvement quite well,

accounting for 42 percent of the variance[12] in religious involvement for Xers, 50 percent for boomers, and 48 percent for pre-boomers. Although this is a complex analysis, several things stand out when we consider only those factors that were statistically significant.

Factors in Generation X Involvement

Considering first the factors affecting generation X's involvement, being African American was positively associated with participation.[13] Having another racial or ethnic identity did not significantly affect the pattern of involvement, although being Asian American was weakly related in a negative direction. Neither did the respondent's gender make a difference for Xer involvement, as it did for the other two generations; however, being married was positively associated. Much to our regret, we made a major oversight in constructing the questions for the telephone interview survey. We neglected to include a question about the number of children present in the home, which much past research has shown to be a highly important factor affecting religious participation. Many young married couples who have dropped out of church or synagogue return when they have young children, concerned that their children receive a religious education. Although we can do nothing about our omission of this important question, we suspect that the positive impact of being married on religious involvement is in large part a proxy for the missing information about children.

Although Xers were reported to have significantly lower religious involvement while they were growing up than the other two generations, such involvement is nonetheless an important influence in their present participation. The same is true regarding the influence of their parents' involvement. If Xer parents were involved in a church or synagogue when Xers were growing up, it is likely that they too are now involved.

Two scales that we constructed from various responses are strongly related to involvement, though in opposite directions.[14] One measures the extent of respondents' self-reported experience of God or a transcendent power in various aspects of life; the other is the previously mentioned measure of individualism in the respondents' approach to religion. As we saw in Chapter Three, a considerable majority of respondents of all generations affirmed belief in God and reported experience of God's presence in their lives. As might be expected, respondents scoring high on the Experience of God scale were significantly more likely to be religiously involved than those with lower scores. In contrast, however, religious individualists—those, for example, who believe (among other things) that individuals should arrive at their religious beliefs independently of any church or religious group—were much less likely to be involved.

As we noted in Chapter Three, friends play an especially important role in an Xer's life. Thus it is not surprising that an important factor positively affecting Xer involvement was having friends present in the congregation. In contrast, having other members of one's household present in the congregation was not important for Xers.

As a last set of measures in our analysis, we also included the several congregational characteristics that we considered previously. Only two characteristics—the congregation emphasizing that individuals should make their own decisions about doctrinal and moral issues, and the congregation emphasizing faith sharing—were statistically significant. The former was negatively related to involvement, the latter positively related.

Factors in Boomer Involvement

Turning to factors affecting boomers' current religious involvement, we found them in many respects to be similar to Xers, with a few exceptions. Among background factors, being Asian American was negatively related to involvement[15]; however, being African American was positively related to involvement. Again, as was true for Xers, being married was important for boomer involvement—perhaps also reflecting the presence of children in the family.

Among variables reflecting religious factors, parental religious involvement and the respondent's own religious involvement while growing up were less important (not statistically significant) in influencing current involvement for boomers in contrast to generation Xers. Both Experience of God and Religious Individualism scales showed quite important influence on boomer participation, as was true for Xers, and as before the two scales work in opposite directions—the former positively related, the latter negatively related. Similarly, having friends as members of the congregation is important for boomer involvement, though slightly less so than for

Xers. As for congregational characteristics that affect involvement, a strict congregation (one with clearly stated rules of morals and ethics) increases boomer involvement. Additionally, boomers are more likely to be involved in a congregation that stresses clear rules of morals and ethics, emphasizes witnessing and faith sharing, and promotes shared leadership.

Factors in Pre-Boomer Involvement

Finally, when we consider the religious involvement of the pre-boomer generation, the profile is somewhat different from the other two. Among background factors, being African American is positively related to involvement. In contrast to the two younger generations, the pre-boomer's level of education also had a positive effect on religious involvement; the higher the level of education, the greater the involvement. Being married or widowed also positively affected pre-boomer involvement.

On matters more directly related to religion, scoring high on experience of God was strongly positively related to pre-boomer involvement (as was true for the other generations). In contrast, religious individualism was a strongly negative factor. Having both household members and friends as members of the congregation was important for participation. As for congregational characteristics that supported pre-boomer involvement, the congregation's denominational affiliation had a positive effect, as did the congregation's emphasis on faith sharing and witnessing. The latter effect was especially strong.

The regression analyses are useful for drawing several conclusions. With regard to background factors, being African American was positively important for participation with all three generations; being Asian American was negatively related to boomer involvement if the responses of the small number of Asian American respondents can be considered reliable (see note 15). Level of education mattered for religious involvement only in the case of the pre-boomers in our sample. Being married was important for involvement with all three generational groups; had we not inadvertently omitted the question about having children present in the home, we suspect this would also have been important in strengthening involvement, especially for married Xers and boomers, who are most likely to have young children. Religious involvement while growing up positively influenced Xer involvement; however, it was less significant for boomers and pre-boomers for whom more years have intervened since childhood and youth.

The strong positive association of the Experience of God scale with involvement is not surprising. Although the strong negative effect on involvement of high scores on the Religious Individualism scale is also not especially surprising, it nonetheless strongly reinforces a point we made in Chapter Two about the impact of religious pluralism, which is reflected in one of the items making up the individualism scale. Pluralism is corrosive when it comes to matters of religious belief (the meaning dimension of religion) but also to religious involvement (the belonging dimension). Belonging remains an important aspect of participation. The finding that having friends present in the congregation increases involvement for all three generations is not surprising. Nevertheless, it is worth emphasizing how important the experience of belonging, social support, and community are for religious participation, not only for Xers—the generation for whom the TV sitcom "Friends" symbolizes their emphasis on relationships—but for the two older generations as well. The effect is reciprocal. One belongs by participating, but one also experiences community and social support as one associates with friends in the congregation. This, in turn, reinforces participation.

The congregational characteristics that proved most predictive of greater involvement have a decidedly conservative flavor. Earlier in our examination of generational attitudes about congregations, we noted that generation Xers tend to be positive about a congregation that emphasizes individual decision making on matters of doctrines and morals, more than boomers or pre-boomers. Yet when it comes to religious involvement, the opposite is true. Highly involved Xers prefer a strict congregation rather than one that is laissez-faire in doctrine and morals. To account for these differences, recall the comparison of involvement by denominational family in Figure 4.2. The comparison revealed that Xers who are members of both conservative Protestant and historic African American denominations (which also tend to hold conservative views on theology and personal morality) are significantly more highly involved than those who are members of mainline Protestant groups, the Catholic church, or

Jewish groups (included in the "other" category). Consequently, although overall gen Xers tend to favor a congregation with a liberal stamp, these congregations do not necessarily elicit their high involvement. In contrast, a congregation that is conservative or strict elicits high involvement.

One other congregational characteristic deserves attention because of its absence in our list of significant influences on involvement: the question of worship and music style. Although, as we have seen previously, generational groups differ in preference for traditional or contemporary worship and music, these differences did not matter greatly in their involvement. Either our measures were insufficiently subtle to capture the real attitude of the respondent, or the respondents are so satisfied with the styles of worship and music found in their congregation that their involvement is not affected one way or the other.

Congregational Type and the Three Generations

Participation in church and synagogue is only one way that people give expression to their religious and spiritual commitment. It is, however, directly related to our concern in this book for how the congregation is affected by generations—how it seeks to bridge generational worlds and the consequences of doing so.

As we said in the Introduction, in stable times generations have few characteristics dividing them. People are not especially self-conscious about being members of a distinctive generation, and members of each succeeding generation are more likely to reproduce the values and standards taught by their parents rather than striking out in a radical direction. Thus generational tension and conflict are not especially significant for social institutions, including congregations. In contrast, in periods of rapid social and cultural change, children and youths are exposed to new and distinctive events and ideas in their formative years that reshape their life world, often leading to discontinuity between their values and standards and those of their parents. This is the kind of fluid situation in which many congregations and other social institutions find themselves today. They are caught in the thick mix of differing worldviews, values, symbols, meanings, and practices that their members bring with them—not least of which are those that reflect their members' generations.

What Holifield called the participatory congregation—the most recent of his four types—responds to this new situation; the same goes for the posttraditional type that we added to the list. In either type, programs and practices are designed to meet the needs of an increasingly diverse and well-educated laity—different audiences—who are self-conscious about their participation, choosing to be involved on their own terms and not necessarily on the terms of a leadership elite. Although the congregation offers space for numerous voices to be heard and responded to, it also opens the door to tension and conflict as diverse perspectives strive to be heard.

Not all present-day congregations are adapting to change in the same way. They may all be participatory to a certain degree, but there are marked differences among them. The nineteen congregations and two campus ministries we studied in depth reflect this diversity. Although they by no means exhaust the ways in which congregations across the United States are adapting to change, they do afford an in-depth look at several options in two distinct regions of the nation.

As we noted earlier, we engaged in participant observation and also conducted more than two hundred in-depth interviews with congregational leaders and members, as well as distributing a questionnaire to members. To make some sense of the data, we created a simple typology for grouping the congregations according to how each has adapted to the generations it seeks to serve. We might think of this typology as subtypes of Holifield's participatory congregation, with a bit of posttraditionalism added in some cases. No single congregation is an exact fit of its type, but we have tried to group them as best we can from observations—our own and those of our research team—and from a close reading of the leader and member interviews. Although we say more as we introduce each type in subsequent chapters, let us briefly characterize them all here.

One set of congregations can be grouped according to what we call an *inherited model*. The programs and practices are those inherited from the past. Although most inherited-model congregations have an intergenerational constituency, and their leaders and members are often aware of generational difference, they do little to change existing programs to address it. Mostly they continue to do what they have done in the past. They follow their inherited practices.

A second set of congregations reflect greater generational sensitivity. Here, the programs and practices reflect a *blended or mixed model,* as leaders and members make an effort to appeal to the generations in their midst. That is, unlike the case of the inherited-model congregation, leaders and members of the blended congregation have more self-consciously sought to adapt their congregational life to the generations in their midst—not, however, without tension or conflict.

Finally, several of the congregations we studied constitute a third type: *generation-specific.* This type has generally tailored programs to what it perceives as the characteristic needs and religious style of a particular generation, even if other generations are present in the congregation.

This tripartite typology is based on our observations and interviews; however, responses to the questionnaire survey that we conducted in twenty-one congregations (as distinct from the general population survey conducted by telephone) also lend some support to the usefulness of the types. Although we can make no claim that the surveys are truly representative of the congregations (the samples responding were for the most part not random), gathering responses from approximately 830 respondents, grouped by the type of congregation to which they belong, adds to the face validity of the types. Here are some examples from the grouped data.[16]

Members of inherited-model congregations are predominantly pre-boomers: six out of ten are in that generation, 29 percent are boomers, and only 11 percent among them are Xers. The inherited-model congregation also has fewer singles, but a greater percentage of divorced and widowed members than is true for the other two. A large percentage of those responding in all three types reported weekly participation in worship, but involvement in blended and generation-specific congregations was 10 percent higher than in the inherited-model congregation. Also members of blended and generation-specific congregations were significantly more likely to say that their congregational involvement has increased over the past five years than was true for the inherited model. When it comes to worship and music preferences, inherited-model members are much more likely to prefer traditional forms of worship or music. Blended-congregation members were in a middle position on worship and music, preferring traditional and contemporary forms about equally. Generation-specific congregations, in contrast, overwhelmingly preferred both contemporary worship and music. The same pattern was true for preference for participatory music over that performed by a choir or soloists.

These various comparisons help to give some indication that the typology has face validity They call attention to the ways congregations take generations into account as they engage in ministry and mission. The descriptive profiles that follow are, however, the major means for demonstrating how congregations differ in their response to the generations in their midst.

In the three chapters that follow, we examine each type and its peculiar dynamics in relation to generational issues. In doing so, we have made a strategic choice *not* to describe all of the congregations and campus ministries that we studied. Instead, we have chosen to give a relatively full profile of a limited number of congregations in each type, drawing from observations, interviews, and some insights from our congregational surveys. We have not neglected the other congregations; they have informed our analysis at many points. Even with the limited number of congregations profiled, we have had to be selective, trying to portray essential information about each congregation while focusing especially on generationally relevant themes.

Also, what we present is a kind of snapshot of the congregations as we observed them at one point in time. No doubt they have changed since the time we concluded our fieldwork. We have changed the names of the congregations and their participants, though we have not disguised their location, since in several instances location is important for understanding the congregation's practices.

In these profiles, we have been guided by six sets of questions that our reading of the data and previous experience in studying congregations suggest are important, not only for understanding congregations generally but specifically for analyzing their efforts to bridge generational worlds:

1. What aspects of the congregation's history, age, and relationship to a denomination are important when considering its relationship to the generations in the mix? Do generational groups differ in the importance they attribute to the congregation's denomination?

2. How important are location and the characteristics of physical space? Does the location of a congregation make a difference? How important are the physical facilities, both symbolically and practically?

3. What are its members like? What are their demographic characteristics? What is their generational mix? How does race or ethnicity interact with generation?

4. What is the religious orientation and style of the congregation? What are the practices and programs in which it seeks to give expression to self-understanding? Do leaders take generational differences into account?

5. What is the congregation's authority or decision-making structure? Who are the decision makers? What is the leadership style of pastors or rabbis?

6. What tensions, conflicts, and challenges has the congregation faced or is currently facing? Are these generationally based? As leaders consider the congregation's future, what are the challenges that they face, especially with reference to generations?

Given these questions, we turn now to the case studies.

Chapter Five

"We've Always Done It This Way"

Congregations and Inherited Traditions

The congregation is a bearer of tradition, as we noted earlier. In its doctrine, liturgy, hymnody, educational programs, and other practices, it gives expression to traditions of faith that have come from the past. Some traditions reflect historic Christian or Jewish perspectives and practices; others reflect a particular denominational heritage; still others reflect perspectives and practices that were an adaptation made in the past in the face of changing social and cultural circumstances. Holifield's discussion of American congregational types, which we summarized in the preceding chapter, offers examples of such adaptation. Other inherited perspectives and practices in congregational life are unique to each one. They represent ways in which the congregation itself has adapted in the past. As the often-heard refrain goes, "This is how we do things here."

Although every congregation that we studied is a bearer of inherited tradition, some are more traditional than others. They are more indebted to, or even wedded to, inheritance from the past, both their own and those of the broader traditions they represent. We have referred to these congregations as reflecting, more than the others, an inherited model. Even if they are diverse generationally (as they typically are), generational difference is often ignored or at least downplayed. There is an assumption, sometimes explicit and sometimes tacit, that the inherited programs and practices are how things should be and therefore appropriate for all generations. They are considered to be what faithfulness to the tradition—whether Jewish or Christian, denominational or local—requires. Such an assumption creates interesting dynamics, as we shall see.

Having said this, we should add nonetheless that the congregations we include here as representing the inherited model are not totally blind in generational terms. Most do, in fact, acknowledge that the generations in their midst differ in preference for programs and practices. The congregational leaders are often discussing and planning ways of appealing to diverse generations. Mostly, however, these plans are still on the drawing board or only partly implemented, and often there is tension surrounding the effort. The tension generally comes from those members and leaders who are wedded to the traditional practices of the congregation, who accept them as normative, and who find considerable meaning in them.

Several congregations fit this type. We have chosen to profile three of them, two from North Carolina and the third in California.[1]

Covenant United Church of Christ

> We affirm our faith in Jesus Christ and in the Church
> that he called into being which, by his grace and mercy,
> welcomes all. We encourage all who join us and confess
> Jesus Christ, regardless of gender, race, sexual orientation,
> social, economic, physical or mental condition, to share
> fully in all aspects of our church life and leadership. We
> believe relationships between individuals, groups and
> nations must be based on love, justice, commitment, and
> mutual respect; and we strive toward such relationships in
> our church, homes, and community.
> WELCOMING STATEMENT[2]

> "To believe is to care and to care is to do."
> BUMPER STICKER ON A MEMBER'S CAR

In the 1960s, Covenant United Church of Christ—founded in 1887 as the Durham Christian Church—was among a small number of congregations in Durham, North Carolina, to take an active role in support of civil rights demonstrators who were, at that time, making their presence felt in the city. Members voted in the mid-sixties to open the congregation to all races—a rarity among congregations in the South at that time. As a result, the congregation lost some members and gained others, with a large number leaving in protest and newcomers joining because of the congregation's activism and commitment to inclusivity.

Several of its current long-time members, who are now the congregation's old guard, were attracted to the church in the 1970s because of the pastor. He was outspoken in favoring racial integration and also served as a member of the Durham City Council. As one of the current copastors told us, "He [the former pastor] was obviously out there in Durham, working on political issues, social issues, and when we talk to people about when they joined this church, a large portion of people joined the church when he was the minister. So they have been here for more than fifteen years. He really drew them in." At the time of our research, a number of Covenant's 260 members—almost all white—spoke proudly of the congregation's heritage of community outreach and involvement in the city.

In the mid-1970s, the congregation changed its name to Covenant United Church of Christ[3] and relocated from the edge of downtown Durham to its current suburban location, near a major thoroughfare and shopping mall and less than two miles from Duke University. Although there are several other United Church of Christ congregations in Durham, they are historically African American and have remained so. The nearest traditionally white UCC congregation is in neighboring Chapel Hill, North Carolina, some ten miles distant.

One hardly sees the church building from the street. Mainly, one sees a sign indicating its presence. The red brick sanctuary and educational facilities are nestled in a wooded area not far from an apartment complex and buildings housing professional offices. Approaching the sanctuary from the parking lot on a Sunday morning, however, one is soon made welcome by greeters standing on the brick apron in front of the building. The greeters invited our researcher into the sanctuary, showed her the guest register, and gave her a pamphlet about the parts of Covenant's worship service designed to make visitors feel at home.

Covenant's sanctuary is small and somewhat stark, an emotional contrast from the friendliness of the greeters. It is a dark room with stained wooden beams, window frames, and cross that hangs from a rafter at the front in the chancel area. The windows lining both sides of the sanctuary are translucent, allowing enough light to tell that a world exists outside while hiding that world from view. The divided chancel, fenced by a wooden rail, has a pulpit on one side and lectern on the other. Both flank a communion table with a marble top. Pew racks hold a Bible (Revised Standard Version), a *Pilgrim Hymnal* (copyright 1938 and 1951), and an *Upper Room Hymnal.* The choir sits in a balcony behind the congregation. On the Sundays we visited, the predominantly white congregation was a mix of old (sixty-five plus) and young (ages thirty-five to fifty), the latter often sitting with their children. Although some married and single gen Xers participate, most of those we interviewed agreed that pre-boomers and boomers are the dominant generations in the congregation and that it is difficult to identify many adult members under age thirty-five.

Copastors of the congregation since 1995 are a couple, Joanne and John Roberts. They came to Covenant from another part of the country, having served separately in congregations that were two miles apart. The Roberts are boomers in their midforties. Joanne's denominational background was Disciples of Christ, but John's was American Baptist. Having met while attending an interdenominational seminary, they decided that "they did not want, as they said, 'to become the other's denomination.'" Following graduation and marriage, they served together as copastors of a congregation dually affiliated with the American Baptist Churches and the United Church of Christ and found themselves attracted to the UCC, a denomination where both felt theologically at home. At Covenant, they share worship leadership and pastoral duties, each preaching on alternate Sundays and dividing responsibility for attending various board and committee meetings. They had been pastors in the congregation for approximately one year when we conducted our research.

Members of Covenant are mostly white and highly educated. More than half have graduate or professional degrees, and they are primarily in professional occupations. Because of its location, many are faculty or administrators at the nearby university. A majority are long-time residents, having lived in Durham for twenty or more years. Among those responding to our congregational questionnaire, 72 percent were pre-boomers, 23 percent were boomers, and 5 percent Xers. One pre-boomer, who described himself as being of the "Depression syndrome," characterized older members like himself as "more conservative in social and financial respects" than the younger generations in the church. He also emphasized his generation's feeling of obligation "to contribute to the congregation's well-being," though he lauded younger members who are doing "a commendable job in picking up the load of the church."

What attracts members to Covenant? For some pre-boomers, especially among the older members of this generation, a lifetime of habit and the opportunity for fellowship with long-time friends are the primary motivation for participation. Other pre-boomers are deeply spiritual, and their participation, as one woman expressed it only half-jokingly, is a means of "studying for the final exam." Younger members, especially younger boomers and the few generation X couples in the congregation, do not look to the church as a primary place for fellowship. Many of them participate because they think their children should be in church. "That's what brought me back," said one boomer, "but then I fairly quickly realized that my behavior is a very big influence in what she sees. If I didn't embody in my daily dealings with people what I wanted her to learn in church, then I was going to be counterproductive to what she would get out of church."

Other boomers told us that they are also attracted by the congregation's emphasis on social issues and outreach. An Xer, a young man who had recently moved to Durham to be with his Jewish girlfriend (a graduate student), emphasized the openness of the United Church of Christ and of Covenant: "One of the reasons I like UCC is that it's a very open church . . . in the sense that they are very accepting of and respect other groups of people that aren't exactly like them. That's one of the reasons I wanted to stay in the UCC. And this particular congregation is a very open church. I've always been the type of person that respects people of other faiths. I had a lot of friends in other faiths." As he and his girlfriend have tried to work out their interfaith relationship, Pastor John encouraged them to explore the similarities as well as the differences in their faiths; he put them in touch with an older interfaith couple. (A rabbi with whom they spoke was not so open!)

In a reflection of the openness that the young man found in the congregation, Covenant is described by other members as a theologically and socially liberal church, much like its parent denomination. "We are open," one said. "We accept various ideas, and while we may not disagree, we can discuss it and allow others their thoughts and actions." About the only thing we agree on, said a woman in her eighties, is "belief in Christ as Lord." But she continued: "We do not have a strong sense of [denominational] identity. Some members don't even know what the General Synod is. I think they know what the United Church of Christ is, and they sometimes applaud the actions of the national church, and sometimes they do not." Expressing a similar opinion, another pre-boomer said, "You can find anything that you're looking for in our church, because we are diverse. Some of us are natives from Durham. Others have joined the church from other places in North Carolina, and we have people from all over that are members of our church. Their reasons for joining have differed. We really are not cohesive except that we all believe that Jesus Christ is the head of the church and that he is Lord and Savior, and [that] it is here that we should worship."

Although some members hold conservative perspectives on various social, political, and economic issues, most view themselves as left of center. The congregation's liberal stance is reflected both in its heritage of social outreach and activism and now especially by an emphasis on diversity. Most members view the congregation as open and accepting of people of different races, sexual orientation, and lifestyles. Paradoxically, however, as one member noted, "the congregation itself is still pretty lily white and economically homogeneous," and more than three-fourths of the members consider themselves moderate or conservative on matters of personal morality and lifestyle.

Nevertheless, the pastors do not hesitate to speak out on lifestyle issues. In one issue of the church newsletter, a message from Pastor Joanne discussed "New Configurations of 'Family,'" changes in marriage and family life patterns, including same-sex union and the growing number of blended families. She encouraged members to discuss the meaning of these changes and speculated, with others, that "the decline of the mainline church may be partly due to the fact that we continue to do ministry and create programs with the old model of the nuclear family—mom, dad and 2.5 children—in mind." Our survey of Covenant members found that almost 40 percent of the boomers responding had experienced divorce.

Tension has arisen on occasion over inclusive language; as an example, a move to purchase new inclusive-language hymnals was voted down, with most resistance coming from older members of the congregation. The same woman in her eighties, quoted previously, was also not shy in expressing her feelings about inclusive language: "I am of a totally different generation from some of these people. . . . They know that I do not like inclusive language, the reason being that I knew all these purple passages of scripture long before anybody thought of inclusive language. I enjoy saying and reading it as it is. If it helps other people [to use inclusive language], let them do it, but leave me alone. And maybe I'm not trying to grow, but I'm just not going to, because I love it the way it is. . . . I guess that's being too opinionated, but I'm not going to change anyway." Another pre-boomer jokingly explained, "For the eighty-year-olds, God is man. There is no question about that: God is man. For the thirty-year-olds, they are not even too sure Jesus was a man. They are arguing about that one." Thus there is considerable diversity of opinion in the congregation.

Covenant's programs are fairly typical of a Protestant congregation. Worship and Sunday school are the mainstay. The worship services are relatively traditional and formal. Hymns rather than praise choruses, and an anthem performed by the choir, all with organ accompaniment, are standard. Responsive prayers encourage congregational participation, and lay members serve not only as ushers but also as lectors. Having lay readers, one pre-boomer told us, "has proved to help a lot of people to feel a bigger part of the church. They not only read the Scripture, but they study the background of it and give a brief background to it before they read." In some services, a lay member may also give the "Children's Word," a sermon for which the children gather on the steps of the chancel area before being dismissed to go to their Sunday school classes.

The copastors share preaching and worship leadership, alternating responsibilities from Sunday to Sunday. When John preaches, Joanne is the liturgist, and vice versa. Both are robed as they lead the services. Adult members' dress at worship is fairly formal—suits or jackets and ties for men, dresses and heels for women. Several older members complained to our interviewer about the casual dress of some children and youths: "They dress like they were at the beach," said one.

The pastors find the more traditional worship style congenial. "We both have a rather traditional style," they say when it comes to worship; however, when they try to introduce things, they are "surprised at how open the congregation has been." One worship innovation has been a twice-monthly contemporary alternative worship service on Wednesday evenings, followed by supper. Although the greatest appeal of the service is to younger families with children, it also has attracted several older members who occasionally have taken part in leading the services. The Wednesday worship and supper have also had another consequence. Some younger families who don't have grandparents nearby "have almost adopted [the older members who attend] as grandparents—have their kids come to know them and spend time with them in that kind of setting."

In addition to Sunday school classes for children, there is an adult Sunday school class that is intergenerational (mostly pre-boomers and boomers); another is mostly attended by elderly women, and a seminar class is issue-oriented. A coffee hour follows morning worship, though it is now called a "cookie hour" since most who attend are younger families with children who enjoy the cookies! Older members typically do not stay for the cookie hour, preferring to leave immediately following worship. A women's spiritual growth group meets on Wednesdays. Youths meet occasionally on Sunday evenings. No programs exist specifically for twentysomethings. A pre-boomer, a long-time member, explained that when his generation had teenaged children the congregation offered a strong youth program; when those young people grew up, the program fell apart. It died, he said, for lack of funding and energy. At the time of our research, the church council had created a new senior high room with the hope that the space would help efforts to strengthen ministry to youth.

Many members are especially proud of the congregation's sister-church relation with two African American UCC congregations in the area. The churches share in three joint worship services annually, create fellowship events, exchange members, conduct some joint programming, and do service projects together. Covenant's social ministries include a number begun by the church some time ago and now operated ecumenically (for example, a food pantry and a program for the homeless). Youths have participated in Habitat programs, and at the time of our research the congregation was exploring participation in the Interfaith Hospitality Network. A number of members are also involved individually in various community programs beyond the congregation, often recruiting others members to join them. The congregation has no programs of evangelism.

When we asked what, in general, brings people together in the congregation, one member expressed it this way:

> It's the food, and there are two types of food. The type that we put out there and have a social event, and the spiritual food we get in the sanctuary there. And I'd have to say that the spiritual food has to come from the sermon more than any one single thing. We can debate forms of service, songs we sing, that sort of thing, all we want to, but the bottom line is the message. We are not a typical church, not even a typical UCC church in this area, in that the educational level is probably at least seven grades higher here than the average church. So what is spoken is listened to and read. If we had a minister that came here and refused to print her or his sermons, I think they wouldn't last.

Although with its congregational polity the entire membership is, in theory, the primary decision-making body, in actuality most decisions are made by the church council, a representative group consisting of elected members plus chairpersons of various boards and committees. In addition to the council, a board of deacons has primary responsibility for the congregation's worship and spiritual life. Current members of the council, deacons, and other committees are, in the majority, boomers or younger pre-boomers. Older members have mostly handed over leadership roles to the younger cohorts, though as one older member put it the senior members serve in a "guidance role." "Many of our [older members] don't want to get elected anymore," she continued. "They feel they have given as much to the church as they can, and they would love to help the younger men and women get a foothold and help run the church and its organizations. And we do have a lot of capable people at Covenant."

The copastors agreed that older (pre-boomer) and younger (boomer) members get along well in the congregation: "I think,"

Joanne added, "that there is a very good relationship . . . and part of that is because the younger group, if we can describe it that way, has been very sensitive to that older group, has reached out to them as far as giving them rides to church . . . or even if they need a ride someplace, to a doctor's appointment or something like that."

Tension and conflict nevertheless arise as these younger leaders propose new practices. Recent issues mentioned in interviews include music (traditional versus contemporary), the proposal to purchase inclusive-language hymnals, how young people and children behave and dress at worship, whether (during the search process for a new pastor) the gender or race of the pastor mattered, whether the congregation would declare itself "open and affirming" (that is, whether it would declare itself open to all persons regardless of sexual orientation), some dislike of the exchange programs with the African American sister congregations, and whether the trustees should permit community groups to use the church's facilities.

The majority of these conflicts reflect generational difference. Most who resist change are older members who prefer keeping things as they are. As one generation Xer put it, "Older people want their hymns, their benediction, their offering, their coffee, and to go home." Change in accepted practices are not welcomed. Nonetheless, despite the predominance of boomers in leadership positions, the opinions of older members are listened to and respected. Because they know their words are considered seriously, they speak their mind but not forcefully enough to buck the system. One congregational leader, however, expressed concern about how much it should permit a small number of older, albeit loved and respected, members to hold veto power on issues of real importance to congregational faithfulness.

Our Lady of Mercy Roman Catholic Church

> Interviewer: *What does this church do really well?*
> Respondent: *Staying true to its community. . . . It's my community's church. It really serves the community and identifies with it.*
> Member of generation X

Located on a side street in the lower east side of Santa Barbara, California, Our Lady of Mercy is a large parish of some twenty-four hundred families (about eight thousand members), of which four hundred to six hundred families are active. Its Latino constituency, almost 90 percent of the membership, is the largest of any of the several Catholic parishes in the area. Latino members are split between Mexican Americans and new immigrants from Mexico and other Central American countries. As we shall see, the distinction between Mexican American and new immigrants from Mexico is a significant one.

The other 10 percent of the membership is Anglo. Most members are blue-collar workers who are maids, domestics, janitors, or service workers in the restaurants, hotels and motels that dot the area, or else laborers in the citrus and farming industries. The Mexican Americans and Anglos are primarily pre-boomers, with only a few boomers and even fewer Xers among them. The immigrant members, in contrast, are cross-generational, with good representation of all three generations. Given differences among these three constituencies, our researcher described the parish as almost being three churches in one.

Dating from the 1920s, Our Lady of Mercy (OLM) was started as a mission church in response to fears that Protestants were making inroads into the Mexican community. (Indeed, a continuing major worry is the loss of younger immigrants to conservative Protestant congregations, mostly Pentecostal in character, but also to the Mormon church.) The church's name, Our Lady of Mercy, is one way of speaking of Our Lady of Guadalupe, the patroness of Mexico. Legend has it that the Virgin Mary appeared to a poor Aztec peasant in Guadalupe, Mexico, in 1531. Within six years of this apparition, six million Aztecs had converted (or been converted) to Catholicism.

The church is housed in a white frame structure. Inside, the large, high-ceilinged sanctuary seats between four hundred and five hundred worshipers. It is both rustic and ornate. The traditional pews are worn from long and frequent use. Ornate statues and pictures of the Virgin Mary and various saints surround the altar. Lining both side walls are intricately carved reproductions of the stations of the Cross. Votive candles are available on either side of the altar, and confessional booths are to the left.

Although symbols of piety and devotion abound, the sanctuary reflects the wear and tear of its years and numerous weekly masses. Other buildings include a large fellowship hall and a rectory, also of 1920s vintage. The fellowship hall is the site of Wednesday night charismatic prayer services, wedding receptions, *quinceañeras* (coming of age celebrations for fifteen-year-old girls), dances, fiestas, and other parish activities. A nearby convent houses four sisters of Bethany (all pre-boomers in age), who live and work in the parish. A former parish school, now rented to social agencies, stands on the other side of the sanctuary. A parking lot between the church building and the school is the site of large fiestas at various times during the year, especially the Spanish Fiesta in early August of each year.

On the street corner in front of the church stands a little shrine to the Virgin, where on most days, and especially on Sunday, Mexican immigrants light ornate prayer candles before the shrine. Some kneel, pray, and make the sign of the Cross before the Virgin Mother's statue.

Two Sunday masses (7:30 and 9:00 A.M.) are celebrated in English, each attended by fewer than one hundred members who are primarily from the Mexican American (approximately 80 percent) and Anglo constituencies (about 20 percent). Most at the nine o'clock service are pre-boomers, though a few families with children are present. After some hymn singing, a lay reader assists with the service, and the assistant pastor, Monsignor John Williams, gives a brief homily before celebrating the Eucharist. Following the communion, an offering is taken, a hymn sung, and the congregation leaves quietly.

In some contrast, the three Spanish language masses celebrated each Sunday (10:30 A.M., noon, and 5:30 P.M.) are well attended, often with standing room only. Outside the church at a ten-thirty service, a sizeable group of Latino men gather but do not go inside. They are mostly Xers and boomers, dressed in Mexican attire—including boots and cowboy hats. They are waiting for parishioners—especially the young women—to leave the service. Vendors selling *dulces* (various sweets), oranges, and tamales have also arrived.

Inside, attendees of all generations are primarily recent immigrants from Mexico and elsewhere in Central America. Music is lively, led by members of a youth choir and accompanied by guitars. Some of the songs (*corridos*) are traditional Latin American folk hymns; others are contemporary praise choruses sung in Spanish. Liturgical dancers sometimes bring the gifts of bread and wine to the altar during the mass rather than having them "walked up."

Lay readers, often women, take part in reading from the Scriptures, during which time there is a buzz of children crying, people talking, and much coming and going. The pastor, Father Herrara, gives the homily in Spanish. When he celebrates the Eucharist, only about 20 percent of the congregation take part. An offering and more singing follow. Many leave straightaway for home, but a number of members stay to interact outside the church building.

In addition to these five Sunday masses, the priests celebrate a number of others during the week, several of which are in Spanish.

For a church the size of OLM, there are relatively few regular programs other than the Mass—no Sunday school or youth programs, for example. The closest thing to a youth program is the choir. Although the church's choir is often identified as a "youth choir," this seems more an accident of who participates than a group or program specifically planned for youth. Connie Velasquez, the director, says that the choir's purpose is not so much for the kids to sing, but "to bring these people into the church and have them actively participating. And it works." She cites the example of one young girl, now a student at a nearby university, who is a catechist in the church: "You plant the seed; you reinforce their self-esteem, and you give them work in the church to do."

The parish also has an Altar Society and a group called *Guadalupana,* both of which consist primarily of pre-boomers and focus on specific tasks, including liturgical celebrations and organizing the various fiestas. *Guadalupana* members are mostly Spanish speaking and described by one member as being "very spiritual." Some members take part in diocesan programs such as marriage encounter retreats and Cursillo, a popular spiritual retreat practice that originated in Spain.

Overall, however, parish programs are relatively sparse. The director's sister, Maria, commented:

> The word *program* is a real Anglo idea! Mexicans, I've found out, are not on time, I mean, it's not something necessarily bad, but they just have a different concept of what time is. When you have programs, they don't respond well to it. What they like to do is socialize, and when they come to the church they expect to socialize in a positive way. . . . I think a lot of the Anglo churches, they go, like, "Well, we're gonna have this youth group and follow the guidelines the archdiocese says that we should follow." But we don't

do things like that. . . . They don't respond well to that—believe me, I've tried!

She also pointed to a related contrast: Mexicans are very family-oriented in their religious participation. Most activities take place in a "family-type environment," she said:

> You don't have this Americanization that says, "Well, you're a kid, so you go off in a corner." In the Anglos' churches, when a kid cries, they take him out of the church. In our church, the kids will be crawling down the middle of the aisle. . . . The kids will be cry-ing, but no one expects the mom to get up and leave. That's just a thing of life. . . . When we come together for fiestas or for anything, it's everybody; it's one and all; and everybody's running around. They don't judge you by your age. It's a family.

A major exception to the sparsity of parish programs is a Wednes-day night charismatic prayer service, a vibrant service conducted in Spanish. Attended on average by a hundred or more members, it is cross-generational and lay-led by several women parishioners and the youth choir. Sonia Rodriguez, one of the leaders, is an enthusiastic boomer who immigrated from Mexico. She told us that her energy comes from a conviction that prayer and faith in Jesus Christ have transformed both her life and that of her husband, a former self-proclaimed Satanist.

The priests give the prayer service leaders considerable latitude in planning and conducting the service. It has a Pentecostal flavor, with loud singing and spontaneous prayer, and people often pray-ing and singing in tongues. Testimonies are given, and one of the women leaders brings a message followed by an invitation for prayer at a makeshift altar. The two-hour service ends with Mass, celebrated by Father Fernando Herrara, the parish pastor. Attendees are mostly from a Mexican immigrant constituency and are primarily boomers and Xers. Because this popular service is mostly lay-initiated and lay-led, it is an important venue for leadership development. It has also spawned other groups in the church—the youth choir, for example, which sings not only at the Wednesday services but also frequently on Sunday morning.

Father Herrara is Guatemalan by birth. He is seventy years of age and has been at OLM for twenty-six years. Conservative in theology, he is described by members as "authoritative but not authoritarian." Though clearly in charge, he seeks lay input to a limited extent, especially from a group of twenty or so key lay leaders. Some older members complain that he caters too much to the concerns and needs of the immigrant members, but other older members believe he listens mostly to pre-boomers. One older Anglo member indicated that efforts to form a parish council were thwarted because the majority of the members preferred to conduct the meeting in Spanish, leaving non-Spanish-speaking Anglos feeling frustrated and excluded. "As the only English-speaking person there, I said my piece and left, because the other hour and a half, I would sit there and know nothing of what was going on."

Father Herrara is assisted by Monsignor Williams, a priest who previously held important posts in the Los Angeles archdiocese but was assigned to OLM for a lighter workload and as a preface to his retirement.[4] He is primarily responsible for celebrating the English-language masses and is popular among the Mexican Americans. With only two priests in this large parish, enlisting and training lay leadership to assist with confirmation training and the Cursillo and marriage encounter groups is a major concern to the pastor. Father Herrara estimates that about fifty laity assist in these tasks.

Theologically and socially, OLM is conservative, shaped by the increasingly conservative bent of official Catholicism and by the traditional values that many Latin Americans bring with them to the United States. Herrara says that the most modern thing they do is the Wednesday prayer service, including "fast music, raising their hands, giving the peace, and praising each other. Those kinds of things we did not do before, and some of the older people do not like it." Herrara frowns on attempts by individual members to interpret Bible, doctrine, and moral teachings on their own: "They know that they aren't supposed to be interpreting it by themselves. If there is a doubt, they have to ask the church, because that is the reason Jesus left the church: to instruct. If each one interprets in his own way, that is why we have confusion." Most parishioners with whom we spoke, especially pre-boomers and boomers, seem to agree. They view homosexuality and abortion as sinful and believe that the priesthood should be limited to males. Gender roles are quite traditional. Despite their forceful and exuberant leadership of the charismatic prayer service, several of the women leaders carry on traditional home life, where the husband is considered the boss of the family.

As much of this description makes clear, ethnicity is a significant factor in the OLM culture, more important in many ways than generational difference. Over the years, there has been an attrition of Anglo members, mostly pre-boomers, as the congregation was perceived to be more and more Hispanic. Such white flight from churches is not uncommon in many southwestern congregations in the face of the increasing number of immigrant members. The building of a nearby, mostly Anglo parish contributed significantly to Anglo flight, as did the closing of the OLM parish school. Now, as one younger Hispanic member commented, Anglo members tend to stick to themselves, avoiding much interaction with Hispanic members. Our researcher noted that many older Mexican American members also reveal an attitude of us (Mexican American) versus them (new immigrants from Mexico). Though celebrating their Latin American culture and heritage, they join some of the older Anglos in criticizing the immigrants for being slow to learn English and embrace American notions and ideals. They also criticize them for being too permissive with their children, allowing them to "run around" during the Mass, talking and giggling. New immigrants, in contrast, find the parish an important haven as they try to negotiate life in a new context. It helps to keep their faith strong, said one: "Crossing the border is hard!"

It would be a mistake, however, to see the ethnic boundaries as overly rigid. Acknowledging the differences in tradition, a pre-boomer Anglo woman expressed admiration for practices that immigrants bring with them—May Day, for example. On May Day, Mexican parishioners bring their children, dressed in their first communion clothes, to lay flowers at the statue of the Virgin Mary: "They do this every single day in the month of May, and I think it's a very beautiful tradition." She also described the Feast of Our Lady of Guadalupe as "unbelievable. They get up at 4:30 in the morning . . . ; the bishop comes; they serve a breakfast to all these people; and it's a beautiful program."

Generational differences exist at OLM, although, as noted, they are often overlaid with ethnicity. Anglos and Mexican Americans constitute a majority of the pre-boomer membership. New immigrants are mostly boomers and generation Xers. Many of the Xers who participate are mainly "passing through," as one member put it; "they are religious people, but they cannot stay here because they have to follow the jobs, the harvesting, the crop pickers or whatever." As we have already noted, many of the key lay leadership roles, such as heading the Altar Society and *Guadalupana,* are held by pre-boomer members. Important exceptions are the Wednesday night prayer service and the choir; boomer and generation Xers are the primary activity leaders. Our researcher suggested that the pre-boomers take leadership in task and service-oriented positions, whereas boomers and Xers, mostly immigrants, seem to find fulfillment in leading more "emotive" groups.

Despite the greater liveliness of the Spanish-language Mass and especially of the Wednesday night prayer service, some Xers who were interviewed complained that the services aren't hip or lively enough. As one said, "When they sing, it doesn't even sound like excitement. And maybe if it was more lively, maybe generation X could get into it. It gets kind of boring . . . and puts you to sleep." Such attitudes trouble Father Herrara. As he talked about the Mass schedule, he expressed some frustration that teenagers "want more fun as part of the Mass. They want music and dancing. They want something very happy. Due to the situation of television, they seem to expect something like a show. But the Mass is not a show," he continued. "It's a question of faith. And that is what they need constantly to be reminded about, that the sacrifice of the Mass is not a show but something dramatic that Jesus left us to do: 'Do this in memory of me.' The music and dancing are good for some other place."

Another line of demarcation between generations is in views about premarital sex. "The older generations," said one Xer, "think, you know, that you should wait until you're married—married by the church—before you can have sex. But a lot of generation Xers—they don't wait." Another young man told us about his unmarried sister's pregnancy. She decided against an abortion: "That was killing God's child." But she had to explain—because she was from generation X—to the older members of the family why it is that "nowadays you can have a baby and, if you still have a boyfriend, not get married. They would always say, 'That's against the church, that's against the Bible. . . .' And it was really hard for us. I had to help her 'cause as times change . . . there's a lot of people having babies at a young age and not getting married right away. She doesn't want to get married right now." He commented, however, that other generation Xers may see things differently and be more in agreement with traditional views.

As for the attraction of Pentecostalism noted previously, another gen Xer reflected on why many of his friends have left OLM to join a nearby Protestant congregation. They find its worship more hip, but also, as he confided, "all the girls are there. . . . I don't know if they are going there for the faith," he continued, "or if they're going there for the girls—if they're soul searching or leg searching!" An older Xer woman also took note of the attraction of the nearby Protestant congregation, but she attributed it in large measure to the "faith" dimension rather than "legs." Because OLM no longer has a Sunday school, she said, Xers are "not really sure about their beliefs"; they are attracted to a congregation that offers clear answers about matters of faith.

In contrast, pre-boomer members find that many of the traditions and practices of pre–Vatican II Catholicism still have great spiritual meaning for them, and they believe younger members are missing an important element of their faith because of the demise in these practices. "We were regulated," one pre-boomer woman told us. "We had monthly confessions; we had fasting on Fridays; we observed all the holy days; and we followed a rule. . . . Today's generation is so much less enforced." Another agreed: "The young people have it too lax. If it becomes too difficult [to follow the rule], they leave." She then spoke with great appreciation for the parish's practice of forty-hour devotions, where the Blessed Sacrament is exposed for forty hours in the church and never left alone: "We go as a group and just sit there and meditate or say certain prayers. It is the most edifying and spiritual time you have with the Lord." The majority who take part, she said, are of her generation. Sadly, she said, few younger members observe the practice.

Despite these differences, younger members find their place in a number of the parish celebrations that have strong Mexican roots, such as observance of Ash Wednesday, where long lines form outside the church waiting to receive the sign of the Cross marked in ashes on their forehead. The youth choir, dressed in purple and black, sings Lenten music, which, says Connie Velasquez, are the best songs—better than those for Christmas or Easter. The Feast of Our Lady of Guadalupe, observed on December 12 to celebrate the appearance of the Virgin to Juan Diego, is another important celebration. "It's just a wonderful, wonderful cultural experience," said one woman. "It's the songs, the procession, the singing of the *mananita*. . . . The youth really get involved in that. That's one thing they really identify with." There are also *Las Posadas,* the celebration just before Christmas of Joseph and Mary's search for hospitality in the inn. The whole church facility—from the parking lot to the kitchen—is used for the celebration, as participants search for and offer hospitality.

For all the enjoyment and importance of these celebrations, Velasquez worries that the parish functions too much as a shelter or haven for young immigrants and does too little to prepare them for their new life in the United States. She recognizes the importance of the parish and its cultural celebrations; "It's a way to go back and feel like you were when you were in Mexico, to have that feeling of family." But she hopes also that the parish will not only help them celebrate their Mexican heritage but also prepare them to become Americans. When her choir members complained about having to sing at a local art museum ("They didn't want these white people looking at them"), "it was like, 'No, Connie, we don't think we want to be American.' Well, you are," she told them, "so stop complaining and get with the program!"

These examples further emphasize our earlier observation that the three ethnic groups—Anglos, Mexican Americans, and recent immigrants—overlap in important ways with generational differences in parish practice. The size of the parish as well as language differences limit the necessity for much interaction between the three cultures and thus reduce to some extent the likelihood of significant conflict, whether ethnic or generational. Where the groups do meet, however, there are rough edges of cultural tradition, attitude, and practice that do not always mesh. For the present, Anglos and Mexican Americans, who are heavily pre-boomer and long-time members, appear to be dominant in shaping parish practices; they are supported by a strong pastor, nearing retirement, who was formed in a pre–Vatican II church. This situation will likely change as the immigrants continue to grow in number, become more residentially stable, and assume more lay leadership roles in the parish. The change, however, may be not so much innovative in forging new parish practices as a substitution of one inherited set of practices (Anglo-Catholic) for another (Mexican-Catholic).

Fellowship Missionary Baptist Church

> *You've got the older group that feels at home . . . by*
> *claiming the tradition. We are here; this is our church.*
> *But the truth of the matter is that this group is out-*
> *numbered. It's continually being diluted by the influx*
> *[of boomers], so there is a bit of anxiety [among the older*
> *members] because on the one hand they want to say, "You*
> *know, this is our church, and we've been here." They want*
> *to define the church based on its past and its history; but*
> *the fact of the matter is that you have a changing mix, a*
> *changing majority, a change in taste.*
> PASTOR ROBERT HENDERSON

Our final example of a congregation that fits the inherited model might well have been classified as blended. As Pastor Henderson's observation indicates, Fellowship Missionary Baptist Church is undergoing change that a growing number of new and young members have brought. Nonetheless, we have included it as representing an inherited-model congregation because the transition is not yet complete, as we shall see. (The same could be said of two congregations that we consider in the next chapter as examples of blended congregations, Temple Beth El and St. Paul's Lutheran Church. Their transition, however, seems more advanced than is the case for Fellowship.)

Founded in 1864, Fellowship Missionary Baptist Church celebrated its 134th year of existence as we conducted our research. A predominantly African American congregation, it was first located in rural Durham County, North Carolina, near one of the largest pre–Civil War plantations in the South. We were told that founding members of the congregation had been slaves on the plantation and that their descendants can be found among the current members of the congregation.

Fellowship Missionary Baptist (FMB) is affiliated with the National Baptist Convention, USA, the largest of the historically African American denominations. It remained in its rural location as a small, family-oriented congregation with a strong focus on mission, as reflected in its name,[5] until it was forced to relocate when construction of Camp Butner, a World War II army base, preempted the church land. Moving to its present site on the northern edge of the city of Durham, the congregation remained small until the coming of its current pastor, Robert Henderson, in 1991. Since that time, it has experienced considerable growth and now has some six hundred members. It also occupies a handsome new church building with a sanctuary that seats five hundred. The old church building was incorporated into the new and is used for educational and fellowship purposes. The city has also grown significantly in the area surrounding the church; its side street location is near a major thoroughfare with offices, businesses, and strip malls.

The church's current membership is a mix of long-time members (many of whom are pre-boomers) and their families and the growing number of new members, the majority of whom are boomers in their late thirties and forties. If those responding to our survey reflect the age distribution of the congregation,[6] 40 percent are pre-boomers and 46 percent are boomers. The remainder are generation Xers. There are also a large number of children and younger teenagers; however, few young Xers—late teens and early twenties—are active in the congregation, a matter about which a number of interviewees expressed concern. Generation Xers who are involved are typically married with small children, or they are single and dating someone with a tie to the congregation.

To judge again from the respondents to the congregational survey (and finding confirmation among several interviewees), we see the older Xers and boomers who have joined the church in recent years are mostly well educated. Sixty-two percent are college graduates, and many have postgraduate degrees, compared to 41 percent of pre-boomers. They are mostly in professional and managerial positions—approximately 70 percent—compared to one-third of the pre-boomers, the majority of whom are in service occupations.

Although overwhelmingly African American in membership, FMB has a small but growing number of whites participating. The newcomers have been attracted by the congregation's senior pastor, Robert Henderson, and his lively, provocative preaching. As John, a generation Xer put it, "Sometimes we have fiery sermons; sometimes we have sermons that are strictly in a teaching mode; sometimes the sermons are motivational." But, he added that what he appreciates most is that Henderson never tries to "tickle your ear"—that is, he never tries to give the congregation only what they want to hear; "His sermons are always challenging."

Robert Henderson has a Ph.D. Along with his pastoral duties (and perhaps appropriately), he teaches preaching at a nearby divinity school. He grew up in the United Holy Church of America, a denomination with Methodist roots and a strong Pentecostal holiness emphasis. He had never had membership in a Baptist church until he became FMB's pastor. In addition to the pastor, fourteen others—five women and nine men—are listed as ministers. They are unpaid but officially recognized as ministers by the congregation and assist the pastor in many ways. One of them is usually responsible for leading the early worship service, including preaching. They also assist in the main worship service at eleven o'clock as liturgists, leading the prayers, and giving the children's sermon.

Among the congregation's numerous programs, the eleven o'clock worship service has a central place, especially for the pre-boomer members. Henderson told us that, though boomers and other younger members are involved in other activities of the congregation in addition to worship, older members are more in the pattern of "we come on Sunday mornings." Upwards of five hundred worshipers attend the eleven o'clock service each Sunday.

One enters the sanctuary through a narthex, where greeters make visitors and regular members welcome and where information about programs is available. Inside the sanctuary, the walls are tan brick with stained glass windows of contemporary design. A vaulted ceiling of light oak matches the oak pews and pulpit furniture. The carpet and pew cushions are a deep red. A center aisle leads to the chancel area, dominated by a large cross hanging against the back wall. Below the cross is the baptistry, a pool surrounded by a low wall and not visible from the pews. In front of the baptistry is the choir area, with room for one or more choirs. An electronic organ, a piano, and on some Sundays drums and keyboard accompany the choirs and congregational singing. The pulpit area is in front of the choir, with a large central pulpit behind which are five chairs, the largest being the pastor's. On either side of the pulpit are planters and fresh flower arrangements. In each pew are Bibles and National Baptist hymnals.

At one of the services that we attended, the sanctuary was three-fourths full, with a good mix of age groups. Dress was relatively formal. Some women, mostly older, wore hats. Men were in suits or jackets. A praise service—primarily singing of a Gospel chorus accompanied by vigorous clapping—preceded the morning worship, which began precisely at eleven. Following a call to worship led by one of the women assistant ministers, we were asked to stand to honor the pastor and choir, who entered down the center aisle. The choir was robed, and the pastor wore a black robe and clerical collar. Following a sung invocation and hymn, a youth member led in a responsive reading, and another assistant minister, a white man, led the morning prayer.

A children's choir sang a medley of songs, which was acknowledged by "amens" and applause from the congregation. A lay woman read several announcements, including acknowledgment of birthdays and anniversaries. The pastor was especially singled out since it was his fiftieth birthday—an event also recognized in a full-page announcement in the Sunday bulletin. Recognition was also given to a member who has been chosen as one of ten national science teachers of the year and would be featured in an upcoming issue of *Time*.

Visitors were asked to stand. The congregation greeted them and each other with handshakes and hugs. Following the greeting, another assistant minister gave the children's message to more than one hundred children gathered around him, emphasizing that the choices which we must make daily have consequences—some good, some harmful.

While the youth choir sang an anthem, the offering was taken. In the tradition of many African American congregations, members filed down the aisle and placed their gifts in one or more of three boxes that the ushers had brought to the front of the church: one labeled Offerings, another Tithes, and a third Missions. Once the offering was completed, the boxes were carried out by the ushers. A hymn and another anthem followed, and then a young white girl, about ten years old and so short that she could hardly see over the pulpit, read the New Testament lesson in a clear voice. When she finished, the congregation applauded.

It was time for the sermon—one hour and twenty minutes into the service. Henderson began quietly, speaking of the post-Easter experience of the disciples and its meaning for Christians today. During the sermon, he often turned to his left and right, and sometimes, with his back to the congregation, he spoke to the choir. But nearing the end of his sermon, he spoke with great force, becoming louder and more animated, punctuating his speech with "Hallelu-jahs!" He spun around on several occasions as if he were a whirling dervish. The sermon concluded with an invitation to all who were hiding from Jesus, whether disciples or not, to open their lives to him. During the sermon, many congregation members joined in with amens and other affirmation of the preacher's message.

Three people came forward during the invitation, two women and a man. They left with the deacons while Henderson continued to invite others to come. The three returned, and the deacons moved their admission to membership in the congregation "on the basis of their Christian experience." The congregation voted to receive them. A prayer time gave opportunity for anyone who wished to come to the altar. Several came, including an elderly woman around whom several members gathered in prayer. Henderson concluded the service at 1:30 P.M. with a benediction and invitation to a fellowship hour.

Although morning worship is central to the life of the congregation, it is only one of a number of programs that include Sunday school classes for all ages, a Bible study program on Wednesday evening, a singles group (mostly older singles rather than generation Xers), six choirs, and a number of mission and outreach programs organized by the missions department. The latter are especially important in the Missionary Baptist tradition. In addition to offerings that support missions, FMB's mission programs include a lay missionary program for men, another for women, and another for young adults. These groups are involved in ministry with the homeless, the imprisoned, those in retirement homes, and various other visitation programs to the sick and shut-in. The church also has a food pantry. We were told that the missions programs are especially important to the older members. Younger members, in contrast, are not particularly interested. "The younger ones," Henderson said, "just don't identify with these things; they don't identify with the seniors in their fifties and sixties."

Theologically, Fellowship Missionary Baptist Church is conservative though not fundamentalist. As Baptists, Henderson told us, members are free to read and interpret Scripture for themselves, but the congregation emphasizes communal interpretation; "I mean, we interpret Scripture as a community and with a clear sense of what is within and outside the boundary, and so we're fairly orthodox—

evangelical orthodox—in our interpretation of Scripture." Evangelical in this sense implies a "personal experience with God, a vital communion with the Spirit," in contrast to a rigid orthodoxy.

On matters of personal morality, the congregation is also relatively conservative. But when it comes to social or public issues, the congregation is "very, very liberal." You might find some antiabortion members (reflecting conservatism in personal morality), the pastor said,

> but you're not going to find antiwelfare people. I mean, there's a certain passion for social justice—issues of education, health care, Medicaid, welfare, prison reform and other "hot button" [social] issues. . . . Almost without exception, the people in this congregation, no matter what their personal means or level of education, are touched intimately, deeply, and closely by issues of poverty. So you may have someone who's doing very well economically, but their mother or father is a Medicaid patient, or they may have brothers, sisters, cousins, and so on who are in prison, without means, and so forth. There is also no intergenerational wealth in the congregation, no [inherited] social, political, or economic status.

On women's roles, the congregation's views are mixed. There are no women deacons; however, the congregation has no qualms about accepting women ministers. On one of the Sundays we visited, a woman preached the early service. No doubt the fact that more than half the women in the congregation are in professional, technical, or managerial positions and are highly educated contributes to the congregation's openness to women taking a leading role in the congregation.

How are decisions made at Fellowship? Most of the members that we interviewed began by mentioning the congregation's Baptist heritage, which is radically congregational in polity and thus gives primary decision-making authority to the membership. It exercises this authority through the church conference, a meeting of all members in good standing who vote on matters that come before them. Church conferences are held quarterly, or more frequently if needed. This, formally and officially, is how decisions are made.

Practically, however, we were told that the real decision-making power rests primarily with the pastor and the deacon board, a small group of men, all pre-boomers and mostly long-time members. It is they who consider the issues that are eventually brought to the church conference. Issues often originate in the various departments that have responsibility for a specific ministry, such as education, music, or missions; but these issues do not come to the congregation until they have been discussed and approved by the pastor and deacons.

Although the conference can go against the deacons' recommendation, it rarely happens. One generation Xer said that the congregation basically "rubber stamps" what the board proposes. Another Xer, a leader of one of the church organizations, made a similar observation, expressing some frustration about the situation: "They [the deacons] are the only ones that have power; they can say yea or nay, and it takes an act of Congress sometimes to get anything done. No one on the board is under fifty. That's a given within this church—within most churches that I've been in. I think there have been individuals who've actually left church because they've said, 'Regardless of what I do or regardless of what I say, regardless of what I can prove, if those eight or nine men say nay, it's not going to go.'" The pastor is sensitive to this situation and told us that he would like to get a broader cross-section of the church involved in setting policy and making decisions.

At the same time, however, most of those we interviewed, including the pastor, expressed belief that the younger members—boomers especially—are actually the dominant group in the congregation. They may not have the decision-making power of the pastor and deacons, but they are increasingly dominant numerically and hold many of the other offices in the church. It is they who run most of the church's organizations, and it is they who often introduce new ideas and practices into the congregation. As Margaret Wilson, herself a boomer and long-time member, expressed it, "the middle group (the younger and more recent members) are the ones that carry the most influence and really run the church."

But the ideas that these relative newcomers bring to the congregation are also at the nub of one of the congregation's significant problems. As the opening epigraph of this section made clear, the older members are quick to say, "You know, this is our church, and we've been here." But things are very much in flux. In the pastor's words, "When people come in, they come with ideas and experiences and knowledge. They've done things here, there, and yonder, and the challenge is how to bring in that knowledge, that vitality, without creating a clash, not only between new and old, but between new and new. 'You got your way; I got my way; he's got his way; she's got her way of doing things. How do we make it all our way?'"

Older members are especially sensitive to this issue, worrying that the younger members are leading the church away from its Missionary Baptist heritage: "The new people coming on board are so excited about joining," said Louis Polk, a pre-boomer and one of the assistant ministers. "As soon as they get here they see things they don't like. They want to change the church because they remember how they were doing it at another church. They really don't understand what Fellowship Church is all about. But," he continued, "since we are a *Missionary* Baptist church, Fellowship *Missionary* Baptist Church [he emphasized the word *Missionary*], we'd like to keep it that way. The older people are still continuing to hold on to the things of the past, holding on to the stability of the church." He cited a new-members class as an effort to attune the younger members to the Missionary Baptist heritage.

"They've been here," Mrs. Wilson said, still referring to the older members. "They've been through it. They know what they're doing and they have a better perspective on how to help." She continued:

> A lot of people that have been in other congregations are coming that have not come out of a Missionary Baptist church. A lot of times they don't stop to look at the structure to see if something is already in place that can meet a need, but rather they think "These people can't do anything. They've never done anything. They don't know what they're talking about . . . I'm going to really help them out." That's like saying, "I can really help these poor folk out, even those [that have] been in existence 134 years. I can really help them out." I'm not saying [that some of it] is not good, but that's what's going on.

Younger members are also aware of this problem, but as might be expected they experience it differently. Many are professionals, and they believe that the congregation could be run much more smoothly, that it could have additional programs, and that it should change to accommodate the time and the people. They call this becoming "more progressive." All the younger group that we interviewed described the older generation as set in its ways and hindering progress. John Abernethy, a generation Xer who is a computer consultant and relatively new to the church, expressed his frustration: "What they [the congregation] can improve on is putting people in positions that those individuals had already had experience doing and not worrying about hurting someone's feelings [by replacing him] simply because he's been in the position for a long time. If I'm the chairman of the budget committee, then I should be a person who already knows how to do budgets."

Louise Mitchell, a thirty-one-year-old professional who works with the church's youth ministry, said "There's a lot of people who have been here a long time, and they want to do things the way . . . that they've been done, you know, for years and years. And I think that sometimes they're just not maybe open to new ideas or fresh insights on things. . . . They're comfortable. And it causes conflicts . . . because people don't get to really use the gifts that they have." When asked to give an example, she cited experiences with the Wednesday Bible study and the youth ministry: "I've noticed that there are people who've been here and who've been working with the youth who don't necessarily want to give the younger people, not control, that's not the word, but responsibility, or, you know, let them have input. I think it's—just to be honest, you know—jealousy, and some of it's just a need to hold on to the past, not thinking that we can do it as well as they can."

These differences among the generations do not always result in stalemate. In some areas, a compromise—or perhaps more accurately, an uneasy truce—has been worked out. Music is the clearest example. Younger members wanted more expressive music in worship, such as contemporary Gospel music, and the use of a keyboard and drums. "That's what we're used to," said one young woman, "and we wanted to hear it in worship." Although the pastor supported the youths, some of the older members strongly opposed the changes. The issue came to a head when a survey revealed that 70 percent of the congregation said they had no problem with the use of drums in worship. But, said, the pastor, "You had a vocal, powerful minority that said, 'We don't want those things in here because we're not that kind of a church.'" Because, however, the opposition was comparatively small, the drums were added. "We persuaded [the opposition's leader] to accept the changes and brought the opposition to a point of toleration" of the changes, said Henderson. "But they still say 'It's not us!'" of the new music and instruments. One way that the compromise has worked has been in continued use of traditional music along with the contemporary. Traditional hymns are always included in worship, but the variety of choirs offers musical diversity—some singing traditional music, others contemporary. "So," said the young woman, "people get to hear what they want to hear."

Conclusion

As we reflect on the three examples of an inherited-model congregation, especially in contrast to those models yet to be profiled, it is tempting to describe them as the most conservative of the three types; in fact, this is somewhat accurate. Yet their conservatism is not necessarily conservative, in the usual contrast between liberal and conservative theological or political views. Rather, they seek to conserve that which they have inherited from their denominational tradition, their own congregation's experience, and their respective ethnic heritage. As a result, their preferred practices and programs come more from the past rather than being an adaptive response to contemporary culture, as is the case with the other two models. Covenant United Church of Christ and Our Lady of Mercy have significant ties to their respective denominations, and OLM also has strong ties to the Latino heritage of many of its members. Being a Baptist congregation, Fellowship has ties to its denomination that are less strong, but the older members' reverence for the Missionary Baptist tradition and African American heritage are strong.

Although Covenant members may at times be unconstrained by the United Church of Christ, they govern themselves by its congregational polity, and for the most part they affirm its progressive stance, commitment to social justice, openness, and inclusivity. Members are also proud of their local heritage as a socially activist congregation, especially involvement in the 1960s civil rights struggle. On the face of things, none of these characteristics precludes the congregation's adapting to generational challenges. Nevertheless, taken together they suggest a congregation that puts greater emphasis on maintaining its history and heritage than on innovation.

For OLM, both Catholic identity and the heritage of ministry to Mexican immigrants are critical to understanding many of its practices and the attraction to a new generation of immigrants. We suspect that the relative lack of adaptation to the culture of younger generations, apart from the Pentecostal prayer service, stems in large measure from pastoral leaders' operating from an orientation that is mostly pre–Vatican II. At the same time, we saw that ethnicity overlaps with generation in contributing to the lack of receptivity (of older and mostly pre-boomer Anglo and Mexican Americans) to the immigrants, who are mostly from the younger generations.

Fellowship Missionary Baptist is in the throes of movement from the inherited model to the blended one. With a rapid growth of younger members, it is no surprise that the boomers and older generation Xers, who bring new ideas and enthusiasm to the congregation, meet resistance from older members for whom the congregation has been a small, close-knit family and who want to hold on to their inherited practices.

In two of these congregations (Fellowship is somewhat of an exception), we do not see much negotiation and contestation among the generations. Traditional practices and programs have staying power. Although younger members—both millennials and generation Xers—are present, they mostly participate on terms dictated by their elders, who are the guardians of the traditions. At Covenant, this is the church council, now mostly made up, as we have seen, of boomers who look to pre-boomers as mentors; at Our Lady, the pastors are the primary guardians; and at Fellowship, it is the body of deacons. Yet, as Fellowship's resolution of the music controversy shows, there are ways to move beyond a generational impasse with a compromise that blends tradition and innovation. Given the support of a pastor who is aware of and understands the generational tension, we expect that this congregation will in time find a way to move to the blended style more readily than the other two. Even so, this involves give and take on either side of the generational divide.

The existence of strong ethnic cultures in both OLM and Fellowship Baptist are a reminder that generational culture is but one aspect of the "thick gathering" that makes up a congregation's identity. The overlapping of ethnic and generational cultures in the two congregations creates at times an additional challenge to congregational leaders as they try to negotiate among the differing emphases. We see this dramatically in Chapter Seven in the case study of Good Shepherd Presbyterian Church, a Korean congregation. The two congregations differ, however, in which generation more strongly emphasizes its ethnic heritage. In OLM, it is the younger generations (who are also more recent immigrants) that most actively celebrate their Mexican heritage. In contrast, at Good Shepherd, as we shall see, the older generations are the guardians of Korean culture. In both congregations, language barriers keep the older and younger generations separated to some degree and help to mitigate some of the potential for contestation. Moreover, as we shall see, at Good Shepherd, the encounter between conflicting ethnic and generational cultures has been further reduced by establishing two relatively separate, generationally specific congregations.

Chapter Six

Seeking the Best of Three Worlds

Blended Congregations

In this chapter, we consider the type of congregation that we label *blended or mixed* in terms of programs and practices. What distinguishes it from the inherited-model congregation is the conscious effort to appeal to the different generations it encompasses. That is, although the inherited-model congregation is also usually intergenerational and often expresses a desire to appeal across generational lines, the blended congregation has backed up its intention with action. Sometimes this means developing programs to appeal to different generations, for example, having one or more worship services with a contemporary liturgy and music along with another or others using traditional liturgical forms and hymns. Or there may be an effort to combine contemporary and traditional elements in the same worship service. The blended congregation may also develop other programs to address the needs of specific generations, or be distinctly intergenerational in character. Blending these various elements, as we shall see, is not without its tension and conflict.

In this chapter, we profile three blended congregations: St. Paul's is an Evangelical Lutheran church located in Thousand Oaks, California; Temple Beth El is a Reform Jewish congregation in Raleigh, North Carolina; and the Catholic Community of St. Clare's is a suburban parish also located in Raleigh.[1]

St. Paul's Lutheran Church

*As members of St. Paul's Evangelical Lutheran Church we
believe that we are a family of God's chosen people. Chosen
by the grace and mercy of God through baptism and
strengthened for our faith walk through His Word and
Sacraments. Further we believe that we have a mandate—
set forth for us in the Great Commission (Matt. 28:19)—
to fully equip ourselves to be "God's Caring People" and to
proclaim His love, justice, and forgiveness through
effective witness and service. To accomplish these goals we
strive to nurture and encourage one another through
worship, study, and prayer.*
St. Paul's Lutheran Church mission statement

Thousand Oaks, California, the home of St. Paul's Lutheran Church, is a moderate-to-high-income bedroom community about fifty miles from downtown Los Angeles. It sits in a hilly basin approximately six miles from the Pacific. Thousand Oaks is a young town, about thirty years old, and has focused on residential development. It is the home of California Lutheran University, a four-year church-related university on the northwest edge of town.

St. Paul's Lutheran Church is the largest of three Lutheran congregations in Thousand Oaks. It is situated on the east end of town on a hillside one block off the main street that runs the length of the town and accommodates most of the retail and service business. St. Paul's new building needed to accommodate more than two thousand members, so it is a large, modern structure quite visible from the main street. It was completed in 1989 and is situated along a residential street, with a public elementary school next door.

The campus is a tight cluster of buildings. There is the new sanctuary with the old one that the congregation outgrew attached at the rear. An L-shaped day school and preschool facility extends from the rear of the old church, and a gym and office building are next to the new sanctuary. Two parking lots and a playground and track for the school complete the campus.

The new sanctuary is a massive, contemporary structure. Its steel-beamed ceiling rises several stories from the sanctuary floor. Along with a balcony, it offers seating for six hundred worshipers. The old sanctuary is used for overflow. Through the use of wood and stained glass, the new sanctuary conveys considerable warmth. There are two primary entrances. Outside one entrance, on a patio connecting the sanctuary to other buildings, members gather for social interaction on Sunday mornings, especially between the 8:30 and 9:45 services. Coffee, information tables, and an open-door library allow lingering, mingling, and movement. One member complained that the socializing on the patio detracts from attendance at adult Sunday school classes and suggested that coffee be served in the classrooms to permit more class time.

Inside the bright and high-ceilinged narthex with its stair leading to the balcony, the volunteer coordinator, one of the lay ministers, staffs an information booth with a variety of literature about the church and the school. She responds to questions and sorts the "friendship slips" that visitors and members fill out during each service. These are taken to the office on Monday and responses to requests are formulated. Ushers hand out bulletins with the order of service and several pages of announcements.

A baptismal font is just inside the door of the sanctuary, symbolizing the newly baptized entry into the Kingdom of God and the beginning of one's Christian pilgrimage. A carved wooden flame sits atop the font, symbolizing the Holy Spirit's presence in baptism. Long rows of padded pews form a semicircle facing the altar. A communion rail fences the chancel, which includes a central altar, a side lectern, and seating for the pastors and lectors. To the far side are a large pipe organ and seating for the choir. A wooden cross and flame hang above the chancel. Behind the chancel wall is a prayer chapel, open and staffed with prayer ministers after each service for those who wish to have personal prayer time.

Four worship services are held each week, three on Sunday morning and one on Saturday evening. The 8:30 and 9:45 services on Sunday follow the traditional Lutheran liturgy. The liturgy and hymns are drawn from the Lutheran Book of Worship (which used to be referred to as the LBW). But because St. Paul's is conscious of drawing in a number of non-Lutherans, it is now referred to as "the green hymnal." These services, especially the 9:45 service, have the largest attendance. When we attended, the six-hundred-seat sanctuary was full, with a cross-section of generations present.

The eleven o'clock service, called the "new worship celebration," follows a contemporary format. A three-piece worship band (guitar, keyboard, and drums) called "company" leads contemporary Christian music. Band members are drawn from the congregation. The service uses some elements of Lutheran liturgy, but not all of it. Although the pastor wears a robe for the service, other participants dress casually. Praise songs replace traditional hymns. The sermon, however, is the same as at the traditional services. Some interviewees criticized the effort to blend contemporary and traditional elements; "It doesn't go all the way," they complained. The service attracts a smaller congregation than the traditional ones, averaging about eighty-five per week at the time of our research. Its appeal is especially strong for those who were unchurched before joining St. Paul's.

A recent innovation has been the Saturday evening service, which has a country-and-western format (one member referred to it somewhat disparagingly as the "hoedown hour"). Country-and-western music is popular in the area, a lay leader told us. "We sort of mooshed it together with worship," he said, establishing the service as an experiment in mission outreach. It's very casual. Some wear shorts and sandals; others are in western wear. Once a month, there is line dancing following the service. Sue and Dick Hart, both in their forties, told us they feel most comfortable with the traditional liturgy and hymnal, but they enjoy going occasionally on Saturday nights. "Somehow the Saturday night one doesn't bother me because it's on Saturday night," Sue said. "It's just OK that it's different."

Pastor Manfred Sauter said that "some who attend like the smaller feel of the service. They have a feeling that it is more spiritual than the Sunday morning services, because we don't necessarily use an order of service. Prayer requests are offered and shared, and the congregation is smaller." Average attendance is about one hundred, mostly younger families, though some older singles and couples attend (especially on the nights when line dancing follows). None of a group of single generation Xers that we interviewed attended. One had tried it, but "I was the only single person under the age of, like, fifty," he said. "I stuck out like a sore thumb!"

Sauter is one of three pastors at St. Paul's. Sixty-one years old at the time of our interviews, he had been at the church for nineteen years. Recently he exchanged some of his responsibilities with Pastor Henry Johnson, who is now responsible for administrative matters as well as confirmation and youth ministry. Sauter is focusing special attention on developing the congregation's small-group ministry. A retired pastor, Jonas Hansen, works part-time in visitation, evangelism, and ministry to seniors.

Membership in the congregation stands at 2,213 (1994 figures), an increase of 25 percent over the previous decade. All generations are represented. When asked, interviewees named three generational groupings in the congregation. The first is the older, retired, "leisure-age" or long-time-members group, which is perceived to be the most Lutheran of all age groups. Next are "school families," young families, or families with small children, who are perceived as least likely to have Lutheran (or any) religious background. Finally, there are "the youth" (eighteen and under), who a survey showed to constitute more than one-third of the congregation.

The only visible presence of generation X is a Sunday evening small group for young adults, whom one of their members identifies as "the misfits." Their age range is twenty-two to thirty-five, and they prefer to call themselves "singles" rather than Xers; they are not so interested in defining themselves as particularly different as a generation. In fact, they resent some of the stereotypes that the media use to describe them. Although they enjoy their participation in St. Paul's, they complain of feeling noticeably single when attending worship, and of having to sit alone while so many others sit in family groups of some type. They perceive that the rest of the church looks at them as singles looking for spouses—which they resent.

In another interview, Eileen Baskin, also a single Xer, similarly reflected the difficulties that singles experience: "Church is a very lonely place as a single person, even when you get to know people." She has gotten involved in a care group, and "that has helped a lot, but I still haven't found my niche yet." She tells of being at church and "getting this warm fuzzy feeling, and then I have to come home by myself." A part of her problem—also acknowledged as problematic by the other singles interviewed—was her work, which took her away a lot.

Boomer members admitted that they belong to the "sixties generation," but none claimed allegiance to what they characterized as boomers' materialistic values. Wilson Bauer, an eighty-year-old pre-boomer, saw a clear difference between his generation and the younger ones in terms of values of honesty and loyalty; he wonders if the church is teaching these values any more. He sees the contemporary church as focusing less on one's relationship to God than on meeting the needs of its constituency's "spiritual questing." In general, however, interviewees tended not to see much difference on issues within the congregation along generational lines. More often, the defining distinction was between those from a strong Lutheran background and those unchurched or from a non-Lutheran background.

In recent years, more and more new members have come from a non-Lutheran background; this describes almost half of the new members since 1990. Despite this change, most interviewees do not feel that the congregation downplays its Lutheran identity. Life-long Lutherans are still present in substantial numbers, especially among the pre-boomers, but also among younger members (many of whom are students, staff, or graduates of California Lutheran University). In the group interview with the generation Xers who meet regularly on Sunday evenings, they spoke of their preference for the traditional Lutheran worship service. Yet the emphasis on Lutheran identity is not monolithic. Both staff and members have a sense of themselves as blending a strong Lutheran heritage with sensitivity and openness to contemporary trends. As one lay member put it, St. Paul's "respects Lutheran history and tradition, but it is not steeped in it."

Pastors and members alike characterize St. Paul's as conservative theologically and family-oriented programmatically. Culturally, on lifestyle issues, the congregation is also somewhat conservative; however, the pastors encourage members to make up their own mind rather than trying to force unanimity. As Sauter says:

> On the more controversial social issues—sexuality, abortion, capital punishment, things of that nature—one of the pastors usually leads [a study of the issue] . . . to share our honest convictions but also to give guidance. I don't think we try to impose our opinion. . . . Committed Christians can take really different positions because of their backgrounds and [bring] their own life experience. Every person has the right to interpret the Scripture for themselves as they live it out in their life. And we are called to accept those persons who may see it differently than I would or one of the other pastors would. A general kind of open acceptance is what our goal is—but our commitment to Christ is central.

Sauter's comment is a good example of what we call "reflexivity." Characteristic of a post-traditional society, members argue with tradition and bring the authority of their own experience as they attempt to respond as Christians to difficult moral questions.

In addition to worship services, St. Paul's leaders give special attention to developing their small-group ministry, the care groups already mentioned. Many of them are intergenerational in composition. Some follow a Bible study format, with resources prepared by Pastor Sauter. Others select their own focus and materials. Parenting skills is a popular topic for some groups, and many with a limited church background select materials that help them grow in their understanding of Christian faith.

A number of respondents commented positively on the effect of these groups in connecting people to a sense of belonging to St. Paul's, and they see the groups as responsible for the "family-like feel" of St. Paul's in spite of its large size. Dick Hart described St. Paul's as "a large church with a small-church kind of atmosphere," he said. "I think that's reflective of the pastors as much as anything. In a church this size, it's very easy to get lost and just come and go without anybody even knowing you were there. But they really make a good effort to be sure people are welcomed and get involved in different things." Sue Hart added, "They have not let largeness in numbers become the issue. Christ is still the center of the church."

Louise Marshall, the council president, commented on two strategies being followed to address generational differences. One is developing some programs that appeal to a particular generation (the country-and-western service, for example) or that address special needs likely to be generationally defined, such as a small group focusing on parenting skills. The other strategy has been to work hard at being inclusive of different ages in as many of the programs as possible, especially on committees. She cites the chancel choir, of which she is a member, as one having a range of ages, "and the variance of age does not make any difference, which is refreshing. There is a common goal. On the committees it is helpful to have the age diversity, so that you have someone who's not afraid to try new things balanced by someone who says, 'Remember when we tried this or that?'" Both strategies are needed, she said, in such a large congregation. "We must address the needs of particular groups and also find ways of bringing the congregation together across age and other lines."

The most frequently cited event that brings the congregation together is the festive "hanging of the greens," which occurs each year in the weeks before Christmas. It involves considerable intergenerational preparation, including decoration and planning for the worship, music, and food. Sauter views such celebrations as a more effective means of Christian education than traditional Sunday school class; he hopes to develop several similar celebrative events at other times during the year.

The preschool nursery and its 380-pupil Christian school (K–8) are another important aspect of the congregation's ministry and regular source of new members among parents, many from non-Lutheran backgrounds. The congregation also makes its facilities as well as its ministry available to the surrounding community: twelve-step programs, SAT preparation courses, singles volleyball and other sports teams, a (non-Lutheran) Hispanic congregation, Jewish festivals, and symphony rehearsals and concerts. The council president, Louise Marshall, characterized St. Paul's as a "seven-day-a-week church. It meets the needs of the people, both traditional and nontraditional, and both physical and spiritual needs."

Leadership, in addition to the staff, is lodged in the church council under the direction of a president, who is elected annually. In recent years, leadership has moved to the younger generations, especially boomers. Council members are a more diverse group than previously, and most are in their forties. A few are in the younger and older age groups. Louise Marshall, the president, is in her fifties and is a single parent. She spoke of the importance of sharing her faith and time with her Christian brothers and sisters, and "being there for my pastors as I know they are there for me, and, you know, supporting them and being honest with them when there are things I don't agree with." Her style of leadership is to allow committees to do their job without micromanagement from the council. Pastor Sauter views the decentralization of authority under her leadership as an important change that is not always appreciated by older, pre-boomer members, who preferred discussion and council approval for all decisions. He also notes a shift to a more "need-centered" focus on local church concerns and less interest in regional or national issues. A decision to participate in a local council of churches was approved when it was emphasized that the council was local and not affiliated with the National and World Council of Churches. The primary area of tension—conflict is too strong a word to describe

it—centers on the effort by the staff and lay leadership to incorporate some megachurch practices into their program without sacri-
ficing the congregation's Lutheran identity. Much of this came to
focus on efforts to incorporate contemporary elements into the worship. Early on, there were complaints that worship leaders were coming in and "setting up their stuff" before the two traditional services,
rather than keeping the boundaries between the types of service
clear. According to Sauter, "We saw that some disliked the contemporary style while others complained that it did not go far enough
in being contemporary."

The Saturday evening country-and-western service also generated considerable discussion. Debate was heated about whether a
country-and-western service would be Lutheran in character, and
if so, how. Some wanted to advertise it as a "country celebration,"
with no Lutheran connection. Others, including the pastors, in-
sisted that it be Lutheran and ensured that it would incorporate
elements of Lutheran liturgy and theology into the service. Others
complained that the contemporary service did not go far enough
in being contemporary; it still embraced too many traditional liturgical elements.

The church leaders' efforts to make the congregation a seven-
day-a-week church also have drawn complaints. We were told that
some members were upset about the cost of using the buildings
during the week, especially use by outside groups that sometimes
abuse the facilities. Council president Marshall, however, echoed
the sentiments of those who favor such use: "One of our goals is
sharing the beauty of the structure we have rather than hoarding
it, . . . and if something gets broken, well, OK. But what a waste of
time, talents, and everything else to have a church only used on
Sunday, or once or twice a week, or only for our members. That has
its price. We have to hire people to make sure things are locked.
Sometimes we get broken into, but if that happens, I can't feel too
bad about it."

In spite of the various complaints, we found general appreciation from all generations for leader efforts to move the congregation
in a more contemporary direction, while at the same time recognizing the difficulty of doing so. Recognition of this tension was best expressed by some of the Xers in the small-group interview. Several of
them told of attending congregations of some more evangelical

megachurches, such as a nearby Calvary Chapel congregation and a Four-Square church that did not appeal to them. They found these churches too demanding of personal disclosure (as in being asked to speak about one's "walk with the Lord" in a small group). With the band, the applause, and the stage lights, they found it geared too much to entertainment to satisfy them, though they also acknowledged that many of their generation found such a church appealing. In reflecting on efforts at St. Paul's to blend some of these practices with traditional Lutheranism, one Xer commented:

> I think that [our pastors] are trying to move in that direction, but they really don't know how it could ever fit in this traditional format. I think small groups is one way. I know that they're very popular in those big megachurches. And the nontraditional services . . . I think [the pastors] are really perplexed on how to do that. . . . It's hard to find a middle ground. You need to have just a totally different radical structure, like Calvary Chapel has done. You know, you open a warehouse and you just start out on a totally different level than most mainstream Protestant churches are at. So to try to do both and think that you're meeting the same needs is really difficult. I can see that. Especially if you're looking at people who've been unchurched and would be very intimidated walking into a Lutheran service for instance.

Temple Beth El

> *[We are] oriented toward transforming traditions to make them relevant for who we are today.*
> RABBI LEAH PREISS

Another congregation attempting to blend traditional and contemporary elements into its practices is Temple Beth El, a Reform Jewish congregation in Raleigh, North Carolina. Nestled in a wooded lot off a busy thoroughfare and near a major shopping mall, Beth El is the only Reform congregation in the city. The temple's contemporary buildings house a sanctuary, meeting rooms, offices, and a weekday school. The congregation was originally founded in 1912 by Jews affiliated with the Hebrew Sunday School Society of Raleigh, who were interested in offering a Reform Jewish education for their children. After meeting in several locations around the city, the society moved to the present location in 1972. Its membership included about 250 families by the late 1950s, never growing too much larger than that until the early 1990s, when Rabbi Leah Preiss became the congregation's spiritual leader—the first woman to serve in this capacity.

Preiss was in her early thirties when she was called to the congregation. A warm, gregarious woman, married and a mother, she is credited by many members with the congregation's rapid growth during the nineties, to 450 families by the time we conducted our research. Preiss demurs and acknowledges that the Research Triangle region's exploding population is also a factor in the growth; nevertheless, members praise her leadership. Said one woman, a boomer, "She's just a very warm, inclusive, interesting person. . . . I find she's very knowledgeable. She's just a real good source for me. She's a good role model. I think it's great that kids see that rabbis can be women and married, have children, and be human and deal with whatever women have to deal with, and yet still be a spiritual leader who has a world bigger than her family to worry about." Her predecessor's style was quite different; he is described as "a really spiritual man . . . very kind, but very quiet and reserved, somewhat 'stand-offish.'"

Like the whole of North Carolina's Research Triangle, Raleigh is increasingly diverse and cosmopolitan, enriched by the arrival of people from all parts of the nation and around the globe. Yet it continues to share in the overwhelmingly Protestant, southern, Bible Belt culture that is its heritage. Jews are still a distinct minority, even in the Research Triangle. When moving to the area, they often experience a kind of culture shock, as expressed in this comment by Jane Weiner, a boomer who moved with her family from south Florida: "It's southern, and it's different, and it's cultural, and it's not south Florida and it's not New York. I think people are still a little bit afraid to say they are Jews and to be Jewish and talk about it. . . . I don't put a sign on the door saying, 'By the way, I'm Jewish.' But they learn who I am real fast. I never hide it. . . . It's a different environment than I've ever lived in. It's a real trip!"

Because of the context, says Rabbi Preiss, "you can't not be part of the non-Jewish community." She estimates that the congregation is the center of social life for 35–40 percent of the members, though most turn to it in times of crisis or for celebrations. Temple Beth El is one of three synagogues in Raleigh, the other two being Conservative and Orthodox.[2]

Membership at Beth El is mixed generationally. Jack Cohen, the congregational administrator, estimated that "under thirty-fives" are about 15 percent of the membership, and "thirty-fives to fifties" and "over fifties" are about evenly split, 40–45 percent each. The eighty-four members who responded to our survey were 31 percent pre-boomers, 52 percent boomers, and 17 percent generation Xers—slightly different from the administrator's estimate for the two older generations, but on target for Xers. Others we interviewed confirmed that boomers seem now to be the dominant group, both in numbers and decision making. Most are long-time members; 75 percent have been members ten or more years. Just more than half of the boomers have joined within the last five years, though almost 35 percent have been members for ten or more years. Ninety-three percent of the Xers have joined in the last five years. The number of young families is growing, especially because of the attraction of a highly regarded weekday preschool that is affiliated with the temple and the congregation's religious school (K–9), which meets on Sundays.

With the membership now at 450 families, the number of active families has almost doubled since the present facilities were built, stretching them beyond their limit. In addition to classrooms and offices, the current buildings house a sanctuary that seats 125–150 people and a downstairs auditorium that can accommodate 200. Current attendance at Shabbat service on Friday evening averages about 120, but it can easily overflow when there is a special celebration. On High Holy Days, multiple services must be held to accommodate the crowd, with the overflow in the downstairs auditorium.

On her first visit, our researcher described the sanctuary as rather formal and uninviting; nor did she herself feel especially welcomed by those in attendance. Members, however, greeted each other warmly and socialized before the services began. Dark mahogany pews, a dark red carpet, and relatively low lighting added to the sanctuary's somber atmosphere. As days lengthened during the spring, the outside light streaming through the windows made its appearance much less foreboding. The semicircular pews are on two levels, a main floor and a balcony. Pews face the raised *bima* or platform area, at the back center of which is the temple's Holy Ark, holding the Torah scrolls. The Ark was built in 1867 for a Detroit temple and was used in two other synagogues before being moved to Temple Beth El in the 1970s. Menorahs stand to either side of it. On one side of the *bima* is a pulpit and on the other is a piano. At the center front is a table holding Shabbat candles and a cup of wine.

Three weeks each month, the Friday evening Shabbat services are mostly geared to adult members, though children and youths are welcome. A family service is held once a month, especially designed for families with children. All services are conducted primarily in English, though Preiss has increasingly introduced Hebrew into the services, often switching back and forth between Hebrew and English in her prayers and blessings. The use of Hebrew is something of an innovation for many older members accustomed to classical Reform practices, which avoided use of Hebrew and of any sort of ritual. "Many of our members," said Jason Hyman, one of the lay leaders, "grew up with that sort of tradition. Now it's moving in the other direction in both the Reform movement as a whole and in this congregation, and some of these people are a little bit disturbed by what they see as an increasing shift in our liturgy toward a more . . . what they interpret as a more Conservative or in some cases Orthodox direction. We've got one sweet little old lady who, every time we add two more words of Hebrew in the service, thinks we're going Orthodox!"

The services are characterized by considerable lay involvement, with laity leading the candle blessing, reciting the *Kiddush,* and singing the music as part of the choir. As the rabbi describes it, "Our worship style as a community is . . . very much a group experience versus a 'me and them' kind of thing. . . . The feel is that we as a congregation are praying together, we are accomplishing something as a group. I'm not doing something for you, but we're doing it together." As she reflected further on the implications of her style for generation Xers in particular, she said she believes "the nature of that kind of inclusiveness is much more comfortable for generation X rather than for them to come in and feel like they are being preached to and told what to do. It gives them much more of an opportunity to become a part of things."

The Friday services also usually include a sermon, sometimes on current events interpreted from a Jewish perspective, at other times on issues regarding Judaism. Rabbi Preiss often uses stories, as in one family service we attended. The story that night was of a gift to a king of a number of precious jewels. One gift was a large but quite rough diamond, which, when polished, was obviously the most precious of all the gems. She then likened the diamond to the temple's children—"diamonds in the rough"—who "are the most precious resource of the Jewish community" and who must be polished and shaped by parents and teachers. Members have responded well to her preaching and teaching. "I don't want it to be so secular," one boomer woman said. "I go there to be Jewish. Not to a watered-down Judaism. I like the history. I like the stories. I like the reminder of why we are who we are and what makes us a different people. I like a little controversy. I like to be different, and I like when our differences are brought out. I think it's important to address the problems of Israel on a regular basis. Leah talks about it very much, which is very good."

The music at the service varies. At one of the services we attended, it was mostly traditional—much the same as what our researcher (who is Jewish) remembered from her childhood. At other times (especially though not exclusively at the family services) the music is much more contemporary and upbeat, accompanied by guitars. At the time of our research, the congregation had no cantor or paid cantoral singers. Instead, music on alternate weeks was led by a choir of temple members ranging from midteens to people in their sixties. Having a choir is an innovation for the temple, and generally it has been well received. Echoing her previous remarks about lay involvement, Preiss says "there is a very different feel to a choir that is from your own community versus professionals who come here to sing songs. Because when [the choir members] are singing they are praying. And that makes a difference. And then the other difference is that it is remarkable in that the choir is totally lay-led, and that's wonderful at times, and it causes all kinds of problems at other times, because there is not as much of a line of authority as perhaps would be advantageous for a choir."

The move to contemporary music was strongly influenced by the most recent cantor, who had resigned sometime before we began our study. One boomer described him as "really great! I mean, it was like having a camp song leader there. . . . He was one of the reasons we joined the temple, and then, like, two months after we got here, he announced he was leaving." Later in the interview, this person turned again to the music: "Well, you have to realize that we came from a Conservative synagogue where they had no guitars or modern tunes. The cantoral soloist [who left shortly after they joined] had cut a tape so we could all learn to sing the songs, and my daughter will not listen to any other music except for the tape. Sometimes I wonder, will my kids actually recognize the traditional? Like, they've never heard the *Shema* sung in the old-fashioned way. I don't think they would know it if they heard it." Although he likes the changes, he says, "I kind of miss the old-fashioned way too. So if I were going to add something to the mix, it would be adding more tradition to it."

Following Friday evening services, members gather in a social for refreshments and fellowship, *Oneg Shabbat* as it is called. Those who stay tend to chat in small groups with others of their own age group. Ironically, although several members commented that welcoming is one of the things the congregation does best, neither our researcher nor one of the project directors was greeted when we first attended a service or at our initial visit to an *Oneg Shabbat*. Members tended to socialize among themselves.

In addition to its worship services, the temple offers a variety of programs. There is the religious school for kindergarten through ninth grade that meets on Sunday mornings and the weekday preschool that uses the temple's facilities, as well as a midweek Hebrew school. The religious school has grown so rapidly in recent years that it has had to resort to multiple classes for the K–4 age group and then to split sessions to solve the space problem. A weekday Hebrew school meets on Wednesdays. For adults, the temple sponsors a variety of educational opportunities. Examples include Torah and Midrash studies, various options for learning Hebrew, an "Introduction to Judaism" class, a course on theodicy (using Rabbi Harold Kushner's book *Why Bad Things Happen to Good People*), another on women and Jewish law, and another on Jewish mysticism.

One program, designed to be cross-generational but with the hope that it will especially appeal to boomers and Xers, is *havurah*, small groups of individuals and families who gather regularly to engage in worship, study, prayer, and fellowship. The *havurah* movement was begun in the 1960s in a number of large cities across the country by Jewish members of the counterculture as an alternative to conventional synagogues, but the movement has now been incorporated into the life of many congregations in the several branches of Judaism.[3]

At Beth El, about ten *havurah* groups were functioning at the time of our research, and leaders praised the groups as an important means of connecting young families with others in the congregation. An older boomer described the group in which she and her husband participate: "We were . . . initially almost instantly—the first time we went into the temple—invited into a group from all different ages. These are people who would not have met otherwise, because we don't have children the same age. There are some single women. There are some older couples. And we have sort of jelled because we are meeting month after month and setting an agenda. And it becomes so that when you walk into the [temple's Friday services] there is a familiar face, someone you can sit down next to . . . and we have created a social life from that." She described the *havurah* groups as a mix of socializing and study: "Occasionally we will go to a concert or to a restaurant. But most of the time, people send ahead an article that they have read or something they are interested in for a discussion. A lot of it is based on something of Jewish importance or political importance. . . . So it's nice. We try to do different stuff. Occasionally we will meet at the temple and have a function for all *havurah* groups."

Life-cycle events—bar and bat mitzvahs, weddings, and baby-naming ceremonies—also occur regularly in the congregation. We were told that observance of bar and bat mitzvahs is relatively new for classical Reform Judaism and reflects the congregation's move to incorporate more Jewish practices and rituals into its life.

Social service and advocacy programs and projects constitute another important dimension of temple life: AIDS awareness services; Habitat for Humanity projects; support of a local food bank, homeless shelter, and community kitchen; hosting a workshop for the Triangle AIDS Interfaith Network, and a candidates' night and voter registration drive are a few of the ways the temple participates in social ministry. A committee on Judaism and the environment also seeks to raise awareness of environmental issues and ground them in Jewish tradition. Several outside groups find the temple hospitable for their meetings: Dancercize and Jazzercise classes, Weight Watchers, a Jewish seniors group, and various social service agencies either rent space or use the temple's buildings at no cost. Although various age groups are involved in these social ministries, several pre-boomers expressed especially strong support of the temple's outside involvement as a reflection of an important tradition in Reform Judaism. One man worried about a trend that he has observed: the broader Jewish community becoming too insulated, developing too many programs that solely involve Jews.

Decision making in the temple is primarily the responsibility of the board, a body of about fifteen members elected by the congregation, plus several who serve ex officio. The nominating committee attempts to make the board representative of the congregation's age and gender makeup, and to that end Leah Preiss has instituted a leadership development course. Although the congregation, by electing the board, is theoretically the primary decision-making body, the board makes most of the decisions, with an even smaller group—the rabbi, temple administrator, and board president—being principal initiators of new directions.

Despite the intention to make board membership representative, membership comes heavily from long-time members, especially from the forty-to-fifty-year-old age group (boomers), but also from the pre-boomer group. One leader commented that the pre-boomers, though not necessarily dominant in numbers on the board, are nevertheless dominant in influence: "They've been here a long time, and they know the history. When they say something, people really listen." Wealth also helps, another boomer added; "I would say that a handful of pretty wealthy older people who donate most of the money to keep the place going have a lot of influence."

What leads people to join and affiliate? The reasons are varied. For many younger families, the preschool and religious school are probably the biggest attraction. For others, participation is an opportunity to meet other Jews. The temple's openness to mixed (Jewish-gentile) marriages attracts others. For others still, it is an important way of linking with and nurturing their Jewish heritage. Several of these reasons are reflected in the comments of an older boomer and her husband who grew up Orthodox. They had dropped out, but

> when our kids were young we rejoined a local Reform temple. Now neither of us had been brought up in the Reform movement, but we felt more comfortable because maybe it put less pressure on us to be entirely devout. And we liked that women were equal. . . . And it was also convenient. It was local. Through our kids, we

started to get pulled in more because we realized that it wasn't fair to expect them to learn something and not be involved ourselves. And by the time we moved here, [synagogue participation] had already become an important part of our lives, and it was a social aspect as well, a way to meet people here—you know, people [with whom] we felt that we had similar interests. So that is how we evolved.

Another older boomer grew up Conservative but rejected it; "conservadox" was her way of describing her congregation. On attending Beth El, she said, "At first I thought this was exceedingly strange! These aren't Jews! But the more I went and the more I studied how the service worked, what was there, what wasn't there, what people were choosing to do as a result of their faith commitments, I felt really drawn in, and I do feel now a very strong sense of deep authenticity of this particular way of understanding Jewish experience."

For pre-boomers other reasons come into play. "I don't think most of us are here so much for spiritual reasons," said one member. "I don't think we are necessarily calling for Judaism itself or Jewish worship so much as for the fellowship and the opportunity to engage in social activities, and I mean social both in the sense of personal social activities (socializing) and also social service—you know charity-type things. But it's like a home and, you know, it's a place where you feel comfortable."

In contrast, Ron Gold, a twenty-five-year-old Xer, tells of moving with his fiancée to the Research Triangle area from California and looking for a synagogue where they could have a traditional Jewish wedding; "I mean, we are both fairly spiritual people." In San Francisco, they had participated for a while in a Christian congregation—"St. John's African Orthodox Church," where *St. John* referred to jazz saxophonist John Coltrane, and where the ministers all played jazz and everyone danced, in addition to doing "more traditional things like Sunday school and Bible teaching."

After visits to several Triangle synagogues, they chose Beth El. The biggest thing that influenced their choice, he said, was the rabbi. "That was the first woman rabbi I had met, and she is just really nice, really down-to-earth and personable." Reflecting further on the importance of spiritual practices in their lives, he continued: "We love those things in our life, and I think we probably would have sought out joining a congregation anyway before we had kids

. . . because of the cultural aspects. . . . Like, there are a number of holidays and things that I have really lost my attachment to . . . and that I would like to learn more about again. And I think that there are probably a lot of people in my boat that grew up with a moderately Jewish faith and have really sort of walked away from that and are interested in integrating it again."

A younger boomer couple, Roger and Myra Simon, had a more calculating attitude about involvement. When they first came to the area, they joined a Conservative congregation because of friends and because the congregation had a lot of older members who reminded them of their parents. They liked the warmth. They had no kids at the time. Although they visited Beth El, they didn't like it because there were too many families with children and they seemed self-absorbed. But about two years ago, they switched to Beth El, primarily because they now have two young children. They found that Beth El made fewer demands regarding Jewish schooling than the Conservative synagogue. It required only one day a week rather than two, which "leaves more time for soccer and other activities. Now, warmth is not what we are after. We just are after taking our children to Sunday school once a week instead of twice a week." One person referred to Reform's lower demands as "Judaism lite!"

This kind of calculating, consumerist approach to involvement is particularly evident in some of the younger families, Xers and young boomers. As temple administrator Cohen told us:

> You know, [it's] almost like joining a club of some kind—that if I pay this much, I get this back; and their expectations of what they want to pay or think they should pay are based specifically on what they think they want to use out of [the temple]. And it's almost like a cafeteria arrangement. They say, "OK, we have all these programs available, and I'm going to use this, this, and this and this." And so, you know, this would seem to be consistent with why I think they are joining. . . . They just want us to be here for a specific reason, and beyond that they don't want to be bothered.

With such diverse reasons for participation, it would be surprising were the congregation not experiencing some tension and conflict. We noted a few complaints about music—the absence of a cantor and the move to contemporary forms. Also, we noted the worry that some older members have over what they think is a move away from classical Reform to more traditional Jewish practices, including greater use of Hebrew in the services. But some younger members also express this same concern. "[The services] are still somewhat out of control to me," an older Xer said in expressing her feelings. "The focus is not spirituality."

Emphasis on gender inclusiveness also raises some hackles. To quote an older boomer, "In traditional Judaism there has always been a strong male voice: the cantor, the rabbi, the hymns. In our temple, it has gone so much to the other extreme to the point that they have ordered new prayer books, because Reform gives you a choice of prayer books. So everything is very gender-neutral. I mean, to me it is not that important. I don't see it as an affront. I am not a militant female libber, but I don't see where they have to make this much of a point. And I know other people that are upset with that too." But according to several others, these are not serious conflicts. As a young boomer said, "Jews are [naturally] a conflicted group of people who, if you put two hundred Jews into a room, you will get four hundred opinions. That is just a fact of temple life. That is not something unusual. Here it's actually less than what I'm accustomed to. I mean, yeah, you'll get these people who they don't want so much Hebrew in the congregation. They are used to a much more laid-back service. They don't like the new music, they don't like the guitar, they would rather have an organ, but to me that's not conflict, that's opinions."

If there is one issue on the horizon that does present a potential for conflict, it is the planned expansion of congregational facilities. The same young boomer who downplayed the seriousness of conflict over Hebrew and the new music admitted that "this new building that they are planning . . . is going to be a killer. . . . I think the building is going to be virtually impossible. That's what my gut tells me, and it bothers me a lot. I don't know if they are going about this building in the right way either. I have my questions about what's truly necessary here and what they can afford and what they can't. But I'm supportive of what they decide to do."

The temple administrator echoed this worry, indicating that opposition was coming from both older members (pre-boomers) and younger families (Xers):

Some of the older members—I guess it's sort of like almost like you call it "school bond syndrome" . . . where a school bond issue is floated and you'll have some resistance from retirees who say "My kids aren't in school. Why should I have my taxes go up?" . . . Then at the other end, with the younger members, we find this sort of resentment where they feel like they are being imposed upon if we ask anything of them beyond what they have already come to us and told us they want to do. They are willing to pay the tuition for their kids at religious school. They are willing to pay, often at a reduced rate, so they request a certain amount of temple dues, but beyond that they don't want to be responsible for providing the resources to build a new building that they might only use a few times a year, or to fund a new program, or to hire a cantor.

How successful is Beth El in blending the generations? Our impression, confirmed by many of the interviews, is that the congregation is moderately successful. The smallest and least successfully integrated generation here is gen X. Although many young families are joining, especially because of the schools, their numbers are small in comparison to boomers and pre-boomers. Single Xers are a rarity in the congregation. Although pre-boomers are pleased with the growth in the number of boomer and Xer families, they are not always happy with the changes that leaders have introduced—partly to attract these younger groups but also in response to wider movements of change within Reform itself, especially the move to incorporate more of Jewish tradition into the temple's practices.

The Catholic Community of St. Clare

> St. Clare's is a gospel faith community baptized into the
> life, death and resurrection of our Lord Jesus Christ.
> PREAMBLE TO ST. CLARE'S MISSION STATEMENT

> For me, this has been the most exciting, vibrant parish
> I have ever been in or worked for. And there's a sense of
> spirituality here that I haven't felt in other places . . . a
> sense of really caring about people. A whole pastoral sense
> of reaching out and touching people's lives and being not
> so much caught up in rules and regulations as being a
> very welcoming place and accepting people where they are.
> LAY STAFF MEMBER

In another area of suburban Raleigh, as one drives along Carter Road, one passes a few farm houses that reflect the area's rural past. They now seem anachronistic. What is most striking are the new subdivisions of large homes that have sprung up along the former country road. There is a sign at a driveway announcing the site of "The Catholic Community of St. Clare." The church is housed in a complex of wooden buildings, stained in a natural finish. It was established in the early 1980s to minister to the growing Catholic population moving into North Carolina's Research Triangle from all parts of the nation. At the time we conducted our field research in 1996, the church's membership consisted of some twenty-four hundred families, or upwards of six thousand members. Average attendance at its seven weekend masses was approximately four thousand. During our field research, the new sanctuary and parish offices were completed and dedicated. The old sanctuary, now incorporated into the new building complex, is used for community gatherings and adult faith formation classes. Another large structure houses children's classrooms and a gym.

Entering the building complex from a large parking lot, one comes into a courtyard incorporating, along one wall, a columbarium and memorial wall—the first of its kind in a Catholic parish in North Carolina. One older member referred to it jokingly as "the final motel" and told her younger friends, "When you come by, just knock on my space." Entering the church indeed means passing the columbarium, and it is not unusual to see family members standing in front of a niche containing the ashes of a loved one, praying and touching a plaque where the person's name is inscribed. Father Frank O'Neill, the pastor, says that the columbarium serves as a visible reminder of the communion of saints, and it also is the site for the observance of All Saints Day and the Easter Vigil.

St. Clare's new sanctuary is a large, modern cruciform space, quite plain, as befits the parish's Franciscan ties (its three priests are Franciscan friars), with a seating capacity of twelve hundred. The only statuary are sculptures of Mary and St. Francis of Assisi. Stained wooden pews have no kneelers. (The lack of kneelers is a "bone of contention" among some older members, an Xer couple told us. "They grumble about not having them and some of the other more traditional things they grew up with.") Windows are opaque glass, specially made for the room by a French glassmaker. The ceiling is high with exposed wooden beams that in part are intended to reflect the former sanctuary, which had a barnlike character. A slightly raised dais has a central altar, a pulpit, and a large baptismal font and pool, all of marble. On the wall behind the altar is a large, gold resurrection cross.

Infant baptisms, of which there are many, are celebrated at the font. At one service we observed, parents, godparents, and children from the congregation were invited to make the sign of the Cross on the baby's forehead, after which the baby's clothing was removed and the priest dipped him into the water, saying that he was being washed of his sin and made a member of God's family. The priest then handed the baby back to the parents after wrapping him in a white garment, signifying the child's status as forgiven and reconciled sinner and new member of the Christian community. Adults are baptized by immersion in the pool next to the font.

The choir sits to the right of the altar. Music is accompanied by guitars, piano, or an electronic organ. The decision to purchase an electronic rather than a more expensive pipe organ was a compromise between those who wanted no organ and those who wanted a pipe organ. Primary objections to the pipe organ were its cost and the belief that the money should be used instead for social ministry. Those supporting the pipe organ gave priority to liturgy. The conflict was heavily, though not entirely, generational: older members were the majority of those favoring a pipe organ and younger members were the majority opposing it.

Dress at worship is casual. Some wear shorts and T-shirts in warm weather. As the community gathers for worship, there is a buzz of conversation with members greeting and catching up on one another's lives: "We all kind of buzz," said a sixty-four-year-old woman, "you know, catching up with each other. How did the chemotherapy go this week? How did the wedding go? This kind of thing. And I think people really like it once they get used to it."

The priests and staff also use this time of gathering, as Father John Wilson told us, "to work the crowd, moving up and down the aisles, talking and greeting." This, he said, "is a deliberate act of community formation. This place is not cold and stiff. It is welcoming. It is a very people place."

Also emphasizing the parish as a community is the practice of having the entire congregation join hands as they repeat the Our Father (Lord's Prayer). Hymns at worship are a mixture of traditional and contemporary. The hymnal, called a Comprehensive Hymnal, combines 30 percent classical hymns with 70 percent contemporary. "Amazing Grace" is a favorite—though one older member says that it "sounds too Protestant." The preaching style of the priests, said one member, relates to people's lives rather than being a theoretical talk; "At St. Clare's, the preacher says 'This is how I live. How do you live?' It's concrete rather than theoretical."

Parishioners often reflect on how different St. Clare's worship practices are from those they experienced growing up. A forty-four-year-old boomer referred to St. Clare's as a "laid-back" church: "Services are not in Latin; you don't have to cover your head; the priest is facing you. There isn't such a, you know, spookiness about going to church that I recall from my childhood. My own children—this is all they know." A thirty-two-year-old Xer added, "No kneelers, no missals in the pews, people talk before Mass begins [which never happened in her childhood churches], and people don't genuflect before the tabernacle."

St. Clare's worship style and overall theological stance are decidedly post–Vatican II. Members agree that the parish is progressive or liberal. "We are encouraged to think for ourselves and use our consciences, along with tradition, of course, and Scripture," said one older woman. Father O'Neill says that members have a responsibility "to listen to the universal teaching of the church and apply that teaching in their life situation." But they must also listen to their own conscience, "and if they, in good conscience, disagree with the church's teaching, then I can't say to that person, 'You're wrong. I can of course say that they are going against Catholic tradition, but this doesn't make them less of a Catholic." In the congregational survey, almost two-thirds of the members—only slightly less in the case of pre-boomers—responded positively to a statement that echoed Father O'Neill's view.

One of the pre-boomers with whom we spoke agreed that the parish is liberal, but he was not sure at all that this was a good thing. "The feeling I get is there is no such thing as sin anymore. . . . Just live your own life. It's not trying to help a person see and form a conscience that can discern between what's right and wrong. Instead, they are more or less accepting wrongdoing on the part of the person. They say, 'OK, we forgive. Just pray a lot and come back in.' But in my sixty-five years, I have found out that this is not the way good things happen in life. You have to struggle."

His views aside, the progressive practices suit the majority of adult members who are generation Xers and young boomers in their thirties and forties. In our survey, 35 percent were boomers, 32 percent Xers. Pre-boomers are also present in significant numbers (one-third of those surveyed). Nonetheless, younger age groups predominate; forty-three is the median age. Bill Hays, an older Xer, describes the presence of so many younger members as a "snowball effect. Just the fact that there are a lot of young people my age, a lot of kids, a lot of family orientation, that draws me and my family." A long-time member commented that younger people—from eighteen to the midtwenties, have been the missing generation in the past and still do not attend in significant numbers, but they seem to be coming back "because they are getting so much more out of church."

Members are well educated: 82 percent of the survey respondents were college graduates, many with graduate and professional degrees. They are also affluent, most with income of more than $75,000. Only 23 percent of the Xers, however, had income this high. Most members are married, and many have children present in the home.

Though the age distribution is weighted toward young members, parish leaders make a conscious effort to develop high-quality programs and practices to address the needs of all generations, and they also work to bridge age differences with programs that are consciously intergenerational. Priority is given to worship and faith formation. "We begin and end liturgically," says Father O'Neill. "That really is the core of who we are. We try to do a fine job in terms of giving people an opportunity to experience the Word preached well and the sacraments celebrated well. . . . I think another big piece is what we call faith formation, the ongoing education of our families and children in the traditions of the faith. If you look at the use of our facilities, almost every day in the week is associated with faith formation, much of it in small groups."

There is no effort to tailor liturgy at the various masses to meet differing tastes, whether generationally defined or not. The only exception is an early Sunday Mass, which is described as quieter and more traditional; however, it does not necessarily attract more traditional Catholics but mostly families getting ready to go out for the day. A seniors program for those over sixty-five, called "Young at Heart," has been quite well received. On the other hand, some single young adults, who are a distinct minority among the married-couple and family-dominated membership, complain that at times they feel excluded by the parish's strong family emphasis despite programs specifically designed for them. As one told us, they had to fight to keep the mission statement from too heavy an emphasis on family. Singles by reason of divorce, however, are quite appreciative of the congregation's support ministry designed especially for them. The parish also has joined the Diocese of Raleigh in a program called "Landings," designed to welcome back inactive Catholics who have recently made the Triangle area their home. St. Clare's offers a class, "Welcome Home," for returning Catholics who have many questions about their faith and about changes in the post–Vatican II church. The diocesan director of evangelization says that "the idea is for people to come in and share their faith story, the good and the bad. We approach the story with reverence. We're not there to fix you or tell you what you did wrong."[4]

Social outreach to the community, both local and global and frequently ecumenical, is extensive and coordinated by a director of volunteers. Examples include involvement in a migrant ministry, AIDS ministry, a program to encourage adoption (especially of children with AIDS), housing for families in transition and for women being released from prison, an Interfaith Task Force on Central America, and work with a sister church in Guatemala. Altogether, an impressive list of more than seventy-five ministries—both for members and beyond the congregation—is published in each week's bulletin. This strong mission emphasis is not an add-on; it is reflected in the worship. The director of music told us that he is conscious in his choice of music to select what supports the parish's mission emphasis: "I think that infuses life into the community when we can sing about where we are, and what we are doing, and how we can live the Gospel." At most of the services we attended, at least one of the songs sung during the service had its origins in Africa, Latin America, or Asia, reminding worshipers of the global church of which they are a part.

Leadership at St. Clare's involves collaboration between the priests, other staff, and an eighteen-member pastoral council. Some on the council are at-large members, elected by the congregation. Others are chairpersons of the various "portfolios," the name given to ministry areas of the congregation (liturgy, faith formation, evangelization, social concerns, building and grounds, and so forth). There are ten portfolios in all, each with a set of goals and objectives established for the year that support the overall goals established by the council and staff. The council meets monthly, as do the various portfolios. Each portfolio is responsible for the work of its area and elects its own chair. The pastor describes governance as "very representative, though within the Catholic tradition, where the ultimate decisions are made by the pastor. I use the parish council. I use the pastoral staff, fourteen people on the staff. We meet weekly. I might run an idea by them first to get some professional sort of input, some exposure at that level, and then it goes to the council. The council deals with it from a different perspective." One lay member, a former council member, describes the pastors as collegial: "If you come forth with an idea that doesn't meet their idea of what should be done but you have a really good case and they see merit in it, they can probably change their minds. And if you don't, they won't [change their minds]."

We have previously noted the complaint by singles, many of whom are young, that at times they are left out or ignored in the parish's heavy orientation toward families. After attending a service on Mother's Day, our researcher wrote in her field notes that "you watch all these families and feel left out somehow, especially on Mother's Day. I think you would have to attend the small-group stuff here to feel a part of the church. Otherwise, you feel left hanging with no way to relate." Parish leadership has attempted to counter this problem, not only by instituting programs for singles but by trying to change the paradigm of family. Said one lay woman: "Family is not just two parents and 2.3 children. Family is very, very diverse and very different today than it was twenty years ago. We emphasize that, as a single, you are still part of a family—your family of origin and the larger family you experience here."

Relatively speaking, the parish is free of the conflict experienced by many other Catholic parishes between older Catholics whose faith and practices were formed prior to Vatican II (mostly pre-boomers) and younger, post–Vatican II Catholics. Boomers came of age during Vatican II, while Xers did so afterward.[5] Because it is a decidedly post–Vatican II parish, one might expect St. Clare's older members to oppose many of its progressive practices, but this is not the case. Most older members, who found the parish too progressive, left and went to a nearby, more traditional parish. Those pre-boomers who have remained mostly like the parish's religious style.

Disagreement has arisen over homosexuality as well as use of inclusive language. To some extent, it has been generationally based, with older members taking the more traditional or conservative position. The director of adult faith formation, however, told us that she is often shocked to find how religiously conservative some younger Catholics—that is, generation Xers—are on such issues as inclusive language. Father O'Neill and others have advocated openness to the gays and lesbians who attend St. Clare's, while not hiding Catholic teachings about the issue. He encourages members to inform themselves about these teachings and then make their own application of them in their lives. There has also been tension over such things as the lack of kneelers, the talking and hugging that goes on prior to the start of the mass, the priests greeting parishioners in the aisles, and crying babies. "No one," said one woman who almost left the parish, "seemed to be engaged in silent devotion. It used to be that people went in and kneeled. I liked the reverence. You entered the sanctuary and did not talk."[6]

Perhaps the greatest challenge faced by the parish is managing growth and assimilating newcomers. With only three priests and a membership now considerably greater than the five to six thousand present when we conducted our research, the parish must increasingly rely on its laity to assume leadership roles. Members marvel at the responsiveness of the priests. As one woman told us:

> I don't know how they [respond to the demands] and stay sane. And yet, when I wanted to talk to a priest and called Father Frank, he was, like, "Well, can you come tomorrow morning at seven or eight?" And I'm like, "Tomorrow?" I mean, I can't get a hairdresser appointment a week in advance, and he's, like, "Well, come on by tomorrow. . . ." So that blows me, and I don't know how they do that, and I don't know how, unless they get a whole lot more priests—which there aren't any more coming. . . . People just aren't becoming priests. I mean, it's not a popular occupation. Nobody

wants to be a priest. It's not a real attractive job. No pay, no marriage, no fun, just a lot of work.

Conclusion

A blended congregation is not easily pulled off in any way that is totally satisfactory to all participants. It involves a precarious stance that both values the inherited traditions of faith while seeking to adapt traditional practices and programs in sensitivity to contemporary culture. The result is a negotiated and often fragile normative order. It is not surprising that a blended congregation is likely to experience tension and conflict over these efforts to be generationally and culturally sensitive while at the same time giving expression to the traditions of the faith community. Of the three congregations that we profiled, perhaps the most successful—that is, most widely accepted—negotiation between traditional practices and contemporary culture is to be found in St. Clare's.

What makes St. Clare's successful in its blending? Several things are at work. First, although it is generationally diverse in its makeup, its members are not only primarily married boomers and generation Xers, but they all (including those who are pre-boomers) have chosen to be in a progressive, post–Vatican II Catholic community. Although some traditionalists remain, the majority of those who prefer traditional ecclesial style have left to join another parish. Thus there is less ideological diversity as a basis for conflict.

A recent study of U.S. Catholics by James Davidson and his colleagues[7] makes clear the potential for division among Catholic generational groups that St. Clare's has so far avoided. The researchers found sharp differences between those whose formative years preceded the Second Vatican Council (roughly equivalent to our pre-boomers), those who came of age during it (boomers), and those whose formative years followed its reforms (Xers). Pre–Vatican II Catholics were more institutionally focused, downplaying individual choice and emphasizing traditional (pre–Vatican II) Catholic beliefs and practices. Both Vatican II and especially post–Vatican II Catholics were less institutionally oriented, placing much greater emphasis on individual approaches to faith and practice—a pattern quite similar to what we described in Chapters Two and Three. Thus by the process of self-selection into the parish—itself a sign of the breakdown of the traditional parish system, where one had no choice but to attend the church in one's parish area—St. Clare's has a relatively homogeneous membership when it comes to accepting Vatican II styles and practices and less potential for conflict.

The second explanation for acceptance of St. Clare's blended style is that the Catholic church itself officially opened the windows (to use Pope John XXIII's metaphor) to modern, even postmodern, culture with the Vatican Council's sweeping ecclesiological and liturgical reforms. Although there have been significant moves by the current leadership to roll back many of the reforms of Vatican II, there is nonetheless official sanction in the council's documents for many of the practices that St. Clare's has put into place.

Third, and quite important, the congregation is relatively new, especially compared to the three inherited-model congregations, but also in comparison to Beth El and, to a lesser extent, St. Paul's Lutheran. Because St. Clare's is relatively young, it is less encumbered by firmly institutionalized cultural practices that lead to the "but we've always done it this way" mentality. We see the importance of congregational age again in the next chapter as we consider the generation-specific congregation.

Finally, St. Clare's, like the other two blended congregations, is large. We speculate that it is probably easier (and more necessary) to blend religious style and practice in a large congregation than in a small one, especially a long-established small congregation. In a large congregation, multiple programs reflecting generational styles of boomers or Xers can be instituted while leaving favored programs of long-time pre-boomer members intact. Doing this is more difficult in a small congregation where size and limited staff preclude multiple, separate programs and where conflict often becomes more readily personalized than in large congregations. It is not impossible for a small congregation to pursue a blended style; it is simply more difficult, requiring leaders with strong gifts of persuasion and skills on conflict management. Of course a new congregation, usually small at its beginning, will not already have developed fixed ways of doing things and is, thus, in a good position to develop blended programs and practices.

There is more evidence of tension over blended styles at St. Paul's Lutheran Church, but this is not surprising. St. Paul's has a strong Lutheran identity, but in recent years it has also attracted a large number of members whose religious background is in some non-Lutheran tradition or in no religious tradition at all. These "switchers," who are mostly boomers and Xers, do not know much about the Lutheran heritage, especially when they join. They reflect the fluidity and lack of boundaries that is characteristic of the two younger generations. The congregation's leaders are thus attempting to appeal to these seekers without losing their Lutheran identity, and they find it to be a delicate balancing act. What helps to minimize conflict is that many of the newcomers are attracted to St. Paul's because it stands in a distinctive tradition, even if they don't initially know much about it. They seek roots that the Lutheran heritage provides. Yet at the same time, they value the congregation's appreciation of generational and cultural differences and its attempt to be culturally sensitive.

A similar phenomenon is to be observed in the growing appeal of worship practices and music from Taizé, an ecumenical community in France that blends traditional liturgical practices (chant and meditative singing) with contemporary styles.[8] For many people today, especially Xers, there appears to be a desire for roots—which the tradition offers, but roots that allow the "tree" to grow rather than have its growth stunted. The blended congregation, though precarious and sometimes conflicted, offers such living roots.

This also seems to be the appeal of Temple Beth El, though it is less far along in its effort to adapt tradition to contemporary culture than are the other two. Like St. Paul's (perhaps even more so), there is a tension between what leaders believe they ought to be doing and the tendency to fall back on habit ("the way we've always done things"). Leaders have to work hard at what they want the congregation to be, even as they often fall short of their vision. Of the three congregations, Temple Beth El is not only the oldest but the most generationally diverse, which adds to its complexity as well as to the difficulty of achieving a fully blended style.

What is of particular interest, however, is that it is the pre-boomers and not the younger generations who most resist drawing sharp boundaries between their Jewishness and contemporary culture—for example, their resistance to use of Hebrew in services or their skepticism about bar and bat mitzvahs. But their resistance to these traditional practices can be explained by their commitment to another tradition, that of classic Reform Judaism, which, as we noted, has often played down those things that sharply set Jews off from the larger culture. Now, however, many young Jews, like their Christian counterparts, are finding traditional Jewish practices appealing, so long as these practices are relevant to their current life and experiences. They want roots and distinctive traditions and practices so long as they do not stunt their growth.

In short, these three congregations show that efforts to blend traditional practice and contemporary culture are neither impossible nor easy. It is difficult to maintain the integrity of the traditions and ensure, at the same time, that they are culturally current. Such living traditions, as the philosopher Alasdair MacIntyre maintains, always involve continuing argument about what it means to live by them.[9] They are always in the process of negotiation and renegotiation. The blended congregation requires hard work on the part of both leaders and followers to maintain its often-precarious normative order.

Chapter Seven

Beyond Tradition

Generation-Specific Congregations

The generation-specific congregation, as the name implies, is one whose programs and practices have been intentionally designed to address the cultural characteristics and needs of a particular generation. This does not mean that other generations are thereby excluded, but rather that the founding leaders had one generation or age group in view as their target audience, to use the language now made popular by seeker churches such as Willow Creek Community Church in Great Barrington (see Chapter Four).

The three congregations that we profile here each had one generation in mind at the founding. Church of the Word in North Carolina, as we shall see, was founded some twenty-five years ago to appeal primarily to undergraduate and graduate students and staff at a nearby university, most of whom happened to be baby boomers. The congregation is now considerably more mixed generationally, but it still reflects much of the character of its original boomer constituency.

Living Waters Church in California had a more recent origin; its target audience was generation X. It too has become somewhat more diverse as time has passed but continues to consider Xers as the primary focus. On visiting, one is immediately aware of this focus (especially if one is the age of the two authors; we were probably the oldest attenders present at the services in which we participated).

Our third congregation, the English-speaking congregation of Good Shepherd Korean Presbyterian Church of Los Angeles, has a different history. Although technically a program of its mother, Korean-speaking congregation, it is in most respects a separate congregation organized to minister to what are called 1.5 ("one point five") and second-generation Korean Americans.[1]

Of course, one might argue that the traditional inherited-model congregation, as profiled in Chapter Five, also fits the generation-specific model, with pre-boomers as the target audience. In one sense this is true. Pre-boomers are likely to find the programs and practices of such a congregation appealing. One difference, however, lies in the intentionality of the leaders of the congregation. Inherited-model congregations are the way they are not so much because they were specially designed to appeal to pre-boomers. Rather, it is because leaders and members tend to assume that this is how things have always been done and therefore should continue to be done. Another difference is that a generation-specific congregation tends to be what, in Chapter Four, we called posttraditional, the next step beyond Holifield's participatory congregation. They ignore or at least downplay inherited tradition.

Church of the Word

We major in the majors and minor in the minors.
PASTOR RON BILLINGSLEY

Chapel Hill, North Carolina, is the quintessential university town, the home of the University of North Carolina, the oldest public university in the United States. Some twenty-five years ago, Ron Billingsley, who was then a staff member of the campus chapter of Intervarsity Christian Fellowship, and several of his colleagues established Church of the Word as a conservative (if not fundamentalist), nondenominational congregation to meet the needs of evangelical students and faculty members.

The students at that time were members of the baby boom generation. The congregation's membership, however, is now intergenerational, though still predominantly boomer in composition. In our congregational survey, 58 percent of those responding were boomers, 18 percent pre-boomers, and 24 percent Xers. Although the 1997 membership was 410, the three worship services on a typical Sunday are attended by four times that number.[2] Now no longer just a university church, Church of the Word draws its members and attenders from the larger Research Triangle area of which Chapel Hill is a part. As the ministries pastor, Jim Jackson, explained, the population attending the Church of the Word on an average Sunday used to be "five hundred students and three hundred from the community. We still have five hundred students, but now we have about a thousand people from the community." The students continue to participate, still coming mostly from Intervarsity Christian Fellowship, but their number has stayed relatively constant. They are now Xers rather than boomers.

Allison Preble, a pre-boomer and long-time member, reflected on these changes. She described visiting the congregation with her husband when it was meeting in campus facilities. They were curious about the "weird church" that their son and daughter, both students at the time, were attending—"whether church members were handling snakes or rolling in the aisles." They liked what they experienced and left their Presbyterian church to become members. In the early years, "the students would just pile in here," she said, "but when we moved into our own building, we began to shift towards young marrieds. Now, of course, those young marrieds are middle marrieds, and they are still there, and we have bushels of those young people. It's an inspiration to me to go to church and not see any gray hairs and see all these families."

Church of the Word members worship in a relatively modern complex of brick buildings erected adjacent to the university almost twenty years ago. Because of the scarcity of parking in the immediate area of the church buildings, many attenders use a nearby university parking lot. The sanctuary, which seats approximately five hundred worshipers, is a low-ceilinged, light and airy room with little that marks it off as a traditional sacred space. Instead of fixed pews, congregants sit in rows of individual plastic and metal chairs. A low stage constitutes the chancel area. The only decorations other than potted plants are two quilted banners, one depicting mountains and clouds and the other a cubist representation of the sun and moon. Both flank a large projection screen on which overhead transparencies are shown. There is no altar or cross. There is, however, an American flag on one side of the stage. A choir (not robed) sits to the right as one faces the front. Musicians who accompany the choir are on the left: a pianist, two guitarists, and a flutist. A small, movable lectern stands beside a table that holds an overhead projector. Non-denominational hymnals are available for worshipers, but they are not much used. The words for hymns and praise choruses are projected on the screen or printed in the bulletin. As the congregation sings, some raise their hands in supplication to the Holy Spirit.

Dress styles vary with age but are mostly informal. Some of the pre-boomers still dress in suits and ties or dresses, but casual attire, including jeans and T-shirts, is the preferred style. "It took a lot of getting used to," Preble said. "I grew up with the generation that says you've got to dress up to go to Sunday school and church. But the interesting thing is that these young couples come in jeans and T-shirts, while their children are dressed fit to kill with the cute little bonnets and fancy dresses!"

Church of the Word offers three worship services each Sunday morning, at 8:30, 9:45, and 11:15. The services are essentially identical, though the sermon, we were told, "may evolve and change" as the services progress. Members told us that the worship is not only something that the congregation does exceptionally well, but it was also named as the primary activity that brings the congregation together. The worship style blends contemporary and traditional elements; in this, it has much in common with a blended congregation. Some Sundays, music consists mostly of contemporary praise choruses. At other times, traditional hymns predominate. There is no fixed order of worship from Sunday to Sunday. Elements of liturgy from various Christian traditions are used. Sometimes the service draws from sacramental tradition; at other times the practice is charismatic in nature. The sacraments are observed periodically, but they are not emphasized. Baptism, we were told, often takes place at a nearby lake.

Members with whom we spoke—especially boomers and Xers—find the lack of liturgical fixity and the informality appealing. "The teaching in the church is that we are all part of Christ's body," said Don Hopewell, a boomer and university professor. "Being exposed to such a mix of traditions forces one's comfort zone to expand." The church's leaders believe that this fluid, regularly changing style creates a freeing worship experience rather than keeping people tied down to the kind of "forced Christianity" that many members remember from their childhood. They want those who visit the congregation to ask, "What's different about this church? What's going on here?" This means, as one pastor said, "that we have to risk 'dancing with the culture' in order to be faithful to the Gospel."

What is at the heart of Church of the Word's worship experience and what draws so many worshipers week after week are the sermons, mostly delivered by Billingsley, the founding pastor, whose title is "teaching pastor." A tall, somewhat heavyset man who is older than most of his congregants, Billingsley wears sport jackets with complementary slacks and a dress shirt and tie when he preaches—no clerical collar, robe, or other symbol of his ministerial office. His sermons consist primarily of teaching: thirty-minute lessons drawn from a passage of Scripture. He does not so much preach as teach the Bible, quite frequently applying the lessons to marriage and family issues, or offering sophisticated, Bible-based analysis of contemporary culture.

A master in using the overhead projector, Billingsley projects his text and outlines his sermon points on the screen as he preaches. For example, on one of the Sundays we were there, his biblical text was from Acts 17, the story of Paul's sermon on the Areopagus in Athens. Beginning with a story of Abdul Rauf (formerly Chris Jackson before his conversion to Islam), the basketball player who refused to stand for the national anthem, Billingsley found himself "in awe at this 'friend of God' with his strong commitment to making this an inclusive society." His act was a witness to the presence of God. "All people," Billingsley said, "have an impulse for peace, love, justice, and the Kingdom of God, believers and unbelievers alike." This led him to the passage from Acts in which Paul was speaking to other "friends of God" and from which Billingsley drew several points, outlined on overhead transparencies: God is Creator engaged in the preservation of the whole creation; God is Sustainer engaged in providential care for the just and unjust alike; and God is Redeemer, offering salvation in Jesus Christ for the sins of the whole world.

Billingsley spent some time elaborating on the first two points before turning to the third, concluding with two messages that Christians must speak to the culture. First, the heart of the Gospel is God's love for all His creation, including those who do not believe. It is not condemnation of the creation. Second, the fullness of God's salvation is experienced through faith in Jesus Christ, but not everyone experiences it. Full salvation is universally available, but it is not universally appropriated.

The congregation, with so many students and faculty in attendance, is drawn to his lecture style of preaching and the logical way that he develops his themes. He is able to teach a fairly literalistic approach to the Bible without being offensive to those who want a more open interpretation. Some members commented that they wish he would "preach" more during the lessons rather than just teach, but the overwhelming sentiment is that Billingsley's preaching is a major appeal of the church. "I didn't feel I was getting fed sufficiently at the church I was going to," said a boomer woman, "and it was Ron's teaching that drew me over here." It is a comment not unlike many others that we heard. "He is a very wise man," said Hopewell, "but he does not set himself up for praise. There is no 'cult of the pastor.'"

In addition to the three worship services, Church of the Word offers a host of other programs. The largest, maintained by a staff of two hundred volunteers, is the Sunday school. It is housed in a building behind the sanctuary and meets only one time period per Sunday, in contrast to the three worship services. The class is not merely a place for study but a social activity outside the Sunday morning time slots. Especially for singles, boomers, and pre-boomers, the class is the niche in which members plug in so as not to become lost in the large congregation. A class designed for college students has not been overly successful in attracting participants, in large part because many of the students are involved in Intervarsity Christian Fellowship and other parachurch organizations on the campus. Many students do, however, attend the worship services.

Weekday programs also abound: small groups, weeknight Bible study, fellowship brunch, "Suppers for Six," men's retreats, and a cross-generational women's study group. The foyer outside the sanctuary is filled with brochures describing these programs. Picnics and other celebrations also bring the church together. During our research, an Easter party in celebration of the Resurrection attracted more than four hundred people dressed in wedding finery to celebrate the marriage of Jesus to his church. A Christmas talent show and an all-church picnic in May are other events that bring the congregation together across generations.

Outreach ministry of the congregation includes a Christian Counseling Center open to members and nonmembers alike. The congregation is also collaborating in an interfaith AIDS ministry, a hospicelike house where people terminally ill with AIDS and with limited financial resources can spend their last days and where others can receive needed care and meals. Because Church of the Word is known as an evangelical congregation, the Interfaith network sought assurance that there would be no proselytizing by members who take part in the AIDS ministry. The congregation also has a Stephen Ministry program and is attempting to offer a Spanish-language ministry (in addition to a longer-functioning Chinese-language ministry).

Although Church of the Word began as a self-consciously fundamentalist congregation, it no longer defines itself as such. It is nonetheless clearly conservative in its theology. Billingsley says that he is often accused of being a fundamentalist: "Well, yes, I do fundamentally believe in the Bible." He often uses a statement (also heard in other evangelical congregations) to define his and the church's stance: "We major in the majors and minor in the minors." That is, there are "majors" about which there is little room for disagreement: the divinity of Christ, the virgin birth, the physical Resurrection of Christ, the sole authority of the Scriptures, justification by faith, and a Trinitarian conception of God. But there are also "minors," many of which are lifestyle issues or what are deemed less important doctrinal issues: infant versus adult baptism, the place of charismatic gifts, divorce and remarriage, women as ministers, or contemporary versus traditional music.

Although most leaders and pastors take a generally conservative approach to the minors, there is room for dissenting opinion. Echoing the pastor, a fifty-five-year-old woman member said, "I think there are certain primary issues that we need to kind of have some agreement on. But what's secondary is secondary—you know, major on the majors and minor on the minors. I think that's very true. I think there is wide latitude on minors within the church, as long as certain basic theological doctrines are adhered to." Another pre-boomer said that she values Church of the Word "because it encourages people to be serious about their faith." Betsy, a twenty-two-year-old generation X graduate student, expressed a similar sentiment: "I like the fact that this church holds to [the majors] hard and fast." But she also likes it that on "some of the minor things the church doesn't give cut-and-dried answers—and to be honest, there aren't any." Her husband, Robert, also twenty-two and a medical student, elaborated: "I appreciate it when the minister is saying, 'I don't know the answers for this; this is how much I know; this is what makes sense to me; there are still areas that I really don't quite grasp yet, but by faith we can go through this.'" He continued, "I don't think a church that has a sort of litany of things that you must accept without any explanation would really fit our generation."

If one does disagree on one or more of the majors, she or he often chooses to leave the church. On the minors, when there is disagreement, leaders often hold a congregational discussion to foster better understanding and, where possible, seek consensus. The staff will also write a "pastoral paper" interpreting a particular big issue as a means of educating the congregation.

On the matter of the overall conservatism of the congregation, one member emphasized that being conservative does not mean being callous to human suffering and need: "I do think [we] have a real heart for the suffering and the needy, and I know that's often put into the liberal feeling—that the heart is with the liberals—but I think there's plenty of heart here."

One area that we were told is out of bounds for discussion in the congregation is politics. Not only do the pastors refrain from addressing political issues in the pulpit, they do not want their members to solicit support for political causes, whether for the political right or left, in any congregational functions. "The leaders of the church believe that we have to have values," said Hopewell, "and we have to make choices, but these are individual choices. We are here in the church to worship Christ, not to be a PAC for Jesse Helms or anybody else. We deal with real-world issues in the congregation, but we don't harangue and exhort each other to take particular real-world political actions."

Leadership at Church of the Word consists of a pastoral staff of five: Ron Billingsley, pastor and teacher (teaching and counseling); Jim Jackson, pastor of ministry (administration, adult education including small groups, and outreach); Sam Sewell, pastor of family education (children and family programs); Will Ritchie, pastor of youth; and Roger Hart, pastor of worship and music. Although Billingsley is sometimes seen as the "head pastor," this is not accurate. "He is the teaching pastor; we don't have a head pastor," said Will Simpson, one of the lay elders.

Twelve elected lay elders and the ordained pastors make up the elder board. They are the congregation's primary decision makers. Elders are elected on the basis of spiritual maturity and the service they have previously rendered in the congregation. Because elders must be members of the congregation, this requirement eliminates from consideration all those who attend Church of the Word without taking membership vows, meaning, the majority of attenders. Elders make decisions by consensus, as is also usually the practice for decision making in the congregation at large.

All elders are male. Women elders are not permitted—a sore point for some of the women and, we were told, the reason that some women have left the congregation. In one sermon that we heard, Billingsley emphasized that everyone, male and female, has a gift for ministry, but holding an "official" position, including the role of elder, "is not necessary for ministry." This we took as a subtle way of saying that women can engage in ministry but not one that is "official" or "ordained." A board of deacons, also elected, is primarily responsible for the buildings and finances of the congregation. Woman can serve as deacon, which is a relatively recent innovation.

Not only are all elders male but with few exceptions they are also boomers, and the same is true of the deacons. Jackson, the pastor of ministry, commented on the preponderance of boomers in leadership roles: "We have an interesting situation," he said, "in which we don't have the white hairs running the church. This is a young church. When the church first started, we even had a twenty-two-year-old elder! That's an oxymoron. So this is a church in which the people in their late thirties and forties are positionally in authority in the church, and now some people in their fifties as well. Our goal has been to get people who are older and people in their twenties to get invested as well in the leadership structure."

So far, however, that has not happened. For both elders and deacons, a nomination is solicited from the congregation as well as suggested by the board of elders. Although this should allow for both Xers and pre-boomers to be considered, they don't seem to be readily included, perhaps, as one elder suggested, because the existing elders narrow the congregation's nominees to those that they consider adequately qualified. This means primarily fellow boomers whom they know best. The final list is submitted to the congregation for a vote at its annual meeting, with an 80 percent favorable vote required for election. The term of office for both lay boards is three years. Once a pastor becomes an elder, the pastor does not rotate off.

Despite the preponderance of boomers both as members and leaders, Church of the Word continues to attract generation Xers, especially students, and a small number of pre-boomers. Several of the pre-boomers with whom we spoke jokingly referred to themselves as "preparing for final exams." Pre-boomers mostly attend the 8:30 A.M. service and a Sunday school class (named "Thirty-Nine Forever") at 9:45 A.M. After the class, many of them leave to eat together at a local cafeteria.

At the time of our research, a potential conflict was brewing over a proposed change in the character of the 8:30 service. Some leaders wanted to give the service a totally contemporary character in both liturgy and music, to make it appealing to generation Xers. A congregational survey had indicated support for such a change. Nonetheless, it was feared that if they made the change, they would probably upset many of the pre-boomers for whom the 8:30 service is the service of choice.

Music, too, is an area where there is mild disagreement. Some, especially boomers and gen Xers, would like more contemporary music and less of what one Xer described as "difficult but pretty" music. A similar disagreement emerged over a proposal to purchase a "really good organ" that became available. The proposal was tabled because people felt that, as elder Will Simpson put it, "if we have a really good organ, our music is going to go a certain way."

The small-group ministry of the congregation is another area where some believe that change is needed. Simpson commented that the groups have lost their focus. He feels it is not clear why they exist. He believes that one reason for this is that they have become too cross-generational. Simpson, who has had considerable experience working with students, says that "the needs of people in their forties and fifties, the needs of young families, and the needs of young singles are all very different, and I think the best way to build an intimate community is to build it around people who have similar needs. I'm not a proponent of a generational church [even as he acknowledged that the Church of the Word is essentially a boomer church], but the basis for intimate community would be people who are like-minded. I do think there should be generational interaction, but there are other avenues for that to happen—potlucks and worship, for example."

At the time of this writing, the Church of the Word is preparing for new challenges. Having outgrown its current facilities, it is in the final stage of erecting a handsome, much larger building several miles from its present site and therefore some distance also from the university campus. What this implies for continued ability to attract students is one of the challenges it faces. But the new location also means increased accessibility to a larger, more diverse constituency, and this presents the congregation with new opportunities as well as new challenges. Will it retain the boomer character, or will it continue to grow into an intergenerational congregation in all respects? These are important questions facing Church of the Word.

Living Waters Church

> *Where the Flock Likes to Rock*
> LIVING WATERS CHURCH WEBSITE

> *I really feel that all we are is just broken people trying to have church.*
> LIVING WATERS' FOUNDING PASTOR

East of Los Angeles on the 10 freeway, one approaches the so-called Inland Empire, which encompasses parts of Los Angeles, San Bernardino, and Riverside counties. Large shopping centers and auto malls line the freeway, and behind them single-story suburbia stretches as far as the eye can see.

About one mile off the freeway in Covina, some thirty miles from central Los Angeles, Living Waters Church holds its weekend services at Elmwood Intermediate School. Its offices are located in a smaller building some ten miles away in a neighboring town.[3] Within a several-mile radius of the school are almost forty colleges and universities, Christian and secular, private and public. Living Waters is a generation-specific congregation whose target audience is generation X.

Living Waters' three weekend services (6:00 P.M. Saturdays, 9:00 and 10:45 on Sundays) are held in the school gymnasium. The classrooms house Sunday school classes. On a typical weekend, the large parking lot is filled mostly with midrange cars and minivans—Hondas, Toyotas, a few Fords and Chevrolets.

One enters the gym to find folding tables on which is displayed basic information about the congregation. Greeters at the door welcome newcomers and regulars alike. Another table holds file boxes with manila folders, each with the name of a staff member or lay leader—an efficient way for members to leave messages for one another. Coffee is available at another table, and at yet another one may purchase Living Waters T-shirts, CDs, and videocassettes. The videos are of recent worship services; the CDs are those produced by the congregation's music ministry.

The space for worship is the gymnasium's multipurpose basketball court, complete with fold-away bleachers. Near center court, a low platform covered with astroturf serves as the main stage for the worship leaders. On either side are six-foot-high speaker sets, and on one side stands a large video screen. Microphones and the complete accoutrements for a five-to-seven-piece rock band are on the platform. White flowers are the only decoration. If someone has "become a Christian" during the past week, a special white rose centerpiece is added to the arrangement. In front of the platform are rows of folded chairs. Overflow participants sit in the bleachers.

Since this space is a gym during the rest of the week, a special team of members and staff set up and strike the entire worship space each weekend. They do the same for the children's ministry, "Kids' Connection," which meets in the classrooms during each weekend service. One member commented that having to set up the worship space each week reminded him of what it must have been like for the first-century church, which had no regular meeting space. Others, however, looked forward to the time when the congregation has its own building and can dispense with the setup. The equipment has to be transported each weekend from the administrative offices.

Living Waters emerged in 1986 from the vision of the founding pastor, Rolf Metzger, who at the time was a seminary intern at a nearby Baptist congregation. Metzger, a charismatic leader and speaker, was pastor of the congregation for eight years before leaving to begin a similar Xer congregation as part of another large congregation that had been founded with boomers in mind. During his pastorate, the congregation's weekly attendance grew to eleven hundred,

His leaving was a crisis moment for the congregation. Some members, for whom Metzger was the principal attraction to the congregation, left when he did. At the time of our research, two years after his departure, the congregation appeared to have weathered the crisis, and a seven-member staff has assumed leadership. Paul Masters, the current lead pastor, was head of the small group ministry during Metzger's tenure. Now he does much of the preaching, which is referred to as teaching rather than preaching. Attendance ranges between eight hundred and nine hundred at the three weekend services. The drop from the earlier high is in part the result of Metzger's leaving, but also because some members left to plant a new congregation, with the blessing of Living Waters leaders. (They hope to spawn additional new congregations in the years ahead.) About four hundred members currently take part in some fifty small groups that meet weekly.

Most members are young. A card for visitors to complete listed eight age categories in a checklist (the oldest of which was forty-six plus!). It is difficult to generalize about the family and church backgrounds of those we interviewed. Some had experienced the divorce of their parents while growing up; several spoke of having had an alcoholic parent; some had no church background; some had engaged in considerable faith exploration in various churches and in other religious traditions; and others were from an intact family with a strong church background.

Generation Xers continue to be the primary focus of the Living Waters ministry. But because the congregation (at the time of our research) was ten years old, many of the earlier Xer members who remain in the congregation are now between thirty and thirty-five. Many who were single when they began their association with Living Waters are now married, with children. Fifty-five percent of Xers in our survey were married; 45 percent were single. Thus the congregation has been pushed to begin children's ministries, including the Kids' Connection.

On one of our visits, we noticed a sign near the entrance to the children's classrooms announcing the start of a support group for children of divorced parents, a type of program that one rarely sees in a traditional congregation. Growth in the number of married members has raised questions for both married and single members. As one of the pastors said, "Singles ask, 'Is this going to become a family church, and will I still feel part of it?' while marrieds wonder, 'Is this really going to be a stable church where I can raise my children?'" Such questions about institutional change as members age can be especially problematic for a generation-specific congregation. Should the church change as members age, and if so, how does this affect its primary vision for ministry?[4] "We struggle with this as a board all the time," one of the elders told us. "How are we going to wear two hats? The singles are still coming, and that was really our original call. . . . How do we do both of these?"

The congregation has, from the start, also attracted a few older members—boomers and even some pre-boomers, some of whom came with their Xer sons or daughters, liked what they found, and stayed. Laurie and Marvin Wilson, a pre-boomer couple, described how they church-hopped among the "smorgasbord" of southern California churches near their home: "We kept coming back [to Living Waters]. I think we responded to Rolf's preaching. It seemed to us that it was real. The faith of this generation seemed very real to us. It was just kind of fresh and new. I can't imagine going back to an organized church again. . . . It's almost like they're all wearing a mask [but] this church is kind of 'unmasked.' And we like the honesty that seems to be here that doesn't appear in mainline—and certainly not in traditional, long-established liturgical—churches." Marvin serves as an elder in the congregation, and with their forty years of marriage they both are important mentors and marriage role models to younger members, many of whom have not known a stable family. "Here we are," says Marvin, "married forty years. And so they look and say 'Has anybody in the world ever been married forty years? Here you are and you're here with us.' They kind of treasure us, and we treasure them. There's a give-and-take of mutual respect for one another."

Living Waters leaders and members describe their congregation as conservative, but not fundamentalist. Masters says that "many evangelical churches would say that we were more moderate, with people on a journey in their faith. We have groups for people dealing with their own sexuality. We have people who are living together . . . and we want to help them in a process of learning why it's important to be apart until they get married. But we do not thump a Bible on their head and tell them they're going to hell. . . . In our dress, we're definitely not conservative. . . . At the same time, our values and our theology would still be very conservative." Several members used the same phrase that we heard at Church of the Word: "We major in the majors, and minor in the minors." Living Waters is denominationally affiliated with the Conservative Baptist Association, but it wears this affiliation lightly. Some participants are unaware of the relationship.

What is it that draws people to Living Waters? Those we interviewed mentioned a number of things, but especially the worship and music. Living Waters's music rocks, and its entire worship service flows around a common theme each Sunday. The contemporary Christian music, much of which is written by the music director and played by a seven-piece worship band, reflects different musical styles: acoustic folk rock, grunge, occasional country-and-western (much to the music director's dislike), and even classical. At one service we heard a lovely rendition of Bach's "Jesu Joy of Man's Desiring" played on an electronic keyboard, a kind of postmodern mixing of codes.

Following an extended jam session by the band, the formal part of the service begins as a singer invites the congregation to join her in worship, referring primarily to singing contemporary praise songs with words projected on the video screen. Some worshipers raise their hands in a bidding to the Holy Spirit to bless their service. Following a brief prayer, there is often a short drama or skit relating to the theme of the service. One week, it was based on the TV sitcom "Cheers"; another, on "Seinfeld." About the "Cheers" skit, Marvin Wilson commented on the use of a bar scene in a worship service: "They were trying to make the point that a bar is a place everybody knows your name. . . . That's what the church should be, a place where everybody knows your name. But if you put a bar set in a mainline church, half the church would leave! But it communicated a point to this generation and to me."

Announcements follow the skit, and the band plays another segment of music chosen to reflect the theme of the service. Then one of the staff—typically the lead pastor—presents the Bible teaching or sermon for the week. Members are encouraged to take notes on the bulletin handout, which outlines the week's teaching and often also contains relevant Bible verses. This twenty-to-thirty-minute teaching often includes or is followed by a video clip from a contemporary film to illustrate some part of the theme. The service ends with the worship band leading an extended jam session as a kind of postlude. Members leave rather quickly. There is no fellowship hour.

At one service, we celebrated the Lord's Supper. We were told that they had begun to observe communion more frequently in close emulation of the practice of the early Christian church. Leaders vary the format, drawing on modes of celebrating the Supper from a variety of traditions. On this night, we pulled our chairs into small circles of ten to twelve and passed the elements (grape juice and Saltine crackers) to each other after brief words of institution from the leader.

The aim of the worship, said one of the staff, is to deal with real-life issues in light of God's Word using ways that "appeal to a remote-control, multimedia generation who are bored by traditional churches." They like things "to flow." Each and every aspect of the service points to the central theme. It is not just preliminaries that lead up to the main thing—the preaching—as in a more traditional church. Several interviewees commented about how the services dealt with issues that they were facing, and did so with honesty and authenticity. In the service on saving a troubled marriage, the lead pastor, Masters, spoke quite openly about difficulties that he and his wife had faced. The video clip for the evening was from the conclusion of the film *Forget Paris,* where the characters split without divorcing and then come back together again.

Another time, Jim Colby, pastor of group life and mobilization, told of being part of a group that used offensive language about homosexuals; it proved troubling to one of the group who was struggling with his sexual identity. The skit that Sunday was a dramatization of the incident. Colby admitted his transgression and warned the congregation not to make the same mistake. At the same time, he did not compromise his belief that homosexuality is wrong, while reminding listeners that they should "hate the sin and love the sinner." He also invited those in the congregation who were struggling with homosexuality to "stay here and find a way to grow out of that . . . to grow into God's best."

"When they [the staff] preach, they share their own lives," said Byron Palka, the director of small-group ministry. "Generation X wants that authenticity, that connection, that [sense that] 'it's working in [the preacher's] life so it can work in my life' kind of thing."

He continued: "They're asking deep questions. They want it real. 'Help me ask questions,' they say. 'Don't give me pat answers. I'm going to question it anyway.'"

Dress at the services is very casual, mostly shorts or jeans and T-shirts. Worship leaders, including the pastors, also often wear shorts and T-shirts. One pastor told us that he had recently worn his hair in spikes. We saw T-shirts of all sorts, some with the letters FDFX across the front (as we mentioned in Chapter Four in opening the discussion of the posttraditional congregation). The letters stand for Fully Devoted Followers of Christ—the goal of Living Waters's ministry as expressed in its mission statement.

One primary way, besides worship, that Living Waters pursues its mission of creating mature disciples is through its small-group ministry. As one document says, a basic conviction is that "a small group of Christians and pre-Christians is the best place for disciple-making, edification, equipping, accountability, and growth"; thus the church "will encourage all aspects of ministry to be cell/team based." The small groups meet mostly on week nights in some member's home or at a nearby college or university. Each group of eight to twelve has a leader who functions more as a facilitator or coach than a directive leader. Discussion flows from the previous weekend's sermon and teaching, using the questions from the "message notes" distributed at the service. Those questions, said Byron Palka, "are designed to say, '[the pastor] talked *at* us about this topic; now let's talk *with* one another about it. Let's . . . make it practical in our lives.' [The small groups] are very relational, not Bible studies."

The relational dimension is important, creating a kind of intimate community that the large worship events do not offer. Leaders recognize the importance, especially for Xers, of such community: "Relationships are huge," one of the leaders told us. "Xers are longing for relationships. For them to come into a relationship with Christ, it's gonna be through a personal relationship they have with a friend, someone they trust, who they see Christ doing something for their life. That's what's gonna convince them. They don't like surfacy chitchat." Once a group grows larger than twelve, or members have been part of the group from nine to eighteen months, they are encouraged to start a new group and are given training to facilitate. This is one strategy of a cell-group ministry: it multiplies by dividing.

In addition to small groups, another kind of cell-group ministry is seen in the ten to fifteen support groups each meeting for a short period of time to deal with a particular issue that participants are facing—sometimes an addiction, sometimes a matter of family or sexuality, sometimes a concern of self-discovery. Support groups are open to others in the community beyond Living Waters and often operate in similar fashion to Alcoholics Anonymous, though their Christian orientation is made clear. Workshops, seminars, retreats, feeding programs for the homeless, missions to Mexico, and similar outreach activities make up other dimensions of the Living Waters ministry. Staff rely on lay leaders for much of this undertaking, meeting with the leaders to provide training and support.

Leadership responsibilities rest on two groups, with Masters, the lead pastor, as the link. One is the executive team, made up of the seven staff members. The other is the elder board, laity nominated by a committee and elected by the congregation. Elders are mostly Xers but also include a few boomers and one pre-boomer. The executive team meets weekly to engage in "vision casting" and planning for the various ministries. Staff members have great flexibility with their respective area. "We are a staff-led church, not a board-led church," one emphasized. "A lot of churches are board-led, but that is ridiculous, because those people are not doing the day-to-day ministry." The elder board meets monthly and hears report of the staff's vision, goals, and plans. Elders are responsible to say "amen" to the staff, or to send back things with which they disagree or have a problem. "We need their accountability," said the same staff member. Elders also review membership, attendance, and finances; they extend prayer, care, and support to any member facing a need such as sickness, surgery, or marriage difficulty. Large issues, such as changing the mission statement or the annual budget, are brought to the entire congregation for a vote.

What concerns, tension, or conflict does Living Waters experience? We noted previously the differing expectations of singles and married members, given the rising number of married members with children. Concern was also expressed for the limited programs available to the older members of the congregation, both boomers and pre-boomers.

A more serious tension exists about the role of women. The executive team includes a woman, though not as one of the primary pastors. "Twice in our history," Colby told us, "we've had a woman teach from the pulpit, and both times we got tremendous flak—from men and women. I'd say that most people really appreciated it, but we got some real flak." The elder board is all male, an issue about which some members, elders, and staff disagree and with which they struggle. Women, however, are allowed to serve in all other forms of ministry. They have recently begun an all-women worship band, the "Chick Band" as they call themselves. Masters admits that the congregation has lost women members because of its views on women's roles: "'When is Living Waters going to begin to live in the 1990s?' they ask."

Another source of tension has been the building: whether to build the new facility or not. (It was subsequently decided to proceed.) What will a building do to the character of the congregation? Some fear that it leads Living Waters along the path of becoming a traditional church—a negative outcome strongly to be avoided. The director of operations, David Parker, worries that a building might negatively affect the cell-church character of Living Waters—the small-group ministry and support groups meeting in homes and elsewhere—which, he believes, contributes to the congregation's vitality. "My concern is that we get this building with twenty rooms, and everybody's going to flock here, and we're going to have to reinforce a no-no. Go back to the homes. That's what we've always been—a cell-based church—so go back. So that's going to be hard, a real challenge."

Parker also added another concern: finances. Raising sufficient money to pay for the ministries, let alone a new building, is a special challenge facing a congregation of young Xers. To quote him again: "So many people will be honest enough around here to say, 'I am so far in debt. I'm twenty-two years old, or I'm thirty, and I have $30,000 debt on my credit cards. I own a boat and a car, and I can't pay for them. How can I give to the church?' I don't know if it's their fault or their parents, but we have a lot of that around here. So, no, they don't really give much—or they give five bucks, ten bucks, twenty bucks. And part of me believes they are really giving. . . . When I get a five-dollar check, I believe that person took that five dollars pretty doggone seriously. It's not a tithe of their gross income, but they're squeezing out what they can."

Then there is the music, which is generally recognized as one of the great strengths of Living Waters. For some of the older members it is nonetheless distracting. Some complained that it is too loud (though the band sees the loud sound as creating more energy for worship); others complain that the music sometimes lacks substance. They would prefer being able to sing traditional hymns on occasion. Ironically, as the music director told us, for gen Xers (for whom Living Waters has been their primary experience of church) the contemporary music—the rock and grunge—*are* traditional! It is all that they have known. As student member Robin Hanson put it, "It's more comfortable for me to have a guitar rocking than to have an organ playing."

Another concern—not so much a tension or conflict—has to do with the mobility of the congregation, which often results in lack of commitment and to losing a large number of members through the back door, that is, through dropping out. Our researcher had an early impression of the congregation as apparently divided between those who seemed highly involved and committed and those who were relatively casual weekend attenders. One young woman among the committed group estimated that only 40 percent of the congregation are involved in a small-group ministry, leaving the other 60 percent without deep roots in the congregation.

Additionally, there is tension over the size of the congregation. Some do not want it to grow larger. The leadership hopes to address this issue by planting new congregations rather than adding members to this one. The issue of growth and starting new congregations also raises the previously noted question of the long-term focus of the congregation. Is it to remain primarily generation X? Or should older and younger generations also be in the picture? If the latter, what does that mean for the congregation's style and practices? Can the congregation become more inclusive, especially of the large number of Hispanics who live nearby?

"I want our church to grow through people that are not from other churches, but from the neighborhood," said Masters, then adding, "We're mostly white, but 80 percent of the people that live just three and a half miles north of us are Hispanic, and we still haven't tapped in."

Despite these concerns and tensions, which in part reflect growing pains, Living Waters is a vital congregation. When asked what it does well, Colby demurred: "I don't know if Living Waters does anything *really* well. We don't feel like we're much of a model for others. But I would say that one of the things that we have done well is that we've not allowed ourselves to stay stuck. We continue to say, 'How can we be fresh? How can we do things differently? How can we adapt our approach?'" One Xer lay member summed up the challenge this way: "If there was one thing that the church in general and definitely Living Waters could do, it would be to take a chance and step out and try stuff that would even more build people up, encourage them to step out in faith, and teach them to pray and share their faith. I think if that happened in the church, you'd see a revolution."

The English Ministry of Good Shepherd Korean Presbyterian Church

> *The vision of Good Shepherd English Ministry is to reach, nurture, equip, and mobilize the next generation of Korean Americans in the greater Los Angeles area so that God may use them most effectively to revitalize the church, to impact the society, and to evangelize the world.*
> GOOD SHEPHERD KOREAN PRESBYTERIAN CHURCH
> ENGLISH MINISTRY WEBSITE

After the U.S. Congress passed the Immigration Act of 1965, Koreans were among the large number of immigrants who came to America. Many were Christians, descended from converts in revivals that swept Korea in the early twentieth century. As they came, often with young children, they formed Korean-speaking congregations in their new country.

Good Shepherd Korean Presbyterian Church in Los Angeles, founded in 1974, was one such congregation. It has become the largest Korean congregation outside of Korea. Although its worship and other ministries were conducted in Korean, one exception was the children's Sunday school, which was taught in English—felt to be needed because the children were attending English-speaking schools and needed English proficiency. As the children grew up, went away to college, and later settled in jobs, many spoke little Korean and found the worship services and adult programs at Good Shepherd not only difficult to understand but also out of touch with the American culture, which they increasingly adopted. The church had no postcollege program to meet the needs of these young adults.

Worried that they would be lost to the congregation either by join-ing Anglo or other Korean American congregations more attuned to American culture or by dropping out of church participation al-together, Good Shepherd leaders created the English Ministry pro-gram in 1989.

The program has in almost all respects become a separate con-gregation. The two are now referred to as the Korean Ministry, or KM, with roughly six thousand members; and the English Ministry, or EM, with approximately seven hundred members. One of its members called the EM "one of the biggest generation X congre-gations in the area" where people "come to grow and be plugged in." Almost all of the EM members are thirty-five or under and English-speaking. KM members are predominantly fifty through seventy and Korean-speaking. Although KM has members older than seventy and younger than fifty who are new immigrants and Korean-speaking, most of those who emigrated from Korea fol-lowing changes in the immigration laws were in their thirties and early forties at the time, and they are now in the age range of fifty through the late sixties.

Generational patterns at Good Shepherd are somewhat differ-ent from what we have considered in most of the other congrega-tions. They play such an important role in distinguishing the two Good Shepherd ministries that they deserve special comment. First-generation immigrants, those who came to this country in the late 1960s and early 1970s, are roughly equivalent to our pre-boomer co-hort; however, their formative years were quite different from those of the other pre-boomers we have considered. Most important for our purposes is that their formative years were in Korea and thus de-cisively shaped by Korean traditional culture and by conflict (World War II and the Korean War). Many of the founding members of Good Shepherd Church were North Koreans who fled to South Korea during the Korean War before coming to the United States. One young man expressed respect for the fact that his parents had experienced so much turmoil and change, including their decision to come to the United States and start a new life of their own.

Despite the changes they have experienced, and perhaps because of them, the first generation values and preserves Korean tradition in the home and in the church. Another interviewee described the first generation's religious practices as "based upon tradition. They do things because it was done in the past; so you just do it, no questions asked." In addition to their strong roots in Korean culture, the first generation's primary language is Korean, with English as secondary. These two traits are important boundary markers between them and the other younger generations.

When they came to this country, first-generation immigrants brought their young children, who, though born in Korea, spent their formative years in the United States and were therefore immersed in American education and culture. This generation refers to itself as the "1.5 generation," standing with one foot in Korean culture and the other in the American (the latter is primary for most). This is also true of language. English is their primary language, though most can speak and understand some Korean. Mary Lee (twenty-six) told us that she identifies "a lot with people of my age, like the eighties generation [that is, gen X], but I think more recently, especially after I visited and lived in Korea for a year, I identify myself a lot more with Korean culture than before."

Samuel Han, also a 1.5 generation member, described his generation as "rooted in tradition but somewhat flexible. We don't throw away everything, but we examine it before we say whether it's good or bad." Their parents, however, see the 1.5s as mostly Americanized. They are college graduates, often with an advanced graduate or professional degree. One of their number described them as "yuppies," very career- and status-oriented; others described themselves as being members of generation X in their lack of strong commitment but different from Xers in their concern for career. The 1.5s constitute the largest group of participants in the English Ministry, although they are joined by some members of a third group, the second generation.

The second generation of Korean Americans are children born to the immigrants since their arrival in the United States. Because they were born here, they have spent all of their formative years in the American cultural context, in contrast to their slightly older 1.5 siblings. As a consequence, they are the most Americanized; said Han, "They are open and flexible. . . . They would say [of Korean cultural traditions], 'Well, that's not mine, or that's not part of me.' They would totally disregard a traditional upbringing."

We have more to say about these generational differences, but first it is important to consider further the origins of the congregation. The Good Shepherd Korean Presbyterian Church in Los Angeles traces its roots back to the Good Shepherd Presbyterian Church in Seoul, Korea, a congregation of between twenty thousand and thirty thousand members and one of the largest and most influential in Korea. The Koreans' worship services are broadcast in the Los Angeles area and are watched by many of this congregation's members, especially those in the first generation who were members of the Korean Good Shepherd before emigrating. The L.A. congregation is affiliated with the Presbyterian Church (USA), the mainline denomination whose missionaries were the primary catalyst for the revivals that played such an important role in establishing Protestant Christianity in Korea. One of the pastors told us with some pride that the Los Angeles Good Shepherd Church is looked to by other Korean American congregations as a pioneer, presenting a model for them to follow.

The congregation is located in downtown L.A. During the three Korean Ministry worship services on Sunday morning, the parking lots near the church fill quickly, and a shuttle bus brings worshipers from a lot some distance from the adobe style church buildings. The large main sanctuary is in a building called Faith Hall. It also houses several offices and another auditorium. The sanctuary is wider than it is deep, with three sections of pews. A dais or raised platform forms a stage on which stands a central pulpit. The choir sits on one side, and a large cross hangs on the wall behind the pulpit. Flowers and sometimes an arc of balloons decorate the stage. For the English service, a praise band is located in front of the dais.

Next to Faith Hall is a long, two-story, L-shaped building housing other offices and educational programs. There are classrooms for all ages. On Sundays and often on weekdays, children are in abundance. Outside of Faith Hall in an adjacent parking lot are several areas with tents, under which are tables and chairs. The area serves as a social gathering place for the Korean Ministry worshipers following service.

Pastoral leadership in the congregation is offered by twelve clergy, four of whom are devoted to the English Ministry congregation: a head pastor, an associate pastor, a missions pastor, and a children's pastor. The head and associate pastors are quite visible in the congregation's activities; however, members have little contact with the other two unless they are involved in missions or in the Sunday school. The head and associate share responsibilities for preaching, acting as liturgist, and teaching in the young adult ministry and couples ministry (see below). At the time of our research, the head pastor had been in his position for approximately one year, the associate for only three months.

Although we are focusing our attention on the English Ministry, it is helpful to contrast its style with that of the Korean Ministry.[5] All of the KM services are in Korean (with simultaneous English translation) and traditional and staid. Dress is formal and conservative. People bow to one another in traditional Korean fashion. The congregation prefers hymns to any kind of contemporary praise music. "When it comes to singing," one EM member told us, "they [the first generation] don't believe in anything that would upset or offend the Lord, that goes against the Bible." A Korean version of the Bible is used, which twenty-six-year-old Mary Lee described as somewhat similar to the King James Version. It contrasts to a considerable extent with the New International Version (a modern English translation that often paraphrases the original texts), which she prefers. The NIV is "very contemporary," she said, adding that "you wouldn't even notice that some passages are from the Bible, because they just sound like good moral statements."

Another member of the EM described the sermons in the Korean service as very serious, never containing any humor. There is little expressiveness in the services. As Jim Wong, an EM member, described it, "The people, they're almost like zombies, sitting and listening, . . . where, instead, they should be coming here to be rejoicing and to be truly giving of what they feel towards God." Also, Lee pointed out that the hierarchy of the Korean Ministry is quite evident in the services; "There are clear distinctions of who are the elders and the deacons [offices in the congregation]."

The worship services at the English Ministry are considerably different even as they follow something of the same pattern as the KM services. Held from 1:30 until 3:00 on Sunday afternoons, there is an average attendance of approximately four hundred. About 70 percent are single; the remainder are married couples. Worshipers come much more well dressed than in the comparable age group at other churches. Many of the men wear suits, and those who don't come in dress shirts and slacks. The women are dressed in blouses and nice slacks or skirts; some wear suits. Only a few wear jeans, but they too, as our researcher put it, "are dressed nicely."

Although held in the Faith Hall sanctuary where the KM also worships, the EM service is much less formal and much more expressive. A praise team, using guitars, a keyboard, and drums, accompanies the singing. The six members of the team dress in contemporary style, and the music complements their dress. Although sounding like pop or rock music, the lyrics have religious themes and are projected on a large screen at the front on the sanctuary. Barbara Hong described the music as "like love songs" in contrast to traditional hymns. One of the KM pastors said that many of the praise choruses come from Vineyard congregations[6] and that the EM services have a Pentecostal flavor—a point of concern for the KM elders, as we shall see.

As worshipers enter the sanctuary, the praise team is singing. This is followed by a call to worship, in which the congregation participates responsively, and an opening hymn. The congregation then joins in a unison prayer of confession and a time of silence before reciting the Apostles' Creed together. Next, the praise team leads in several choruses, with the congregants actively participating by singing, swaying, and clapping their hands to the beat. One of the ministers then leads in prayer, and another hymn is sung. A lay reader is called up to read the Scripture lesson for the day. A choral anthem follows; then comes the sermon. In contrast to the sermons of the KM service, which were described as never having any humor, the EM preacher frequently uses humor to make his point. The sermon themes also differ. Korean Ministry sermons focus on history and tradition, Margaret Kang told us, while the EM sermons focus on contemporary issues and trends: "You know, like, Pastor Joshua . . . will deal with issues that he knows that we're going through, whether relationships, or careers, or the struggle we have with a lot of the factors that are out there—you know, with temptations."

The sermon is followed by a prayer and often another solo by one of the choir members. The offering is taken while the praise team sings. A prayer of thanksgiving follows. The minister makes announcements during which he reads the names of newcomers to the church. Newcomers are asked to stand while the rest of the congregation applauds and welcomes them. Congregants then greet their neighbors. A closing hymn, the Lord's Prayer (recited while participants hold hands) and a benediction end the service.

Although a number of worshipers leave following the service, many stay for either the young adult ministry (YAM) for singles or the couples ministry for married couples. These are basically Bible study but also include singing of praise choruses, prayers, some social time, and food. After one of the ministers introduces the Bible study for the day, the two larger ministries break into small groups for intense discussion of the passage. Other courses are also offered as a part of SALT, an acronym for Sunday afternoon leadership training. The courses focus on such topics as dating, marriage, child rearing, or basic Christian beliefs. Both the YAM and couples ministry organize worship and social activities for members during the week, for example a singles Wednesday praise gathering and a couples' date night. Marriage and family seminars and retreats are also offered by the couples ministry. During these meetings, a children's ministry offers a full range of Sunday school classes for toddlers through elementary school age.

Home fellowship groups offer another important point of contact with fellow members of the EM congregation. Since many live some distance from the church buildings, and since the congregation is quite large, the home fellowship groups offer intimate community nearer members' homes. Groups consist of six to twelve people, often mixing singles and couples. They share a meal and study and pray together. "What's really good," said Linda Jee, "is they pray for each other. They take prayer requests. I think that's really good, because at a big church, if you don't have anyone really kind of watching out for you, you feel like you're not part of it, and I think you tend not to come back. But knowing that there are people praying for you, then that really helps." The groups are led by members who are trained and supported by the church's pastors. One member said there were twenty to twenty-five of these groups meeting either weekly or biweekly.

Since the majority of the English Ministry congregation are singles, the young adult ministry plays an especially important role. The president of YAM, Samuel Han, laments the fact that in the past some have treated it as a "meat market" in their search for a spouse, and others who are highly career-oriented have used it as a place to "check out the competition." But this has changed, he says, and YAM is fulfilling its primary purpose of offering 1.5 and second-generation young people "a place to fit in, a place to belong and have friends who are fellow Christians, fellow Koreans, and they can come and worship and praise God together."

A major concern of all that we interviewed is the high dropout rate among members of the English Ministry—as much as 60 percent annually, one leader estimated. Some attributed it to lack of commitment among the younger generations, a trait they said that both 1.5 and second-generation Korean Americans share with other generation Xers. Others felt that the size of the EM congregation is a contributing factor. Jee, a member of the newcomers' committee, said that if one does not make friends quickly in a new church, he or she is much more likely to leave. Thus her committee works hard to establish friendship with new members, learn their names, give orientation to the congregation, and invite them to dinner or Sunday school class.

On rare occasions, the Korean and English Ministries come together. Bilingual services are held at Thanksgiving and Christmas; there is an annual all-church picnic; and there are occasional joint missionary activities. The KM head pastor also occasionally preaches at the EM service, and KM members are invited when there is a musical or some other special event of the EM congregation. In general, however, the two ministries don't interact, and most of the EM members that we interviewed did not know any KM members and could not name any activities that the two groups do together.

One new area of contact between the two ministries is the deacons board. As a Presbyterian congregation, the primary governing body of the congregation is the board of elders or church session, the latter being the major policy-making body. The board of deacons, in comparison, has primarily a service role, caring for members' needs. It has also served as a kind of training ground for elders. At the time of our study, the elder board had just approved election of seven deacons from the English Ministry, to create a channel of communication between the two congregations.

This change, however, did not come without struggle. It took five or six years for the elders to agree to the appointment of the young deacons. According to YAM president Han, the elders were not sure that the younger members were mature enough for the responsibility. Also, as Pastor Jonathan Yang told us, there are a number of first-generation Korean Ministry men who are waiting in line to become elders and deacons, and there is some resentment that the younger members of the English Ministry are being given a "fast track" to the board of deacons. One new deacon, for example, is several years younger than an older brother, a KM member who is one of those waiting in line to become a deacon.

Both boards at Good Shepherd, elders and deacons, are all male, even though the Presbyterian Church (USA) allows and encourages election of women to these offices. Good Shepherd elders (thirty-six in number) are not only male but also older first-generation members of the congregation, mostly sixty and above. Deacons, except for the seven from EM, are mostly in their forties or older and are also first-generation.

There is a third group besides the boards of elders and deacons, consisting of approximately fifty older women, all first-generation, who are called *Kwonsa,* a term of respect in Korean. Although they are not a part of official Presbyterian polity, they are found in many Korean congregations, much as the "church mother" is a recognized position of respect in African American congregations. Yang told us that the *Kwonsa* are "sort of in between ordained elders and deacons." In general, he said, especially in the Korean Ministry, women are busy and active in serving the church, but the roles he mentioned were mostly traditional: cooking, baby sitting at church, serving meals, and so on. Men, he said, take care of most of the administrative responsibilities. Han added that "even the seven deacons elected from EM are all males and all established family men. Women in the English Ministry cry out for more strong female role models."

The rather strong control exerted by the board of elders is seen not just in their reluctance to appoint deacons from the EM. Representing the sentiments of many of the older KM members, they also have refused to allow younger members to openly express charismatic gifts, and for a considerable length of time they also resisted use of drums and praise music in EM worship services. The EM members explained their side and their style of worship, but it took some time before the board of elders finally agreed to changes in the music. Han described the conflict this way:

> The drum sets were taken away [by the elders] because they thought the drums were not appropriate to praise, especially when it comes to praising God. That was a big debate. . . . They're slowly seeing that the second generation and 1.5 generation (my age group) need to have the freedom and mobility to express ourselves. One fear that the Korean older generation has is that the younger generation—if they were to let us go about expressing the way we do—we would break up the church, break up the body, that we would break off and create our own individualistic, more liberal church. That is not the case. We are in a constant struggle to understand and to mutually get along with the older generation.

"You know, you *have* to compromise," Lee added, "even if drums are horrible to the ear for some members. Well, we're sorry," she said, "but the world is changing and so is the church." Such compromise, however, is a constant struggle for a church as steeped in tradition as is Good Shepherd.

Conclusion

The generation-specific congregation takes us one step further from the blended in its embrace of the cultural style of a specific generation. The three cases we have presented in no way exhaust the possibilities for the generation-specific congregation, nor do they represent all of the strengths and liabilities of such a church. But what are some of the commonalities, differences, and issues that this kind of congregation exemplifies?

At least two of the congregations (Church of the Word and Living Waters) were new at the time of their founding. To some extent, this was also true for the English Ministry at Good Shepherd. By this, we mean that they started out as a new congregation without the encumbrance of a shared past, without inherited tradition and practice. Living Waters leaders at least implicitly reflect a form of "primitivism," a belief that their congregational life emulates characteristics of the practices of the earliest churches. In doing so, they have bypassed the accretions added over the years in various denominational traditions.

Clearly, part of the appeal of each of the three congregations to boomers and Xers is that they are different, they are not like ordinary congregations that have turned them off in the past; participants fear nothing more than a return to that kind of church. We see this in the music they prefer (praise chorus but not hymns, guitars and drums but not organ), in their preferred style of architecture (either lacking traditional symbols or preferring no fixed building at all), in their dress styles and the expressiveness of their worship, and in their willingness in various ways to "dance with the culture," as one of the leaders put it. Good Shepherd's English Ministry is less a totally new congregation than the other two. It is still under the strong control of the older, Korean Ministry congregation, and it has its roots in Presbyterian traditions. Yet its relative separation from the older congregation has allowed it to be highly innovative in many of its practices.

In short, the absence of strong, inherited traditions, especially in Church of the Word and Living Waters and to some extent in the English Ministry, give these congregations a posttraditional flavor. They are the kind of congregation one might expect in a society that has become posttraditional, as we discussed in Chapter Two. At the same time, however, the question with which each congregation struggles is how far can it go in neglect of inherited tradition without losing its Christian identity. How much can the congregation dance with the culture without allowing the culture to write the music? A similar question could be asked of innovative congregations in other traditions.

That both leaders and members wrestle with such questions is evident in other ways in all three congregations. Especially in the worship practices of the Church of the Word, and in a more limited way through introduction of frequent celebration of the Lord's Supper in Living Waters drawing on different communion practices, we see what we called earlier a kind of reflexive reappropriation of inherited tradition, which moves them toward the blended model. We saw a somewhat similar growing appreciation of inherited Korean tradition and practice by the 1.5 generation. None of these congregations is likely to appropriate the inherited tradition whole-cloth. Instead, they adapt tradition to make it appropriate to their experience, as we saw in all three churches.

In adaptation, these churches, more so than most blended and certainly more so than inherited-model congregations, recognize the importance of sensory experience and feeling for both boomers and generation Xers, the latter in particular. Although they do not neglect the intellect, participants are seeking more than a "head trip." Thus the congregations encourage great expressiveness in worship, emphasis on feeling, music that sounds like "love songs," videos and drama to illustrate sermon points, and various other nontraditional artifacts that appeal to those who have been immersed in a sensory culture, a generation looking for a "felt" religion.

The novelty of many of these practices, however, has another liability. Though they help some to experience a deeper faith, they also attract the curious. Thus in all three congregations there are more attenders than members, and for at least two of them (Living Waters and Good Shepherd) there is what both called a back-door problem, a high turnover of participants with many coming in the front door but rather quickly exiting through the back, unwilling to make the commitment necessary to stay.

There is a further problem that the generation-specific congregation faces, one that has been an issue both for the Church of the Word and for Living Waters. (Good Shepherd's English Ministry is too young to have experienced it yet, but it will come in time.) We refer to the obvious fact that members age and mature, and they don't always do a good job of making room for or relating to new generations that come after them—or for that matter, to preceding generations that might also be attracted to the congregation. They become multigenerational but fail to recognize it, or in some ways fail to take advantage of it. In the process of aging and maturing, they also develop institutions and traditions of their own, despite constant reference to being novel and different. "How we do things here" becomes "how we've *always* done things here!" Ideas and practices are infused with value. Charisma becomes routinized, to use the description of the sociologist Max Weber. Having to construct buildings is an additional maturation issue that further institutionalizes the congregation's practices and reduces its ability to be fluid and flexible.

Finally, the generation-specific congregation risks missing the rich interaction that comes through the give-and-take of generations trying to find ways of living together faithfully. Fortunately for each of the three congregations we profiled, there was evidence of at least limited cross-generational contact, where, for example, pre-boomers could serve as mentors for boomers and Xers, and where the younger generations enlivened the experiences of their elders. Ironically, given the rather steep language and cultural barriers that separated the Korean and English Ministries at Good Shepherd, there was probably *less* cross-generational contact in that congregation than at the two predominantly Anglo ones. We suspect, however, that family life and the filial respect inherent in Korean culture offer other occasions for substantial intergenerational interaction outside the congregational context.

Epilogue: A Consciousness Beyond Complacency

Social analyst Ken Dychtwald, a popular writer and lecturer on generations and cultural change in America, concludes his recent book *Age Power: How the 21st Century Will Be Ruled by the New Old* this way: "The rise of age power . . . poses a new and perplexing problem. Living in an era when life expectancy was thirty-five and less than 2 percent of the population was more than sixty-five, our founders never anticipated the challenges of managing the relative contributions and demands of three to four living generations—particularly when the elder generation had grown so large and powerful."[1]

Because of increasing longevity, he envisions a society where three or four generations are living with one another and the proportion of elders is quite large. The "new old" is the large boom generation soon to face retirement. He goes on to write, "Our social institutions and policymakers must learn a new and complex skill: how to manage a *multigenerational melting pot.*" It is an intriguing notion, one that forces us to think creatively about the challenges before us.

Focusing mainly on finances, medical services, and caregiving, he thinks that as a society we must establish new ground rules for intergenerational relations. Opportunities are greater now than ever before for extended sharing, mentoring, and friendship across age and generational lines. If we do not seize the opportunity for building new and supportive relationships, the alternative is likely to be, to one degree or another, "age wars," or a situation where political action lines are drawn between the generations. Current rumbling about the future of Social Security as voiced by many boomers and whether there will be a sufficient number of young Americans working to sustain the government program, make clear that this scenario of rising tension between the generations is by no means far-fetched.

Dychtwald does not look at religious institutions, but clearly the same concerns apply. On theological grounds, it might be argued, in fact, that pressure is greater upon the congregation than on other social organizations to model a multigenerational order. As a gathering informed by religious ideals of equality and fairness, a congregation (of any faith tradition) is in a position to lead the society—not just to proclaim but to implement those ideals and teachings. Of course, the congregation is a complex reality and cannot always lead the society so easily; to a considerable extent it is a mirror of society, reflecting age-based and generational values as well as many other local influences. But it also exists as an institution whose mission is to reflect upon, and to engage theologically, its social and cultural contexts. Local cultures and theologies mix in every congregation subtly and interactively, creating a distinctive normative system; each one is, as one writer says, a "negotiated order"[2] built up over time and through social interaction, and peculiar to a particular place and circumstance. Thus the challenge for any congregation—whether inherited, blended, or generation-specific—is to cultivate awareness of its mission and how it came to exist in the institutional form that it does, and consciously to try to model the social ideals and teachings for which it stands. If a congregation fails in this level of self-understanding, it risks losing the very quality that by definition distinguishes it from secular institutions.

Beyond Complacency

But how likely is it that a congregation will cultivate such self-understanding? As we have seen in this book, many pressures are upon the congregation, working against it becoming a genuinely multigenerational institution. Trends toward greater religious pluralism and privatism in society limit opportunities for shared faith, except in the narrowest and shallowest sense. Lack of broadly shared faith means that people can easily turn inward and live in a religious world limited largely to their own social experiences. Expanding levels of education and computer literacy, and the rise of the so-called knowledge class in contemporary society, all give rise to diverse worldviews and new divisions in religious interpretation. Metaphorical as opposed to literal understanding of symbols and texts is greatly amplified under these conditions, resulting in a proliferation of interpretations and ideological stances.

Changing patterns of family life pose yet another important challenge for the congregation, one of the most important of which is the reduced possibility for intergenerational transmission of beliefs and values. Aside from the high level of disruption within families, the growing number of mixed-faith marriages works against strong religious socialization for children and the likelihood of parents and their children having common beliefs and practices. Even among intact families of the same faith, it is not unusual for parents to feel frustrated about the values and beliefs their children hold, and for them to worry about exposure to influences from outside the family. Issues vary for the several generations, but family concerns generally are widespread today.

Then there is the rapid pace of technological change. It continues unabated in contemporary society; indeed, it seems to accelerate by the decade and is a driving force shaping the signs, symbols, and experiential frames by which successive age groups understand themselves and the worlds in which they live and express themselves. If, as many communication theorists say, life is constituted in the very act of human communication—that is, people "live in communication"—then the universe of meaning and the epistemology on which they rest are ever shifting, especially for the younger generations most exposed to this intensifying pace of change. The implications for the congregation are considerable and likely to increase in importance in the years ahead.

Taking into consideration these current trends, the inherited-model congregation clearly faces serious challenges as it tries to hold on to younger generations. Members of these generations may be present within the congregation at any given time, but as we saw in Chapter Five they participate largely on terms dictated by their elders, not because of any serious effort at negotiation across generational lines or willingness to adapt programmatically. This is an example of what Dychtwald means by "age power." Some younger people will stick with the congregation throughout their adult lives, becoming in time the "new old," guardians of religious tradition themselves. Others not brought up religiously will no doubt be drawn to the history and heritage of the congregation, if nothing more because it offers a bastion of continuity amid so much social and cultural change. But we would expect many younger members to switch to another congregation or simply drop out of active participation in the years ahead. Lack of voice and agency, except for the most traditionally minded, will drive many with open, flexible views away. The challenge for the congregation is to break out of blindness to its cultural captivity and to make a genuine effort at bridging the generational gaps that already exist. The inherited-model congregation can and does build such bridges, but doing so requires much deliberation and effort. Even when successful, the bridges often turn out to be rather precarious.

The generation-specific congregation faces problems of another type. We would expect this type of congregation to proliferate in the years ahead as new generations emerge. There is no reason to think that the pace of cultural and technological change will decline, and every reason to think that the face of religion will continue to shift in form and style with generational experiences. But the major function of this congregational type may be more to introduce or reconnect people to a religious heritage—or, as in the case of the Good Shepherd Church, keep them from deserting their ethnic heritage—than to be an ongoing fellowship that sustains people over the entire adult life span. This itself is not an unimportant function, especially in a society where so many Americans have little grounding in religious tradition and are best served by gradual introduction into a faith community.

Yet the fact remains that what is the primary strength of such a congregation—religious styles and structures that attract because they are culturally current—is also a weakness in the long run. As observed in Chapter Seven, it is an open question what will happen to the people who make up the generation-specific congregation as they themselves age. Will they continue wanting to be with the same age group? What happens once their children grow up and forge a generational identity of their own? At some point, pressure is likely to mount in favor of a multigenerational congregation, as has occurred in Church of the Word. Deeply entrenched in its own generational culture, the congregation faces serious challenges bridging the gap between itself and the children's (or elder's) world. These congregations have to ask themselves—as many are already beginning to do—what they will be like in the years ahead when their original membership has aged and priorities are no longer as they are now. We simply do not have sufficient experience with such congregations.

The blended congregation, or one that is consciously trying to become multigenerational in program, style, and structure, best reflects not just the values of the great religious traditions but also the goal Dychtwald holds forth as so important for us in the twenty-first century: caring, sharing, and mentoring across all age groups. This does not mean, however, that the blended congregation is without considerable challenge itself. As we have seen, this congregational type is fragile in ways, subject to tension and conflict that can easily erupt. The normative orders within it are at best precarious, seemingly held together by only a thread.

Definition of social reality rests, it is sometimes said, upon meaningful conversation among people; within the congregation, where norms of expected belief and practice play so crucial a role, it is difficult to sustain shared interpretation unless people consciously attempt to build bridges through dialogue and exchange of ideas and concerns. We cannot escape the fact that multigenerational community is problematic even for a congregation seeking it. Churches, synagogues, and temples speak a great deal about the human family and indeed champion community as a basis for spiritual well-being and for what is best in life. Yet the very structure of most congregations often stands in the way of making it easy to embody community in keeping with its ideals. Addressing this situation within the Christian context, Wuthnow writes:

> The church, as it has evolved in the twentieth century, is in many ways ill suited to create community. It brings people together once a week, drawing them from broad geographic areas, and expects them to forge some intimate bond when they probably will not see each other again for seven days. It adds people to its membership rolls—the more the better—until most of them have no idea who their fellow members are. It places a speaker up front and expects everyone else to sit in rows facing that speaker, much as they would at a concert or athletic event. If interaction happens before or after the service, it does so informally, *despite* everything else that has gone on. In short, the church is an administrative convenience, created unwillingly by a combination of its history and the programs planned by its leaders. If community is going to take place at all, it must occur against high odds.[3]

The congregation has little choice but to "work at" creating community, if in fact it is to overcome such a legacy and compete with other social agencies. In today's diverse and fluid society, community often takes form around human experiences and concerns—that is, people come together to address problems of environmental responsibility, in support of gay and lesbian rights, through sharing stories of abuse within families, by caring for one another as cancer survivors. The congregation can be, and often is, a social space giving rise to communal support and action on behalf of one or another cause, yet often too this occurs in the venue of just a small group that happens to meet within the congregation. Small groups serve people in useful ways but work against a broader sense of community.

Frequently missing in worship services and congregationwide programs and activities is a unity of purpose and intentionality that can only arise out of shared experience. Already, blended congregations have gained some skill at addressing intergenerational concerns, but now they must take what they have learned and attempt the most difficult bridging of all: breaking out of the staid, familiar complacency that characterizes many congregations and transforming worship opportunities, programs and activities, and institutional structures such that people experience a broadly based, enlivened community. This is unlikely without a serious look at how the generations themselves can be brought together.

The Generationally Conscious Congregation

Earlier in this book, we spoke of the importance of reflexivity, or of cultivating awareness of ourselves in social and historic religious contexts. Reflexivity involves, in the words of one writer,[4] a "contemplative act of stepping back from one's own perspective and recognizing that it, too, is situated" in a plurality of possibilities. It is a serious act of self-understanding arising out of sociological imagination, recognition of one's own views, values, and identity in relation to others. It presumes a sense of human agency, a capacity to define the self, and a sense of the relation of the self to the past and to all we know as tradition and culture. With just a little stretch of the imagination, we can grasp how reflexivity might work not just for individuals but for congregations too. With this in mind, we ask, What principles might inform the generationally conscious congregation?

Of course, every generation lives to some extent by cultural and religious fictions. Boomers have skepticism about social institutions and expect the congregation to earn their trust to a greater degree than pre-boomers or generation Xers do. The latter have profound concerns about finding close, familylike relationships within a congregation, born less out of lack of trust than perception of the congregation as cold and unresponsive to their needs. As a start toward a more reflexive consciousness, the congregation should recognize that the generations have varied, and at times conflicted, views about the meaning of religious involvement itself. The words that Americans use to designate involvement in a congregation—*to affiliate, to join, to participate, to become a communicant, to be part of a fellowship*—all mean various things, and those meanings are shaped by the experiences people have had growing up in a religious setting or in any other voluntary organization. Meanings shift as generational experiences change.

For better or worse, all such religious definitions are colored as well by a highly subjective cultural ethos that easily leads to a disconnect between the individual and the congregation. Robert Bellah and his colleagues point out in *The Good Society* that we Americans have trouble understanding social institutions and tend to perpetuate misperception of our social reality. Typically, we think of institutions as constraining, as if they were objective—distant and removed from our own everyday lives, which presumably are free and autonomous. Thus Bellah and colleagues point out that "we form institutions and they form us every time we engage in a conversation that matters, and certainly every time we act as parent or child, student or teacher, citizen or official, in each case calling on models and metaphors for the rightness or wrongness of action."[5] Equally true, we often fail to grasp our own power to form, or reform, the institutions that sustain us.

Far from being fixed and reified entities, institutions have the capacity to evolve as clientele and circumstance change. The congregation too has a responsibility in making this possible. Where there is consciousness about how and why it goes about practicing a shared faith and life as it does, the congregation helps people understand that institutions are adaptable, and thus enabling. From the standpoint of the "problem of generations," the congregation helps by communicating awareness of how religious styles are culturally conditioned by particular age-based social experiences. Such awareness becomes a basis for renewed bonding.

This is at once liberating theologically and programmatically. People come to recognize that congregational structures exist first and foremost in relation to goals, and that religious teachings and programs may be cast in more than one cultural medium. People grasp how faith is lived in, through, and in response to a variety of religious and cultural idioms, not the least of which are the various moral and religious vocabularies forged out of generational experiences, in which case the act of faith comes to be understood as arising out of a conversation with tradition as well as contemporary culture and is expressed not in any singular style but in multiple ways. The generationally conscious congregation thus encourages a creative space for exercising human agency and recognizes the appropriateness of multigenerational styles of moral and religious action—even for the most fundamental of religious practices, such as in the many expressions of charity and caring for others, in cultivating a deeper spirituality, in worshiping together, or in grappling with social injustice and the moral dilemmas of our time. People of all ages are likely to be drawn to a congregation where they sense a connection between their own feelings, sensibility, and inclination to act and the structures established within the congregation allowing meaningful expression of those responses.

Despite the proliferation of how-to manuals about bridging the generations, in churches and elsewhere, there is no simple formula for doing so. Hence we resist that temptation here. Each congregation poses its own distinctive opportunities and challenges. St. Paul's Lutheran Church is successful in attracting boomers to a Saturday evening worship service with country-and-western music, though less successful in that regard with generation Xers, who prefer the traditional Lutheran service. In contrast, what seems to account for the blending of generations at St. Clare's Catholic parish is not so much generational-based worship as the fact that the parish is relatively young and fairly homogeneous in accepting post–Vatican II styles and practices. Generation-specific programming is the key to the multigenerational congregation in one setting, but in another it is the age of the parish and its ethos. Congregation history, local community demographics, leadership styles, and many other factors all bear upon the creative possibilities in any specific setting.

Aside from being practical about what they can do in bringing the generations together, religious institutions must be reflexive in the sense of institutionalizing a level of deliberateness within their structures, engaging in planning and strategizing broadly, and then carefully monitoring whatever they do. This is a major challenge for congregational leaders in the years ahead. As the St. Paul's Lutheran example shows, what works for boomers may not work for generation Xers. In this case, the responsible strategy was not to try to impose the country-and-western service on the younger generation but to establish a new, or as it turns out in this instance perhaps an old, worship format. Reflexively speaking, there is no absolute standard by which to judge the appropriateness of the worship format; each such format is a cultural medium, and each presumably is as capable of communicating religiously with its own audience as is another with a different audience.

To be sure, there are standards of judgment that come out of religious Scripture and tradition. St Paul's looked to its Lutheran heritage for guidance. Such traditions, however, do not set absolute, unchanging standards. Instead, if they are *living* traditions, they are constantly being renegotiated and retraditioned through a reflexive conversation with the culture.

Because it works at negotiating and planning across generational lines, the blended congregation inevitably must experiment and risk failure. In our judgment, this does not make it weak, but strong. Terminology about a congregation being weak or strong has often in the past focused upon doctrinal commitment—as if the sectarian or orthodox version of faith were the one true standard against which to judge all faith—and organizational strictness the primary basis on which to claim a congregation's well-being.[6] Real strength within a congregation, we maintain, lies in its capacity to accept others, their beliefs, and their values, even as they differ from those presently in control of the institution, recognizing that all our many interpretations of faith and practice are just that: interpretation, born out of biography and the historic encounter of our community with the tradition by which we name ourselves.

This is not to argue for total relativism. Every one of the historic faiths has a Tradition (capital *T*) to which it looks as a final authority. But this Tradition has, through the years, generated traditions (lowercase *t*) that are historically and contextually bound expressions of the Tradition as the religious community has engaged in the reflexive process of retraditionizing. The temptation is always to turn tradition into Tradition.

Acknowledgment of this fundamental grasp of religious reality augurs for a somewhat relaxed approach to alternative religious styles, as problematic as that may be for many congregations; it also implies appreciation for conflict management and resolution. Perhaps the test of a strong religious institution in times of great social change is not its diversity of theological and cultural styles, but how well it handles that diversity. The challenge ahead for the congregation is to create an environment that not only accepts and respects this internal pluralism but institutionalizes creative ways of dealing with it theologically and programmatically. Shared decision making across the generations and other like-minded constituencies is a beginning; beyond that is the need to cultivate a theology of culture that recognizes both the possibilities and inherent limitations of any singular religious style or mode of expression.

Religious researchers can help by giving more attention to generations as carriers of culture and religious styles than they have done in the past. It would be especially helpful to conduct research within congregations that draws attention to generations as major players in the process of religious reformulation. Traditions are not only carried forward by generations, they are reshaped in the process. The congregation is a "divided religious world," but boundaries between generational cohorts are also points of contact that make reformulation and renewal possible. Division between generations poses an opportunity for recasting faith and practice in ways that may be newly meaningful across generations. We need a better grasp of the retraditionalizing process itself within the congregation and of the importance of consciously addressing generational values and priorities. Of course, the task mentioned in the Introduction of sorting out the complexities of generational cohort, life-cycle, and period effects is crucial to a refined analysis of changing patterns of congregational life.

In the final analysis, we do not want to overstate the case for generational change. It is but one among many important aspects of religious transformation in the contemporary world. Religion in America is now drawn toward two extremes, in the direction of absolutism or relativism. Neither is what we argue for here. Ours is a middle position that looks upon the congregation as engaging the culture theologically, but not for the sake of any particular ecclesial form or doctrinal system.

Western faith traditions jealously affirm loyalty to the Ultimate Authority, above and beyond all earthly authorities—including institutional form and theological framework. Inevitably, the congregation is caught up in a dialectic between structure and freedom, finding itself, as Peter Berger, says, "in the dilemma of reconciling [its] nostalgia for certainty with a social reality in which such certainty is very hard to come by."[7] It is a dilemma no religious tradition escapes in the modern context. It is also a dilemma that should be embraced and creatively dealt with.

To be sure, life within such an in-between space is not easy, either for individuals or congregations, given the human quest for certainty and closure. Yet it is a space that Jews, Christians, and believers in other faith traditions have long claimed generates radical trust—or as Protestant Christians say, living by faith alone. Although radical faith as such is not easy to affirm, much less to live by, nonetheless it is the challenge that may yet save the congregation willing to take on the venture. Perhaps what the generations and their shifting cultural and religious styles pose for the congregation in some final sense is just that: yet another test of faith.

Appendix

Methodological Notes

Data for this study came from two sources. First, during 1995 and 1996, we engaged in participant observation and interviews with members of twenty congregations and two campus ministries in North Carolina and southern California, evenly divided between the two states. Second, we commissioned a telephone survey of a random sample of residents of the entire state of North Carolina and the eleven counties that make up southern California.

We begin with the congregations. Since we have chosen not to use the actual names of congregations and their participants, we are unable to list them here. We do wish, however, to indicate some of the criteria used in selecting them.

First, we were interested in possible regional differences, but since we wanted to be able to do field observation on site in the congregations, we chose to limit ourselves to two regions, focusing our work in the two states in which the principal researchers reside. This gave us congregations in two sites with regional contrasts. North Carolina, as part of the so-called Bible Belt, has until recently been almost monolithically Protestant and heavily influenced by the preponderance of Southern Baptist and other evangelical Protestant congregations. California, by contrast, is the most religiously pluralistic state in the nation.

Within the two states, we narrowed our congregational focus to two subregions. In North Carolina we studied congregations in the Research Triangle area, concentrated primarily in three counties (Wake, Durham, and Orange); in California, we chose churches primarily from among the eleven counties that make up southern California. To be sure, the Triangle area of North Carolina is somewhat atypical compared to much of the rest of the state; however, as noted, the telephone survey covered the whole state.

Second, in selecting the congregations, we realized that we could in no way represent all possible types of congregations with a sample of twenty plus the campus ministries. We did, however, attempt to select a diverse group: Jewish, Catholic, mainline Protestant, and evangelical Protestant. We also achieved racial and ethnic diversity by including predominantly African American, Caucasian, Korean, and Latino congregations.

After securing permission from the congregations to include them in the study, we assigned a member of our research team to each congregation. They were given an observational protocol as well as interview guides for pastors and members. Each field researcher made multiple visits to the assigned congregation, observing worship, educational events, meetings of the governing board(s), and other congregational events. Following each visit, researchers recorded their observations in field notes. They also were instructed to interview the principal pastor or rabbi of each congregation plus at least twelve lay members and leaders. Some also interviewed other staff members where possible.

The interviews, though following a common set of questions, were open-ended. They were tape recorded and later transcribed. The researchers also prepared a paper summarizing what they had learned about each congregation from their observations and interviews. In addition to the interview and observational data, we distributed a short questionnaire to congregational members. The distribution was not randomly done, and in some instances we received too few back to merit analysis. We have made limited use of the questionnaire data for illustrative purposes for those congregations for which there was an adequate number returned; however, in no case can we claim a random sample.

Once the interviews were transcribed (running to more than two thousand single-spaced pages of text), we entered them into a qualitative, searchable database (ASKSAM). Each interview was coded according to a set of categories that reflected themes in which we were interested. The codes enabled us to select text reflecting specific themes.

As we noted in the Acknowledgments and in Chapter Four, we decided not to attempt to create a profile of each congregation and campus ministry. We chose instead to profile nine congregations in some depth. We did, however, read and make use of the interviews and observational data from all twenty congregations and campus ministries.

The telephone survey was the second major source of data for the book. It was conducted for us in February 1997 by FGI, a survey research firm in Chapel Hill, North Carolina. The questions covered such issues as denominational affiliation, religious participation while growing up, current religious participation, various religious beliefs and attitudes, valued congregational characteristics, and respondents' demographic characteristics. Interviews took just over fifteen minutes each. They were conducted with a random, computer-generated sample of 1,102 persons, evenly divided between the two states. We asked to speak with an adult over age eighteen in each household called. If we did not reach the number called, or if the person answering refused to be interviewed, the computer selected a replacement at random. Survey responses have a margin of error of plus or minus 4 percent.

The data from the survey have been deposited in the American Religion Data Archive at Purdue University and may be accessed online (at http://www.thearda.com/).

Table A.1
Summary of Survey
Responses by Generation

	Generation X	Boomers	Pre-boomers
	n = 330	n = 411	n = 261

Religious Participation in Childhood

How involved in church/synagogue
was mother when you were growing up?

Not at all involved	13.5%	12.3%	13.5%
Not very involved	17.4	14.3	14.0
Somewhat involved	30.6	33.9	27.2
Very involved	38.5	39.6	45.3

How involved in church/synagogue
was father when you were growing up?

Not at all involved	29.0	26.5	23.7
Not very involved	20.7	18.3	20.1
Somewhat involved	25.8	27.1	24.3
Very involved	24.5	27.9	31.8

How involved in church/synagogue
were you when you were growing up?

Not at all involved	8.2	7.3	5.0
Not very involved	13.0	9.5	13.3
Somewhat involved	43.9	38.6	28.6
Very involved	34.8	44.5	53.1

	Generation X	Boomers	Pre-boomers
	n = 330	n = 411	n = 261

Your participation in worship services when growing up?

Never	11.9%	7.3%	6.4%
Few times a year	11.0	9.8	5.6
Once/twice monthly	18.9	13.9	13.7
Weekly or more	58.2	68.9	74.3

Your participation in Sunday/Sabbath school when growing up?

Never	17.0	11.3	12.9
Few times a year	11.2	9.3	4.5
Once/twice monthly	15.2	12.8	8.1
Weekly or more	56.7	66.6	74.5

Your participation in church/synagogue youth group

Never	27.6	24.1	26.3
Few times a year	15.2	13.1	7.4
Once/twice monthly	14.8	19.0	18.1
Weekly or more	42.4	43.8	48.2

Present Religious Participation

Worship services

Never	33.9	27.1	25.1
Few times a year	13.6	12.2	7.0
Once/twice monthly	16.1	17.6	10.6
Weekly or more	36.4	43.2	57.3

Sunday/Sabbath school

Never	57.9	48.3	45.5
Few times a year	6.1	6.8	4.2
Once/twice monthly	10.3	11.5	5.9
Weekly or more	25.8	33.4	44.4

	Generation X	*Boomers*	*Pre-boomers*
	n = 330	*n = 411*	*n = 261*
Private prayer or meditation			
Never	16.8%	10.0%	10.4%
Few times a year	3.7	5.9	2.5
Once/twice monthly	12.5	6.8	4.8
Weekly or more	67.1	77.3	82.3
Bible study (other than Sunday school)			
Never	50.2	44.0	41.1
Few times a year	8.8	10.0	7.3
Once/twice monthly	10.9	9.5	10.6
Weekly or more	30.1	36.5	41.1
How religious are you?			
Not at all religious	6.7	5.5	5.7
Not very religious	14.3	10.5	7.2
Somewhat religious	53.0	47.9	37.8
Very religious	25.9	36.2	49.3
How important is religion in your life?			
Not at all important	4.8	4.4	4.7
Not very important	8.5	7.4	3.9
Somewhat important	27.3	24.7	12.8
Very important	59.4	63.5	78.6
How spiritual are you?			
Not at all spiritual	4.8	3.2	3.2
Not very spiritual	9.7	7.7	5.7
Somewhat spiritual	49.4	47.0	42.2
Very spiritual	36.1	42.1	48.9
What best expresses your belief about God?			
Don't believe in God	1.2	2.0	1.1
Uncertain, lean toward not believing	6.1	2.0	2.2
Uncertain, lean toward believing	8.8	7.6	6.7
Definitely believe in God	83.8	88.5	89.9

	Generation X	Boomers	Pre-boomers
	n = 330	n = 411	n = 261
Do you feel that God is personally involved in your life?			
Yes	92.5%	91.3%	93.2%
No	7.5	8.7	6.8

How Often Do You Feel God's Presence in:

Nature

Never	14.6	7.9	9.6
Some of the time	31.9	33.2	27.7
Most of the time	21.6	22.8	25.3
All of the time	31.9	36.1	37.3

Worship services

Never	11.5	8.2	9.1
Some of the time	25.1	25.3	18.8
Most of the time	21.9	25.8	30.6
All of the time	41.6	40.8	41.6

Reading Bible/sacred texts

Never	16.6	11.7	11.6
Some of the time	23.8	24.7	22.9
Most of the time	20.0	20.6	24.7
All of the time	39.7	43.1	40.9

Reading inspirational books

Never	18.3	11.9	13.5
Some of the time	41.7	37.4	31.8
Most of the time	19.3	22.0	25.4
All of the time	20.7	28.7	29.3

Private prayer

Never	8.1	6.4	6.7
Some of the time	23.6	22.8	24.6
Most of the time	25.3	21.8	19.1
All of the time	42.9	49.0	49.6

	Generation X	Boomers	Pre-boomers
	n = 330	n = 411	n = 261
Meditating			
Never	18.1%	10.2%	9.0%
Some of the time	28.0	28.8	28.9
Most of the time	21.4	24.0	23.9
All of the time	32.5	37.0	38.2
When serving others			
Never	15.9	9.9	13.8
Some of the time	34.5	36.4	30.4
Most of the time	23.0	24.4	24.2
All of the time	26.7	29.4	31.6
During experiences of joy?			
Never	11.2	8.6	9.1
Some of the time	37.3	33.4	27.6
Most of the time	22.1	23.5	27.6
All of the time	29.4	34.4	35.6
In sorrow or tragedy?			
Never	8.9	7.2	8.5
Some of the time	36.3	29.0	24.4
Most of the time	21.5	19.2	25.9
All of the time	33.3	44.6	41.2
Experience of God			
In shrines/sacred places			
Never	18.3	14.2	18.8
Some of the time	28.7	34.6	30.5
Most of the time	22.2	21.8	22.8
All of the time	30.8	29.4	27.9
In dreams/visions/paranormal experiences			
Never	33.9	27.7	42.0
Some of the time	41.9	49.7	35.3
Most of the time	12.5	10.7	11.7
All of the time	11.8	11.9	11.0

	Generation X	Boomers	Pre-boomers
	n = 330	n = 411	n = 261
Most congregations have lost the real spiritual part of religion			
Strongly disagree	3.8%	8.9%	7.4%
Disagree somewhat	17.9	17.3	19.1
Neither agree nor disagree	9.4	7.2	6.2
Somewhat agree	32.9	38.1	34.0
Strongly agree	36.1	28.5	33.3
Morality rules preached by most religious groups are too restrictive			
Strongly disagree	19.4	31.5	39.9
Disagree somewhat	28.9	29.0	27.2
Neither agree nor disagree	9.5	10.1	5.6
Somewhat agree	27.7	19.9	18.0
Strongly agree	14.5	9.6	9.3
An individual should arrive at religious beliefs independent of church groups			
Strongly disagree	8.6	16.3	21.4
Disagree somewhat	13.1	13.6	14.6
Neither agree nor disagree	5.5	5.9	4.2
Somewhat agree	26.0	24.4	25.9
Strongly agree	46.8	39.8	33.9
One should follow his/her conscience even if contrary to religious teachings			
Strongly disagree	14.6	18.5	25.9
Disagree somewhat	17.7	16.3	16.6
Neither agree nor disagree	6.8	5.7	5.1
Somewhat agree	28.6	28.6	22.3
Strongly agree	32.3	31.0	30.1

	Generation X	Boomers	Pre-boomers
	n = 330	n = 411	n = 261

People who have God in their lives don't need a church or religious group			
Strongly disagree	29.3%	33.1%	44.2%
Disagree somewhat	19.8	21.2	17.1
Neither agree nor disagree	7.4	5.9	4.0
Somewhat agree	21.9	20.2	17.1
Strongly agree	21.6	19.5	17.7

All great religions are equally true and good			
Strongly disagree	31.2	32.3	36.2
Disagree somewhat	17.6	16.5	17.2
Neither agree nor disagree	9.3	9.1	5.9
Somewhat agree	24.7	23.2	20.5
Strongly agree	17.3	19.0	20.2

Most importantly, religion teaches the good moral life			
Strongly disagree	7.0	9.3	8.0
Disagree somewhat	6.7	7.6	6.8
Neither agree nor disagree	4.9	4.7	2.3
Somewhat agree	26.8	24.3	17.4
Strongly agree	54.6	54.1	65.5

Is it better to explore many religions or focus on the teachings of one faith tradition?			
Explore differing traditions	64.0	59.3	54.1
Focus on one	36.0	40.7	45.9

	Generation X	Boomers	Pre-boomers
	n = 330	n = 411	n = 261

Congregational Characteristics Important for Respondent's Involvement

Congregation belongs to a particular denomination or religious tradition

Very negative impact	4.6%	4.8%	6.0%
Somewhat negative impact	16.3	15.2	17.1
Somewhat positive impact	49.2	51.9	39.6
Very positive impact	30.0	28.2	37.3

Congregation teaches clear rules of morals and ethics for all to follow

Very negative impact	6.8	9.5	6.2
Somewhat negative impact	18.8	13.4	14.7
Somewhat positive impact	36.1	34.3	28.2
Very positive impact	38.3	42.8	50.9

Congregation makes sharp distinction between religious and secular

Very negative impact	8.4	14.4	11.7
Somewhat negative impact	25.4	27.8	29.9
Somewhat positive impact	46.7	36.4	28.5
Very positive impact	19.5	21.4	29.9

Congregation emphasizes social action and social justice issues

Very negative impact	5.6	5.4	8.9
Somewhat negative impact	13.2	12.9	20.7
Somewhat positive impact	50.5	47.9	37.6
Very positive impact	30.7	33.8	32.8

Congregation emphasizes helping needy people

Very negative impact	.9	.7	.6
Somewhat negative impact	.3	1.2	1.4
Somewhat positive impact	20.8	18.4	18.6
Very positive impact	78.0	79.7	79.4

	Generation X	Boomers	Pre-boomers
	n = 330	n = 411	n = 261
Congregation emphasizes personal witnessing and faith sharing			
Very negative impact	3.7%	6.1%	6.8%
Somewhat negative impact	8.6	12.2	11.0
Somewhat positive impact	41.4	32.5	29.4
Very positive impact	46.3	49.2	52.8
Congregation emphasizes making one's own decisions about doctrine and morals			
Very negative impact	10.7	13.9	20.4
Somewhat negative impact	11.6	14.4	15.9
Somewhat positive impact	37.7	39.0	30.5
Very positive impact	39.9	32.8	33.2
Congregation emphasizes shared leadership between clergy and laity			
Very negative impact	4.7	2.6	4.5
Somewhat negative impact	10.1	9.7	7.1
Somewhat positive impact	51.0	44.9	35.1
Very positive impact	34.2	42.8	53.2
Prefer worship that is:			
Emotional and uplifting	59.7	59.6	55.1
Intellectually challenging	40.3	40.4	44.9
Prefer worship that is:			
Traditional and formal	42.4	38.8	46.2
Contemporary and informal	57.6	61.2	53.8
Prefer music that is:			
Traditional	54.1	53.0	74.1
Contemporary	44.9	46.5	24.0
No music at all	1.0	.5	1.9

	Generation X	Boomers	Pre-boomers
	n = 330	n = 411	n = 261

Confidence in Social Institutions

Public schools

	Generation X	Boomers	Pre-boomers
No confidence	15.2%	12.7%	10.9%
Some confidence	31.6	37.9	27.8
Moderate amount of confidence	33.1	34.2	37.0
Great deal of confidence	20.1	15.2	24.4

Churches and organized religion

No confidence	10.8	8.2	9.2
Some confidence	27.8	30.1	23.4
Moderate amount of confidence	32.4	35.1	29.2
Great deal of confidence	29.0	26.6	38.2

U.S. Congress

No confidence	23.1	21.9	16.9
Some confidence	45.2	44.2	37.2
Moderate amount of confidence	24.3	27.3	35.8
Great deal of confidence	7.4	6.6	10.0

U.S. Supreme Court

No confidence	11.8	11.9	13.1
Some confidence	35.6	36.4	28.6
Moderate amount of confidence	34.7	38.6	35.7
Great deal of confidence	18.0	13.3	22.6

Organized labor

No confidence	15.0	25.1	28.5
Some confidence	34.9	40.5	31.0
Moderate amount of confidence	30.2	25.8	28.2
Great deal of confidence	15.0	8.6	12.4

	Generation X	Boomers	Pre-boomers
	n = 330	n = 411	n = 261

How Would You Describe Your:

Religious beliefs?

Conservative	42.5%	43.5%	55.2%
Moderate	31.9	34.0	29.1
Liberal	25.6	22.5	15.7

Views on personal morality?

Conservative	46.9	53.7	65.0
Moderate	29.4	31.8	25.7
Liberal	23.6	14.5	9.4

Views on social issues?

Conservative	31.8	39.2	45.6
Moderate	42.6	37.2	40.0
Liberal	25.6	23.6	14.4

Views on economic issues?

Conservative	39.8	47.3	52.5
Moderate	38.5	38.9	36.7
Liberal	21.7	13.9	10.7

Views on political issues?

Conservative	39.2	41.2	52.4
Moderate	33.5	36.8	36.0
Liberal	27.3	22.0	11.6

Registered to vote?

Yes	78.4	88.3	93.0
No	21.6	11.7	7.0

Party affiliation?

Republican	38.1	40.1	40.1
Democrat	36.1	46.4	50.5
Independent	19.0	9.5	7.5
Other	6.7	4.0	1.9

	Generation X	*Boomers*	*Pre-boomers*
	n = 330	*n = 411*	*n = 261*
Did you vote in the last national election?			
Yes	57.5%	78.5%	84.3%
No	42.7	21.5	15.7
Are you a born-again Christian?			
Yes	37.0	46.3	52.4
No	63.0	53.7	47.6
Are you an evangelical Christian?			
Yes	12.8	25.9	30.6
No	87.2	74.1	69.4
Are you a member of the religious right?			
Yes	14.7	16.0	14.9
No	85.3	84.0	85.1
How important is your present congregation in your life?			
Not at all important	3.8	2.7	1.5
Not very important	9.9	11.3	4.6
Somewhat important	34.0	35.8	27.9
Very important	52.4	50.2	66.0
How involved are you in your present congregation as compared with five years ago?			
More involved	43.5	42.6	28.6
Less involved	36.9	28.0	27.1
About the same	19.6	29.4	44.3
Do your family members share your religious views?			
Yes	79.6	88.2	88.9
No	20.4	11.8	11.1

	Generation X	Boomers	Pre-boomers
	n = 330	n = 411	n = 261

Before Age Eighteen, Did You Experience:

Divorce of parents/caregivers

Yes	27.3%	17.5%	11.9%
No	72.7	82.5	88.1

Separation of parents/caregivers

Yes	21.1	10.5	5.7
No	78.9	89.5	94.3

Being raised by a single parent?

Yes	30.4	18.8	17.8
No	69.6	81.2	82.2

Do you come from an intact family?

No	44.7	27.1	22.9
Yes	55.3	72.9	77.1

Gender

Male	45.8	39.7	35.7
Female	54.2	60.3	64.3

Highest level of education

Less than high school	7.6	4.1	17.4
High school graduate	27.4	22.1	24.1
Some college/vocational school	37.4	35.3	32.8
Four-year college degree	21.3	22.6	13.7
Graduate or professional degree	6.4	15.8	12.0

Income

Less than $10,000	8.8	3.4	11.9
$10,000–19,999	14.1	8.2	17.2
$20,000–34,999	25.7	16.2	21.9
$35,000–49,999	28.5	25.0	18.2
$50,000–74,999	11.9	27.1	17.5
$75,000–99,999	6.3	11.3	6.0
$100,000 or more	4.7	8.8	7.3

	Generation X	Boomers	Pre-boomers
	n = 330	n = 411	n = 261
Race or ethnicity?			
African American	11.9%	13.5%	12.2%
Asian American	5.0	3.6	1.7
Caucasian	64.1	73.1	77.6
Latino/Hispanic	16.3	7.4	2.0
Native American	2.8	2.5	6.4
Current marital status			
Single	51.5	20.3	7.0
Married	41.8	62.3	59.9
Divorced/separated	6.7	15.4	10.9
Widowed	.0	2.0	22.1
State of residence			
Southern California	56.1	50.1	44.6
North Carolina	43.9	49.9	55.4
Denominational family in which raised?			
Mainline Protestant	14.8	22.4	27.7
African American Protestant	1.2	1.7	1.9
Conservative Protestant	31.5	37.5	41.0
Catholic	31.2	19.7	11.9
Other	13.6	13.6	12.5
No preference	7.6	5.1	5.0
Current denominational family			
Mainline Protestant	16.7	20.9	27.4
African American Protestant	3.0	3.2	2.5
Conservative Protestant	32.7	38.9	39.3
Catholic	21.5	12.2	11.1
Other	7.9	8.0	7.2
No preference	18.2	16.8	12.5

Table A.2
Regression of Current Religious Involvement Across Three Generations

	Gen X		Boomer		Pre-boomer	
	Beta	Sig.	Beta	Sig.	Beta	Sig.
Racial-ethnic:						
African American	.100	.029	.083	.032	.153	.000
Asian American	−.080	.071	−.079	.034	.008	.847
Hispanic or Latino	−.023	.638	.004	.914	.043	.279
(Excluded categories: white and other)						
Gender: female	.040	.381	.038	.329	.036	.399
(Excluded category: male)						
Marital status						
Married	.100	.036	.126	.008	.170	.020
Divorced	.061	.177	−.031	.479	.103	.069
Widowed	—	—	.055	.139	.184	.007
(Excluded category: single)						
Education	−.021	.646	−.008	.833	.108	.015
Parents' religious involvement	−.008	.869	.009	.837	.069	.104
Religious involvement growing up	.147	.004	.082	.055	.082	.060
Experience of God	.221	.000	.213	.000	.233	.000
Religious individualism	−.233	.000	−.290	.000	−.211	.000
Number of household members in congregation	−.008	.868	.014	.721	.107	.010
Number of friends in congregation	.157	.001	.081	.032	.139	.001

	Gen X		Boomer		Pre-boomer	
	Beta	Sig.	Beta	Sig.	Beta	Sig.
Congregational emphases						
Particular denomination/ tradition	−.016	.749	−.029	.472	.084	.049
Clear rules of morals/ethics	.035	.497	.111	.010	.017	.707
Distinction between religious and secular	.061	.180	.048	.237	.022	.587
Social justice and social action	.005	.914	−.020	.587	−.027	.524
Helping needy people	−.046	.328	.061	.114	−.027	.514
Witnessing and sharing faith	.119	.017	.207	.000	.240	.000
Individual decision making	−.126	.012	−.035	.388	−.037	.372
Shared leadership	.047	.318	.123	.001	.052	.209
Preference for contemporary worship/music	.007	.880	−.030	.431	−.059	.137
Adjusted r^2:	.418		.496		.480	

Items Used to Construct Various Scales

Religious Involvement Growing Up

(alpha = .76)
("Never" to "Weekly")
    Attendance at worship services
    Attendance at Sabbath or Sunday school
    Participation in church/synagogue related youth group

Parents' Religious Involvement

(alpha = .72)
("Not at all involved" to Very involved")
    Mother's involvement when respondent was growing up
    Father's involvement when respondent was growing up

Current Religious Involvement

(alpha = .82)
("Never" to "Weekly or more")
    Attendance at worship services
    Attendance at Sabbath or Sunday school
    Pray or meditate privately
    Bible or Scripture study
    Participate in spiritual growth group
    Participate in church-sponsored women or men's group

---

* The reliability coefficient, Cronbach's alpha, indicates the degree to which the items "hang together" consistently around a common theme, based on interitem correlation. The coefficient can vary between 0 and 1. The higher the coefficient, the more reliable the scale.

Religious Individualism

(alpha = .66)
("Strongly disagree" to "Strongly agree")
The rules of morality preached by most religious groups today are just too restrictive
An individual should arrive at his or her own religious beliefs independent of any church or religious group
A religious person should follow his or her conscience, even if it means going against what his or her religious tradition teaches
People who have God in their lives don't need a religious group

Experience of God

(alpha = .90)

How often, if ever, do you feel the presence of God or spiritual power?

("Never" to "All of the time")
    When experiencing nature
    During worship services
    While reading inspirational books
    During private prayer
    While meditating
    When serving others
    During experiences of joy
    During experiences of sorrow or tragedy
    When visiting shrines or sacred places
    In dreams, visions, or other paranormal experiences

Preference for Contemporary Music and Worship Styles

(alpha = .59)
    Adding scores for two items asking for preference for traditional or contemporary music and traditional or contemporary worship style

Notes

Introduction

1. Strictly speaking, the term *cohort* refers to people born in the same year. *Cohort group* refers to people born within a particular span of time, say a five- or ten-year period. A *generation* is usually thought of as consisting of cohorts, but it is common to speak of a *generation cohort*. See Chapter Fourteen of MacManus, S. A. *Young v. Old: Generational Combat in the 21st Century*. Boulder: Westview Press, 1996.

2. There is a substantial body of evidence to support this generalization. On Roman Catholic trends in the United States, see Davidson, J. "Generations Have Different Views of the Church: Vatican II Is the Dividing Line," *National Catholic Reporter*, Oct. 29, 1999. Davidson points to the big divide as being between pre–Vatican II and Vatican II generations, or pre-boomers and boomers. More broadly, General Social Survey data on the American population from the National Opinion Research Center confirm major differences in religious patterns between those born prior to 1946 and those born afterward. See Machacek, D. M. "Generation X and Religion: The General Social Survey Data." Unpublished paper, Department of Religious Studies, University of California at Santa Barbara, 1996.

3. For a comparative analysis of generational changes in religion in eleven countries (United States, Australia, and nine European nations), see Roof, W. C., Carroll, J. W., and Roozen, D. A. (eds.) *The Post-War Generation and Establishment Religion: Cross-Cultural Perspectives*. Boulder: Westview Press, 1995.

4. By no means do all researchers agree with these cutting points. Strauss, W., and Howe, N. *Generations: The History of America's Future, 1584 to 2069*. New York: Morrow, 1991, is perhaps the best-known, most comprehensive study of generations historically in this country; those authors define the birth years for boomers as 1943 to 1960, and for "thirteeners" (generation Xers) as 1961 to 1981.

5. Mannheim, K. "The Problem of Generations." In Kecskemeti, P. (ed.), *Essays on the Sociology of Knowledge.* New York: Oxford University Press, 1952, p. 304.

6. Strauss and Howe (1991).

7. For an analysis of how national and international events in people's formative years can make a lasting impression, see Schuman, H., and Scott, J. "Generations and Collective Memories." *American Sociological Review,* June 1989, *54,* 359–381.

8. Strauss and Howe (1991), p. 63.

9. Porterfield, A. *The Transformation of American Religion.* New York: Oxford University Press, 2000, p. 12.

10. See Smith, T. W. "Changes in the Generation Gap, 1972–1998." (GSS Social Change Report no. 43.) Chicago: National Opinion Research Center, University of Chicago, Oct. 2000. This conclusion was reached by looking at 101 trends at three points in time, plus an additional 52 trends for two periods of time (1973, 1985, 1997). The generation gap is measured by contrasting the difference between the eighteen-to-twenty-four age group and the sixty-five-and-older age group at the several points in time.

11. Wuthnow, R. *After Heaven: Spirituality in America Since the 1950s.* Berkeley: University of California Press, 1998, p. 12.

12. Ryder, N. B. "The Cohort as a Concept in the Study of Social Change." *American Sociological Review,* Dec. 1965, *30,* 843–861.

13. Lindner, E. W. (ed.) *Yearbook of American and Canadian Churches 2001 (69th Edition).* Nashville: Abingdon Press, 2001.

14. Wolfe, A. *One Nation, After All.* New York: Viking, 1998.

15. Chesterton, G. K. *Orthodoxy.* New York: Lane, 1909, p. 85.

16. Schaller, L. E. *Tattered Trust.* Nashville: Abingdon, 1996, pp. 45, 51.

17. Both of us have written recently on the role of reflexivity within religion. See Carroll, J. W. *Mainline to the Future: Congregations for the 21st Century.* Louisville: Westminster John Knox Press, 2000; and Roof, W. C. *Spiritual Marketplace: Baby Boomers and the Remaking of American Religion.* Princeton: Princeton University Press, 1999.

Chapter One

1. Mahedy, W., and Bernardi, J. *A Generation Alone: Xers Making a Place in the World.* Downers Grove, Ill.: Intervarsity, 1994, p. 10.

2. Cote, J. E., and Allahar, A. L. *Generation on Hold: Coming of Age in the Late Twentieth Century.* New York: New York University Press, 1994, p. 39.

3. For a discussion of the impact of post–World War II generations on participation in the congregation and other types of voluntary organization, see Putnam, R. "Bowling Alone: America's Declining Social Capital." *Journal of Democracy,* 6 Jan. 1995, pp. 65–78.
4. Smith, H. *Rethinking America.* New York: Random House, 1995.
5. See Cote and Allahar (1994).
6. Peter L. Berger was one of the first to address the rise of a "new class" and the implications for religion. See his essay "American Religion: Conservative Upsurge, Liberal Prospects." In R. S. Michaelsen and W. C. Roof (eds.), *Liberal Protestantism.* New York: Pilgrim Press, 1986.
7. See Hunter, J. D. *Culture Wars: The Struggle to Define America.* New York: Basic Books, 1991.
8. Kosmin, B. A., and Lachman, S. P. *One Nation Under God: Religion in Contemporary American Society.* New York: Crown, 1993, p. 226. The data reported in this paragraph are taken from the same book.
9. The phrase comes from Thomas, D. L. *The Religion and Family Connection: Social Science Perspectives.* Provo, Utah: Religious Studies Center, Brigham Young University, 1988.
10. See Dinges, W., Hoge, D. R., Johnson, M., and Gonzales, J. L. "A Faith Loosely Held: The Institutional Allegiance of Young Catholics." *Commonweal,* July 17, 1998, p. 13.
11. MacIntyre, A. *After Virtue: A Study in Moral Theory.* (2nd ed.) Notre Dame, Ind.: University of Notre Dame Press, 1984, p. 216.
12. Data are taken from Roof (1999).
13. Sweet, L. I. "Communication and Change in American Religious History: A Historiographical Probe." In L. I. Sweet (ed.), *Communication and Change in American Religious History.* Grand Rapids, Mich.: Eerdmans, 1993, p. 5.
14. Beaudoin, T. *Virtual Faith: The Irreverent Spiritual Quest of Generation X.* San Francisco: Jossey-Bass, 1998, p. 71.
15. Postman, N. *Amusing Ourselves to Death.* New York: Penguin, 1986.
16. See Buttrick, D. G. "Preaching to the 'Faith' of America." In Sweet (1993). He cites a good example: "in a talk on ecology it might be possible to describe a woodland hacked by unrestricted lumbering in one paragraph and then, in a following paragraph, to describe the same forest tract in its original unspoiled condition before the lumber camps arrived. The connective logic might be represented by 'but,' though a speaker would likely add the word 'imagine': 'but imagine the tract before lumbering began.' In consciousness we can visualize the lumbered forest and then, in an instant, imagine the same forest lands in pristine, untouched beauty" (p. 316).

17. Berger, P. L. *The Heretical Imperative: Contemporary Possibilities of Religious Affirmation*. Garden City, N.Y.: Anchor Press/Doubleday, 1979.

Chapter Two

1. Wuthnow (1998).
2. Bass, D. C. "Faith and Pluralism in the United States." *On the Way*, 1985, *3*(1), 12ff.
3. For an elaboration of the "third disestablishment" thesis, see Roof, W. C., and McKinney, W. *Mainline American Religion: Its Changing Shape and Future*. New Brunswick, N.J.: Rutgers University Press, 1987, Chapter One.
4. See Melton, J. G. "Another Look at New Religions." *Annals of the American Academy of Political and Social Science*, May 1993, *527*, 97–112.
5. Hunter, J. D. *Evangelicalism: The Coming Generation*. Chicago: University of Chicago Press, 1987, p. 152. His is a commentary on John Murray Cuddihy's influential book *No Offense: Civil Religion and Protestant Taste*. New York: Seabury, 1978.
6. Thiemann, R. F. "Public Religion and Pilgrim Citizenship." In *Religion and Values in Public Life*. Cambridge, Mass.: Center for the Study of Values in Public Life, Harvard Divinity School, 2000, p. 44.
7. Berger, P. L. *The Sacred Canopy*. Garden City, N.Y.: Doubleday, 1967.
8. Berger, P. L. *A Far Glory: The Quest for Faith in an Age of Credulity*. New York: Free Press, 1992, p. 68.
9. Gallup, G., Jr., and Castelli, J. *The People's Religion: American Faith in the Nineties*. New York: Macmillan, 1989.
10. Baggett, J. *Habitat for Humanity: Building Private Homes, Building Public Religion*. Philadelphia: Temple University Press, 2000, pp. 213–214. Baggett draws from Gallup and Castelli (1989) and Wuthnow, R. *Sharing the Journey: Support Groups and America's Quest for Community*. New York: Free Press, 1994.
11. The findings discussed here are taken from Roof, W. C. *A Generation of Seekers: The Spiritual Journeys of the Baby Boom Generation*. San Francisco: HarperSanFrancisco, 1993.
12. There were four generational cohorts in this analysis: pre-boomer, born from 1926 to 1935; pre-boomer, born from 1936 to 1945; boomer, born 1946 to 1954; and boomer, 1955 to 1962.
13. Wuthnow, R. *Christianity in the 21st Century*. New York: Oxford University Press, 1993, p. 108.
14. *The Unchurched American*. Princeton, N.J.: Princeton Religious Research Center, 1978, p. 9.

15. This theme is developed in many of Giddens's works, but perhaps most explicitly in *Modernity and Self-Identity: Self and Society in the Late Modern Age*. Stanford, Calif.: Stanford University Press, 1991.

16. Carroll (2000), p. 15. Much of the discussion in this section is taken from this recently published book.

17. Giddens (1991), p. 14.

18. Lifton, R. J. *The Protean Self: Human Resilience in an Age of Fragmentation*. New York: Basic Books, 1993.

19. Ford, K. G. *Jesus for a New Generation*. Downers Grove, Ill.: Intervarsity, 1995, p. 174.

20. Wuthnow (1998), p. 3.

21. Swidler, A. "Culture in Action: Symbols and Strategies." *American Sociological Review, 51,* 273.

22. Carroll (2000), p. 28.

23. Gallagher, W. *Working on God*. New York: Random House, 1999.

24. For further discussion of the emerging "spiritual marketplace," its varied dynamics, and its institutional structures, see Roof (1999).

Chapter Three

1. Strauss and Howe (1991), p. 37.

2. Schuman and Scott (1989).

3. Skolnick, A. *Embattled Paradise: The American Family in an Age of Uncertainty*. New York: Basic Books, 1991, p. 2.

4. Smith (2000).

5. See Marler, P. "Lost in the Fifties: The Changing Family and the Nostalgic Church." In N. T. Ammerman and W. C. Roof (eds.), *Work, Family, and Religion in Contemporary Society*. New York: Routledge, 1995.

6. Flory, R. W. "Conclusion: Toward a Theory of Generation X Religion." In R. W. Flory and D. E. Miller (eds.), *Gen X Religion*. New York: Routledge, 2000, p. 238.

7. For a discussion of "family congregations," see Becker, P. E. *Congregations in Conflict: Cultural Models of Local Religious Life*. Cambridge, UK: Cambridge University Press, 1999, Chapter Four.

8. See Miller, D., and Miller, A. M. "Introduction: Understanding Generation X." In Flory and Miller (2000), pp. 1–12.

9. See Smith (2000).

10. See Davidson (1999), p. 18.

11. See Greeley, A. M. *Religious Change in America*. Cambridge, Mass.: Harvard University Press, 1989. Commenting on Protestant switching

trends, Greeley observes that "only about half of those who have converted away from the mainline accept the literal interpretation of the Bible, a phenomenon which suggests that the enthusiasm of the changers is not quite the same as that of television evangelists" (p. 39).

12. For evidence of such patterns for baby boomers, see Roof (1999).
13. Beaudoin (1998), p. 74.
14. Bellah, R. N., and others. *Habits of the Heart: Individualism and Commitment in American Life.* Berkeley: University of California Press, 1985.
15. Flory and Miller (2000) argue that Xers differ from boomers in the greater stress they place upon community, belonging, and authenticity.
16. See Roof, W. C., and Hoge, D. R. "Church Involvement in America: Social Factors Affecting Membership and Participation." *Review of Religious Research,* 1980, *21*(4), 405–426.
17. Beaudoin (1998).
18. Gallagher (1999), p. 51.
19. The term is associated with Donald E. Miller. It describes churches characterized by openness and creative adaptation to secular cultural practice. See his *Reinventing American Protestantism: Christianity in the New Millenium.* Berkeley: University of California Press, 1997.
20. Beaudoin (1998), p. 84.

Chapter Four

1. Holifield, E. B. "Toward a History of American Congregations." In J. P. Wind and J. W. Lewis (eds.), *American Congregations, Vol. 2.* Chicago: University of Chicago Press, 1994, pp. 23–53.
2. See Carroll (2000) and Miller (1997).
3. A theologian interviewed for an article in an evangelical publication accused Willow Creek of "selling out the house of God." See Mauldin, M., and Gilbreath, E. "Selling Out the House of God." *Christianity Today,* 1994, *38*(8), 21–25.
4. Trueheart, C. "The Next Church." *Atlantic Monthly,* Aug. 1996, p. 36.
5. See Wuthnow, R. *The Restructuring of American Religion.* Princeton, N.J.: Princeton University Press, 1988.
6. See Kelley, D. M. *Why Conservative Churches Are Growing.* San Francisco: HarperSanFrancisco, 1972; and Stark, R., and Finke, R. *Acts of Faith.* Berkeley: University of California Press, 2000. The quotation from Kelley is on page 56.
7. Ammerman, N. T. "Golden Rule Christianity." In D. Hall (ed.), *Lived Religion in America.* Princeton, N.J.: Princeton University Press, 1997.

8. We grouped the denominational families following the pattern of Roof and McKinney (1987). Because there were only twenty Jewish respondents in the survey, we grouped them, along with those who did not fit one of the other denominational family categories, into a "Jewish/other" category; it is so mixed that we have made little of it in our analysis.

9. The reliability coefficient (alpha) for the index is .60.

10. In constructing the index, we summed the responses to the four involvement items and then divided by four (the number of items) to get an average involvement score for each respondent. The reliability coefficient (alpha) for the index is .82.

11. It is important to emphasize that statistical significance is not necessarily the same as substantive significance; however, it is a useful way of sorting out those relationships that would have occurred by chance in 5 percent or fewer cases.

12. The variance is a statistical measure of the variation or dispersion of scores—in this case, of religious involvement—from the average or mean score of the entire group. The percentage of variance explained for the three generations is quite large, especially in a survey such as this with a large number of respondents.

13. In the regression table (Table A.2 in the Appendix), note the use in several places—as with race, for example—of "excluded categories." Because regression analysis assumes continuous variables, it is necessary, when the measure is categorical, to create dummy variables by using only one category at a time while treating all other responses as zero. It is also necessary to exclude one or more of the categories from the analysis. We indicate in the table the category (or categories) excluded.

14. Ten items having to do with the frequency of experience of the presence of God or a spiritual power in various settings were summed to construct the Experience of God scale. The reliability coefficient for the scale is .90. Four items were used to construct the Religious Individualism scale, with scale reliability of .66. See the Appendix for the list of items for each scale.

15. There were only 38 Asian Americans in our total sample; thus the findings about Asian American involvement are likely to be unreliable. Of the 38, 30 percent were Catholic, with 22 percent indicating that they were mainline Protestants and the same percentage having no religious preference.

16. When we grouped the congregations by type, both inherited-model and generation-specific congregations comprise approximately 30 percent of the respondents each. The other 40 percent are in blended congregations. Given the lack of random selection of respondents, it

is technically inappropriate to use a test of statistical significance. We have done so nevertheless, using the chi square test as a rough indicator of important differences. We mention only differences that were significant at .05 or less and report them here.

Chapter Five

1. Field work and interviews for Covenant United Church of Christ were done by Jennifer Berentsen Williams, for Our Lady of Mercy by Gaston Espinosa, and for Fellowship Missionary Baptist Church by Michelle Wolkomir.
2. From the Covenant United Church of Christ website.
3. The Congregational Christian Churches, reflecting an earlier merger of Congregational and Christian Churches, united with the Evangelical and Reformed Church in 1957 to form the United Church of Christ.
4. Both priests were due to retire in the summer following our field research.
5. In the Baptist tradition, some Baptists were strict Calvinists with a strong belief in the doctrine of predestination—the belief that God has already foreordained who will be saved. Such a belief makes missionary work, especially when defined as evangelism, irrelevant. Most Baptists, however, have rejected belief in predestination and given strong emphasis to evangelism and missions. A number of African American Baptists (those at FMB included), stand in this broader Baptist tradition and have symbolized their belief in missions by including *Missionary* as part of their name.
6. As we have indicated in the Methodological Notes at the end of this book, we were unable to use random sampling methods in getting responses to our congregational survey; nor was the rate of return for some congregations especially high. For Fellowship Missionary Baptist, we received fifty-nine responses to the one hundred surveys that were distributed—a reasonably respectable return.

Chapter Six

1. Field work and interviews for St. Paul's Lutheran were done by Lynn Gesch. Michelle Wolkomir was responsible for the fieldwork and interviews at Temple Beth El and St. Clare's.
2. Conservative and Orthodox are the two other major Jewish "denominations" in addition to Reform. A fourth branch, Reconstructionist, is much smaller than the other three.

3. See Schwartz, S. *Finding a Spiritual Home.* San Francisco: Jossey-Bass, 2000.
4. Shimron, Y. "Spiritual Journey Leads Back to Catholic Church." *News and Observer* (Raleigh, N.C.), Apr. 23, 2000.
5. Davidson (1999), p. 18.
6. Quoted in Shimron (2000).
7. Davidson, J., and others. *The Search for Common Ground.* Huntington, Ind.: Our Sunday Visitor, 1997. See also Williams, A., and Davidson, J. D. "Catholic Conceptions of Faith: A Generational Analysis." *Sociology of Religion,* Fall 1996, *97,* 273–289.
8. Others also report a growing tendency among generation Xers to adopt and adapt traditional religious practices such as the lectio divina, a meditative reading of Scriptures. See Wimmer, L. "Gen X Revisited." *Christian Century,* Nov. 8, 2000, 1146–1148.
9. MacIntyre (1984), pp. 221–222.

Chapter Seven

1. Field work and interviews at Church of the Word were done by Jennifer Berentsen Williams, at Living Waters Church by J. Shawn Landres, and at Good Shepherd Korean Presbyterian Church by Ellen Posman.
2. Having a much larger number of people attending church services than are actual members is characteristic of many newer congregations, especially evangelical ones. These congregations typically have relatively strict membership requirements, and many people choose to attend their services and other programs rather than take the required steps into membership.
3. As with Church of the Word, Living Waters is currently erecting a new church building that will consolidate the scattered ministries, moving out of its elementary school home.
4. It is not unlike "young adult" Sunday school classes in the traditional congregation. Some carry the name *young adult* with them well into the older adulthood of their members!
5. The description relies heavily on the perception of 1.5 and second-generation interviewees, since we did not interview members of the Korean congregation other than one of the pastors.
6. Vineyard Christian Fellowship churches are relatively new on the ecclesiastical scene, beginning in California in 1974. They are Pentecostal in theology and have pioneered use of contemporary music styles in worship. For a fuller description of Vineyard churches, see Miller (1997).

Epilogue

1. Dychtwald, K. *Age Power: How the 21st Century Will Be Ruled by the New Old.* New York: Tarcher/Putnam, 1999, p. 203.
2. Fine, G. A. "Negotiated Orders and Organizational Cultures." *Annual Review of Sociology,* 1984, *10,* 239–262.
3. Wuthnow (1993), p. 214.
4. Paden, W. E. *Interpreting the Sacred: Ways of Viewing Religion.* Boston: Beacon Press, 1992, p. 3.
5. Bellah, R. N., and others. *The Good Society.* New York: Knopf, 1991, p. 12.
6. Kelley (1972).
7. Berger, P. L. "Protestantism and the Quest for Certainty." *Christian Century,* 1998, *115*(23), 782–785, 792–796.

Bibliography

Ammerman, Nancy Tatom. "Golden Rule Christianity." In David Hall (ed.), *Lived Religion in America*, pp. 196–216. Princeton: Princeton University Press, 1997.

Barna, George. *Baby Busters: The Disillusioned Generation*. Chicago: Northfield Publishing, 1994.

Beaudoin, Tom. *Virtual Faith: The Irreverent Spiritual Quest of Generation X*. San Francisco: Jossey-Bass, 1998.

Berger, Peter L. *The Heretical Imperative: Contemporary Possibilities of Religious Affirmation*. Garden City, N.Y.: Anchor Press/Doubleday, 1979.

Carroll, Jackson W. *Mainline to the Future: Congregations in the Twenty-First Century*. Louisville, Ky.: Westminster John Knox Press, 2000.

Celek, Tim, and Dieter Zander. *Inside the Soul of a New Generation*. Grand Rapids, Mich.: Zondervan, 1996.

Cote, James E., and Anton L. Allahar. *Generation on Hold: Coming of Age in the Late Twentieth Century*. New York: New York University Press, 1994.

Coupland, Douglas. *Generation X: Tales for an Accelerated Culture*. New York: St. Martin's Press, 1991.

Coupland, Douglas. *Life After God*. New York: Pocket Books, 1994.

Davidson, James D., and others. *The Search for Common Ground*. Huntington, Ind.: Our Sunday Visitor, 1997.

Flory, Richard W., and Donald E. Miller (eds.). *Gen X Religion*. New York: Routledge, 2000.

Gallagher, Winifred. *Working on God*. New York: Random House, 1999.

Hoge, Dean R., Benton Johnson, and Donald A. Luidens. *Vanishing Boundaries: The Religion of Mainline Protestant Baby Boomers*. Louisville, Ky.: Westminster John Knox Press, 1994.

Holifield, E. Brooks. "Toward a History of American Congregations" pp. 23–53. In James P. Wind and James W. Lewis (eds.), *American Congregations*, Vol. 2. Chicago: University of Chicago Press, 1994.

Long, Jimmy. *Generating Hope: A Strategy for Reaching the Postmodern Generation*. Downers Grove, Ill.: Intervarsity, 1997.

MacIntyre, Alasdair. *After Virtue*. Notre Dame, Ind.: University of Notre Dame Press, 1984.

Mahedy, William, and Janet Bernardi. *A Generation Alone: Xers Making a Place in the World.* Downers Grove, Ill.: Intervarsity, 1994.

Miller, Craig Kennet. *Postmoderns: The Beliefs, Hopes, and Fears of Young Americans (1966–1981).* Nashville, Ky.: Discipleship Resources, 1996.

Miller, Donald E. *Reinventing American Protestantism: Christianity in the New Millennium.* Berkeley: University of California Press, 1997.

Porterfield, Amanda. *The Transformation of American Religion.* New York: Oxford University Press, 2000.

Roof, Wade Clark. *A Generation of Seekers: The Spiritual Journeys of the Baby Boom Generation.* San Francisco: HarperSanFrancisco, 1993.

Roof, Wade Clark. *Spiritual Marketplace: Baby Boomers and the Remaking of American Religion.* Princeton, N.J.: Princeton University Press, 1999.

Roof, Wade Clark, and William McKinney. *American Mainline Religion.* New Brunswick, N.J.: Rutgers University Press, 1987.

Schwartz, Sidney. *Finding a Spiritual Home: How a New Generation of Jews Can Transform the American Synagogue.* San Francisco: Jossey-Bass, 2000.

Smith, J. Walker, and Ann Clurman. *Rocking the Ages: The Yankelovich Report on Generational Marketing.* New York: HarperBusiness, 1997.

Strauss, William, and Neil Howe. *Generations: The History of America's Future, 1584–2069.* New York: Morrow, 1991.

Thau, Richard D., and Jay S. Heflin (eds.). *Generations Apart: Xers vs. Boomers vs. the Elderly.* Amherst, N.Y.: Prometheus Books, 1997.

Wuthnow, Robert. *The Restructuring of American Religion.* Princeton, N.J.: Princeton University Press, 1988.

Wuthnow, Robert. *Christianity in the Twenty-First Century: Reflection on the Challenges Ahead.* New York: Oxford University Press, 1993.

Wuthnow, Robert. *After Heaven: Spirituality in America Since the 1950s.* Berkeley: University of California Press, 1998.

The Authors

Jackson W. Carroll is the Ruth W. and A. Morris Williams Jr. Emeritus Professor of Religion and Society at Duke University Divinity School. He has written extensively about congregations, pastoral leadership, and theological education and is currently Director of Pulpit & Pew, a major research project on pastoral leadership at Duke Divinity School.

Wade Clark Roof is the J. F. Rowny Professor of Religion and Society and chair of the Department of Religious Studies at the University of California at Santa Barbara. He has written widely on generational change in American religion and is currently conducting a study of religious pluralism in southern California funded by the Ford Foundation.

Index